Also by Patricia Cornwell

A TIME FOR REMEMBERING
POSTMORTEM
BODY OF EVIDENCE
ALL THAT REMAINS
CRUEL AND UNUSUAL
THE BODY FARM
FROM POTTER'S FIELD
CAUSE OF DEATH
HORNET'S NEST
UNNATURAL EXPOSURE

Ruth, A Portrait

THE STORY OF RUTH BELL GRAHAM

by

Patricia Cornwell

Galilee
DOUBLEDAY
New York London Toronto Sydney Auckland

A GALILEE BOOK
PUBLISHED BY DOUBLEDAY
a division of Bantam Doubleday Dell Publishing Group, Inc.
1540 Broadway, New York, New York 10036

GALILEE, DOUBLEDAY, and the portrayal of a ship with a cross above a book are trademarks of Doubleday, a division of Bantam Doubleday Dell Publishing Group, Inc.

First Galilee edition published November 1998 by special arrangement with Doubleday.

The Library of Congress has cataloged the hardcover Doubleday edition as follows:

Cornwell, Patricia Daniels.
Ruth, a portrait: the story of Ruth Bell Graham / Patricia Cornwell. —1st ed.
p. cm.
Includes bibliographical references and index.
1. Graham, Ruth Bell. 2. Baptists—United States—Biography. 3. Evangelists' spouses—United States—Biography. 4. Spouses of clergy—United States—Biography. 5. Children of missionaries—Biography. 6. Graham, Billy, 1918– . I. Title.
BX6495.G666C67 1997
269'.2'092
[B]—DC20 96-41961
CIP

ISBN 0-385-48900-5

Printed in the United States of America

10 9 8 7

To
the wise old woman

Contents

The Beginning

MAY 2, 1996

CAPITOL ROTUNDA

WASHINGTON, D.C.

The Hendersonville High School band, of western North Carolina fame, played on the lawn, cool air warmed by the sun, while Secret Service watched. Celebrities and senators and old friends like Tricia Nixon Cox and Lynda Bird Robb, and Paul Harvey, and a crime novelist whose first book had been Ruth Bell Graham's biography, took seats inside. They assembled in good spirits amid oil portraits and marble, on this National Day of Prayer, when the Reverend Billy and his wife, Ruth, were to receive the Congressional Gold Medal. George Washington had been honored thus in 1776. Two hundred years later, the first clergy couple followed.

I was there, in truth, to take notes. It had been suggested that I update the biography I had decided to write long ago when I was twenty-four and too young to have any business asking. As I sat in a section near the front, among Ruth Graham's vast relations, I was struck by how time has spent itself. I was sweetly sad, and amazed that some people are never a disappointment, no matter where journeys take us or how well we finally know those we chose to emulate and love.

Neither Billy nor Ruth had shifted in a way that counts. He was still tall and a bit befuddled by all the attention. His eyes were no less blue, but they were not as much here as there, and most of all they were kind. Hers typically didn't like being noticed and didn't miss a trick. She still plotted practical jokes and would rather chat with ushers and housekeeping staff. Vice President Al Gore gave her a chair when she was escorted to the front. When Billy was led in, he gave Ruth a kiss.

I sneaked ahead of Newt Gingrich to hug Ruth in all her magenta. She thought I was sweet to come all this way from Richmond, Virginia, and hoped I might find time to stop by the Renaissance afterward and visit. She asked me if I were still doing my work in morgues, and I assured her I was and all was going fine. She would get room service, something Chinese, if the hotel had it, she promised. If that would suit?

She did not know if the Gold Medal was really gold or *something else*, but she suspected something else when a granddaughter persisted in knowing a little later in a room of the Renaissance, where she and Billy briefly rested. I was certain Ruth did not care about the medal's composition, nor was she especially impressed when the four major television networks let the world know that the Grahams would be dining with the Clintons at the White House this night.

That's interesting, Ruth commented from her bed, as she dipped into a dish of Chinese food. "Honey?" she called out to her husband, who was stirring cream of broccoli soup, wondering if it was cool enough. "Did you agree to something you didn't tell me about?"

"What's that?" He cupped a hand behind an ear, from his couch.

A striking teenage boy, who wore a small earring, pointed a camera, intending to take another photograph of his legendary grandfather. "I don't have a *good* picture of you." The grandson was having fun.

"You can get one in my coffin." Grandfather Billy leaned forward and dipped into his soup.

"What?" The grandson guffawed.

"Bill!" Ruth chided her husband as misinformation on the evening news went on. "What a dreadful thing to say!"

The journey that led us here, or at least my humble few miles of it, opened with rain. The night was cold and interminable and blew over eaves and in billowing sheets through an open stadium, shrouding lamps in milky light, on June 5, 1982. I was still young and newly married, and unknown, and on a budget. I had attended but one Billy Graham crusade prior to this, in Asheville, when I was too young to precisely remember the decision I made.

At one end of Boston's muddy Nickerson Field was the wooden platform, this moment occupied by four rows of empty folding chairs and several tall amplifiers and a baby grand piano enveloped in heavy plastic. Bundles of thick cable snaked across the wet plank floor. The podium was covered with a small square awning flapping loudly like a wind-ripped flag. It was 7:00 P.M. I had never been so cold and wet and hungry in my life, and I let my then-husband know this more than once.

For the past hour some thirteen thousand people cocooned in slickers, trench coats, hats, plastic bags, and galoshes had trickled through the field house for the 7:30 service. It would not be televised because of the weather. Wide wooden boards bridged puddles leading to tiers, and rainwater was an inch deep on the seats. The Reverend Billy Graham had been urged to cancel and as usual had refused, leaving his hotel with plastic-laminated sermon notes and his large-print black leather Bible. Wearing a Greek fisherman's cap, a khaki trench coat, and tinted glasses, he arrived in the flashing blue of a light attached to the roof of his rental car.

No one seemed to notice the figure slipping out of the backseat. She left him at the field house door and skated across the muddy tile floor, Sheraton trash can liners over her feet and fastened at the ankles with rubber bands. She wore black kid gloves and a fuchsia plastic rain cloak with a matching cap that was an umbrella from her crown to the tip of her nose. Looking like a psychedelic version of the Morton Salt girl, Ruth gave me a wet hug.

In no hurry to file outside to find a seat as there would be plenty to choose from this raw, dreary night, we sat in folding chairs against a cinder block wall, watching the crowd slog by. Outside, propagandists were passing out tracts accusing Billy Graham of being a Communist sympathizer, and buildings and buses near the stadium boasted anti-Graham signs and banners. A deranged man less than ten feet from us loudly asked a security guard if he was Billy Graham disguised as a cop.

Ruth seemed impervious to it all, unaffected by the confusion that seemed to eddy around her husband everywhere he went. She missed little. An amused smile tugged at her lips from time to time as her brain processed images, expressions, snatches of conversations here and there. With dignity, she sat. Her Styrofoam cup of steaming coffee disappeared at intervals beneath her voluminous hat.

At close to 7:30, she slogged through the mud, dragging her trash bag-covered pumps over makeshift boardwalks and puddled artificial grass. She chose an empty row on the playing field, several hundred yards from the platform, in front of the back tiers. She tilted a gray metal folding chair to spill rainwater from it, and demurely seated herself, tucking her skirt and bright pink rain cloak around her. She proceeded to remove her wet black kid gloves one finger at a time, and wormed her hands up her sleeves, kimono-style.

Regal and unflinching in the bone-chilling downpour, she sat erect, the steady thrumming of rain muffling her husband's voice as it echoed off the stands.

Swathed in a heavy khaki trench coat and now hatless, Billy preached, slightly bent against the blustery wind and rain. The awning flapped wildly above him. He could see little but the hazy white glow of the lights clustered on poles bordering the field high above him. He was oblivious to the bird that had alighted on a nearby lamp to sing lustily for the duration of the service. From Billy's vantage, the crowd was dark and formless.

To Ruth he was a faraway figure, sometimes obscured by umbrellas tilting in her line of vision. Soberly she listened, her eyes riveted straight ahead. She smiled when he leaned close to the microphones and began teasing her about the bright new rain outfit she had just purchased, cracking the usual jokes about wives and their outrageous shopping habits, adding that she was sitting "somewhere out there among you, but I don't know exactly where."

That was the way she liked it, in the middle of the masses and invisible. The pathos, the motion interested her. Anonymous, she became animated like a child. She became pensive and reverent, relieved to keep her public self folded up and in her pocket like a dime-store rain bonnet.

"And if people start recognizing me after this book," she let me know in 1981 when this research began, "I'm going to dye my hair and move to Europe."

Not long before she made this threat, on a January morning, I telephoned to ask if I could drive up for a visit. She was in bed with the flu but said to come anyway since it seemed I had something very important on my mind. It was bitterly cold, and the sky was lead as I made the two-hour trip from Charlotte, North Carolina, to Montreat, where she lived on the side of a ridge in a house built of century-old logs.

She was alone, split wood smoldering quietly in the fireplace in front of her hand-built bed. She was propped against several pillows and surrounded by letters, stationery, books, pens, cassette tapes, napkins, Kleenex, and her large black leather-bound King James Bible. She smelled faintly of Rose Milk. A woman of regal beauty, she was thin but shapely, her features flawless, as though chiseled with love. She was intense and soothing, like the fire on her hearth. Her movements were graceful, her presence hypnotic, even on this day when her bones ached and her eyes were glazed with fever.

"I want to write a book about you," I said to my hero.

"You want to do what, honey?" she asked in a voice distracted and weary.

"You know, I want to write your biography," the twenty-four-year-old police reporter announced.

"Well, sure. That's fine," she said with a weak smile. "But I don't think it would be very interesting."

Several days later, Ruth and Billy flew to Mexico and rested for a month. Her health and senses restored, she telephoned me one afternoon at the *Charlotte Observer*, where I was working on my latest crime story.

"Patsy," she said, "no way you're going to write a book about me."

I met Ruth through her parents, Nelson and Virginia Bell, whom I grew to love shortly after my mother moved my two brothers and me from Miami to Montreat in 1963, when I was seven. Homesick for my own grandmother, I visited Mrs. Bell several times each month, entering without knocking through the screened-in back porch that led into the warm, fragrant kitchen. Beneath a layer of wax paper on top of her refrigerator there were always cups of homemade custard, generously sprinkled with nutmeg and deliciously moist.

I'd find her in the same place each time, sitting in her favorite chair beside the living room couch, a pink baby blanket over her knees, a battery-powered magnifying glass in her lap.

"Go get a custard," she'd chirp before I could sit down. For the next hour she'd spin colorful and exotic tales about her missionary days in China while we played games like Rook or Scrabble. She always won or made me think I had.

It was during these visits that I became acquainted with Ruth, when she would glide in with dinner for her parents, or perhaps for a chat. I was struck with her beauty, her gentleness, and her spontaneous laughter. Other encounters came when I was in the local red brick grammar school and would spot her car idling out by the endless line of orange buses wrapped around the school. She was there to pick up her younger son, Ned. I would conspicuously walk back and forth in front of her Oldsmobile, searching with mock gravity for bus #91, until Ruth noticed me and asked if I wanted a ride. It was a shame if Ned, much less empathetic than his mother, spied me first. Once he rolled down his window and said, "You can quit walking around the car 'cause we're going to Asheville."

When I was nineteen, Ruth and I began to become friends. In April of 1976 she invited me out to lunch. Invitations to her house, which was two miles up the mountain from mine, followed. Usually she was alone. Husband Billy was delivering lectures at major universities and preaching throughout the world. After three decades of international acclaim, his pace was more, not less, frenetic. My earliest memories of him are when he sat with his family near the back of the Montreat Presbyterian Church on the infrequent Sundays when he was in town.

Back then I wasn't aware of who he was, but I surmised, based on all the head-turning and ogling, that he was very important. After the service, people flocked around him to shake his hand, ask him to autograph their Bibles or bulletins, or wonder if he might pray for them. I remember a woman pointing out that the price tag was still dangling from his suit jacket. She asked if she could keep it as a souvenir.

In later years, when I would see Billy in his own home during my visits with Ruth, I was surprised that he did not seem affected by the adulation and criticism. He just seemed tired. She would attempt to shield him when anyone else appeared. "Bill, why don't you go sit up there in the sun and rest," she would say as he greeted people, a slightly bemused expression in his eyes when she repeated the suggestion two or three times.

More often than not, he would amble out onto the lawn or into the living room with Ruth and the guests. At home, he didn't look so austere. He usually wore a tennis sweater, jogging shoes, and baggy blue jeans. Sometimes his socks clashed with his shoes or half his shirt collar was crumpled inside. His eyes didn't have that steely gleam. They were soft, far away in thought. They became softer when they looked at her.

Ruth seemed virtually untouched by the pressures of living in his wake while conducting a significant ministry of her own. Her eyes were vulnerable. After all these years of being exposed to the public, she had not slammed and latched the door to her emotions. She had always been an excruciatingly private woman, sensitive to others and fiercely protective of her family. She could not see what good could come of my writing her biography. It was difficult convincing her.

"Ruth," I told her in May of 1981, after she had repeatedly rejected my idea throughout the spring, "I haven't changed my mind."

"I know you haven't," she said, discouraged.

"If you don't let me write this biography, it will be the only selfish thing I've ever known you to do." I was out with it.

"That's really hitting below the belt," she fired back.

"Not because you'll be denying me the privilege," I was quick to add, "but because you'll be denying those who have never met you and never will."

Several days later she telephoned me.

"OK," she said.

"It will be painless," I promised.

It wasn't.

"We'll have fun." I was sure.

We didn't.

"What a great way to spend time together," I encouraged.

After it was finished, we did not speak for eight years.

1
CHAPTER

Before Ruth

Courtesy of Ruth Bell Graham Personal Collection

THE YOUNG COUPLE IN CHINA

North Jiangsu, China, December 5, 1916. The Grand Canal meandered through the frozen lowlands like a muddy snake and carried the launch and its barge past dozens of sampans, tugboats, and junks.

Nelson Bell was a twenty-two-year-old medical doctor. He buried his chin deeper inside the flipped-up collar of his wool coat, buffering himself from the cold air and the sour smell of dirty feet on the deck outside a window that had no glass. His wife, Virginia, wrote letters at a small table behind him, glancing up each time her husband briefly retreated from frigid air. He was captivated and repulsed as he watched their arrival into a new life. Across murky water rose an ancient city surrounded by high gray brick walls, and heads of criminals impaled over the gate stared with dull, blind eyes.

Lemuel Nelson Bell was a witty, intelligent young man with a character as sturdy as his Scotch-grain leather shoes. Handsomely built, he had wavy brown hair, even teeth bright as a blade, a square jaw, and a patrician nose. He was six feet tall, a solid hundred and ninety pounds, and looked more like a matinee idol than a missionary. Bell was a professional baseball recruit when he forsook his dream because he longed to share the Gospel with those who had never heard it. As he stood in his cabin, it seemed the Grand Canal beneath his feet and the faith of his forebears were moving together, carrying him to his destiny.

He was born July 30, 1894, in the iron-laced Allegheny Mountains near Clifton Forge, Virginia, where his father, James Bell, headed the commissariat at the Longdale Mining Company. Nelson Bell's ancestors were Scotch-Irish immigrants who had begun farming and lumbering some eight hundred acres of fertile land in the Shenandoah Valley in the early 1700s. He was probably most like his great-great-grandfather John McCue Jr., whose father had immigrated to America from Northern Ireland around 1731. Young McCue, born in 1753, was educated at Liberty Hall, which would later be renamed Washington and Lee University. He set his heart on becoming a Presbyterian minister and briefly wavered when Thomas Jefferson offered to train him as a lawyer and let him live at Monticello, as legend has it. But McCue refused and set about evangelizing the territory. By 1791 he was ordained and settled in the small parish of Tinkling Springs in Augusta County, Virginia.

A flamboyant man, McCue galloped through the countryside in his two-wheeled gig, his long brown hair streaming back from a high forehead. He spoke his mind from his hogshead pulpit and was subsequently chastised from time to time at the presbytery meetings he was consistently tardy in attending. During heated arguments he was known to threaten to remove his parson's coat and resort to his fists, and "he could tell comic stories in a manner irresistibly ludicrous," wrote an acquaintance. He died Sunday morning, September 20, 1818, when he was thrown from his horse on his way to preach. He left eleven children. A son, William, one of the county's first physicians, died soon after, and William's widow, Ann Barry McCue, married pioneer John Allen in 1821. Three years later, Allen and Elisha Rumsey, who also had a wife named Ann, founded a small settlement on the Huron River in southwest Michigan Territory which they christened "Ann's Arbour," now Ann Arbor, Michigan.

Nelson Bell's maternal great-grandfather, a classmate of John McCue, was the Reverend William Wilson.[1] His daughter Elizabeth married John McCue's grandson Thomas, and they built a plantation in Augusta County which they named Belvidere. The modest, two-story brick house, where Nelson Bell's mother, Ruth Lee "Cora" McCue, was born, was used as a Confederate hospital during the Civil War. In 1864 when Sheridan stormed the grain- and cattle-rich Shenandoah Valley to burn the Confederacy's breadbasket, Elizabeth McCue slipped a gold coin from her shoe and paid the Union officer in charge to leave the property without burning the barn.

Family lore has it that thirty-three years later Elizabeth McCue saw a photograph of this man and recognized him as the new president of the United States, William McKinley. Her daughter Betty immortalized herself in the valley when another band of Union soldiers appeared at Belvidere and an officer moved from room to room dropping lighted matches in the closets. Betty followed close behind, stamping them out. When the officer then demanded the brooch she was wearing, she slapped it into his palm, pin first.

"Madam!" he exclaimed as he returned the brooch and bowed, "I admire your spunk!"

Elizabeth McCue's daughter Cora was a strong-willed, practical woman who as a child had a bit of a temper. The living room door at Belvidere still bears the scars young Cora inflicted when she beat it with fire tongs after spats with her brother William. In 1882 Cora married distant cousin James Bell, as handsome as he was impractical, with more of a penchant for spinning colorful yarns than minding his store. Cora handled the family finances. She supervised their three children and indulged her interest in world affairs and foreign missions through reading and entertaining furloughed missionaries.

A bit of a daredevil, Cora decided on one occasion when a missionary was visiting to make an impulsive visit to Belvidere. Since her husband had taken the horse-drawn wagon to work, she had no transportation to the train station at the foot of the mountain. Cora recalled that there was a handcar at the mine, and she and the missionary, who knew nothing about such contraptions, hopped aboard. The track ran past the store and James Bell looked up just in time to see the runaway car streak by, its handle seesawing madly.

"That looks like my wife!" he exclaimed as the car derailed, propelling both Cora and the missionary into a thicket.

When Nelson Bell was six, his mother moved the children to Waynesboro to begin school. Her husband joined them later and began working as a salesman at a local shop. From the start, young Nelson showed that he had inherited the best qualities of his ancestors. He was a devout Christian and unshakably loyal to the Presbyterian tradition of his family. He was a talented athlete, whose intelligence and agility produced maddening spins and intricate strategies on the tennis court and baseball field. As he matured, his fondness for baseball grew into a passion, and by age sixteen he was the captain of his high school's champion team.

He quickly distinguished himself as a pitcher with his own version of the knuckleball. The ball was gripped firmly in his fingertips, and he stood perfectly straight and still, the shadow of his cap hiding his eyes as he cut them left and right, checking the bases. Slowly, he cocked his body like a catapult and snapped forward, sending the unspinning cowhide sphere floating toward the plate where it either jumped over or dove under the befuddled player's bat. In every cheering crowd, a willowy, gray-eyed blonde watched, her milky complexion flushed beneath a sweeping hat.

Virginia Leftwich was born April 12, 1892, in Richmond. She was the oldest of four children, two boys and two girls. Her father, Douglas Lee Leftwich, was a traveling salesman and an expert cabinetmaker with a magnificent baritone voice. Shortly after Virginia's birth, her family moved to Charlottesville, then to Waynesboro, where she lived five blocks from the Bells' three-story house.

Her ancestors included high-ranking military officers, scholars, and physicians. She was descended from William Wertenbaker, whom Thomas Jefferson had appointed in 1826 to head the library of the University of Virginia. Her uncle was the prominent Princeton University historian Thomas Jefferson Wertenbaker. Another relative was novelist and foreign editor for *Time* magazine Charles Christian Wertenbaker, who would scandalize the family when he was told in 1954 that he had incurable cancer. Rather than suffer the physical and mental ravages of a slow death, Charles Wertenbaker slashed his wrists in his home off the Bay of Biscay in southern France. He watched himself bleed to death while his wife, Lael Tucker, dripped morphine into his wounds to dull the pain. She published several accounts of her husband's suicide.

Though Virginia Leftwich and Nelson Bell had been acquainted as children, it wasn't until high school that they fell in love. Fragile in body, Virginia was stubborn and valorous in spirit, with a sensitivity to stress that would make pain an integral part of her life. After graduation, Nelson entered Washington and Lee University while she studied nursing in Richmond. He had intended to study law, but his plans were dramatically altered by a seemingly insignificant event. On a winter's evening in 1911 when the air was sharp and stars shone like pin pricks in black, Nelson and a friend strolled across campus spinning their career plans as young people do. Abruptly, his companion slowed his pace and turned a shadowed face to him.

"Nelson," he asked, "did you ever think of becoming a medical missionary?"

As the two figures paused on the frosty grass, words emerging in smoky puffs, Nelson knew without equivocation that come morning he would switch from law to premedical. He had been caught in the wake of the Student Volunteer Movement for Foreign Missions, launched by American evangelist Dwight L. Moody in 1886. Since that time, thousands of America's most intelligent and attractive young men and women had enlisted to achieve the evangelization of the world in their generation.[2]

Nelson had heard his mother's missionary friends tell of their experiences in China, a land of mystery on the dark side of the world, polarized by squalor and opulence. Few Westerners had dared go there, save the importers of opium or Christianity. Nelson had his mind made up, but baseball would almost scotch his plans. In 1913, while a student at the Medical College of Virginia in Richmond, he signed a baseball contract with the professional Virginia League after it was agreed that he wouldn't have to play on Sundays. Two years later the team was sold to the

Baltimore Orioles. To play in the major leagues had been a passion he had held in his heart since childhood.

For weeks his conscience and ambition waged a silent struggle, and he resigned from the league. In May of 1916 the executive secretary of the Southern Presbyterian Foreign Mission Committee cabled him, inquiring if Nelson could leave for China immediately. One of the two American doctors at the Qingjiang General Hospital in North Jiangsu had died after a few months of service. Nelson and Virginia agreed to accept the offer, providing their departure could be delayed three months to give him an opportunity to get at least a little experience as a physician.

Virginia abandoned her Baptist heritage and became a Presbyterian. Nelson received his medical license, and on June 30, 1916, they were married. They began their lives together in the coal fields of West Virginia where he served a residency. In early November, they hauled their few belongings to Seattle, Washington, and sailed to the Far East. Two of the dozen Southern Presbyterians to join the China mission field that year, they docked in Shanghai's International Settlement after nineteen days of turbulent waters and horrendous seasickness. They were met by Jimmy and Sophie Graham, veteran missionaries who would become two of the Bells' closest friends.[3]

"Poor Virginia Bell," muttered one missionary woman to another as they eyed the slender blonde standing on the quay beside a small mountain of boxes and trunks. "She won't last a year."

Dressed in tailored woolens, hats, and gloves, the Bells gripped the sides of the rickshaw and squinted in the late morning sun. Tins of cheese, a Virginia ham, bolts of cloth, and medicines were secured by ropes on all sides, and the couple bounced through the crowded streets to the train depot. From Shanghai the train clattered slowly a hundred and fifty miles northwest of Zhenjiang, where a ferry carried the newlyweds across the muddy Yangtze River to the Grand Canal.

On December 5, the Bells boarded a launch that took them the remaining one hundred and twenty-five miles north to Qingjiang. Traveling this distance along the Grand Canal would take as long as two weeks when the water was low or choked with ice. But their sail lasted a brief forty-eight hours, the dank cabin below the deck full of Chinese chattering like magpies until dawn. Wretched on their slivers of sleeping shelves, the Bells had spent the noisy night hours stretching out and tucking their legs as they vacillated between being cramped and being cold.

They disembarked at the Qingjiang quay and were surrounded by bartering rickshaw coolies tugging at their baggage to the shrill music of foreign tongues. Women nursing infants eyed the Americans with mild suspicion, and other Chinese squatted on the shore washing rice in the filthy water.

The 170-bed Qingjiang General Hospital had been built two years earlier by Dr. James Baker Woods, a medical missionary in China since 1894. The small gray brick complex occupied a six-acre tract of land less than a mile from the canal and, as was true of every other settlement and city in China, was surrounded by a wall. Absalom Sydenstricker, father of Nobel Prize-winning novelist Pearl Buck, had founded the mission station in 1887.

Beyond the north wall of the compound were barren fields where peanuts and sweet potatoes had been harvested two months earlier. In every direction, the expanse of bleak earth was interrupted by thousands of tan, conical grave mounds, kept clear of grass and weeds by filial caretakers who feared the wrath of the ancestors they worshiped. In this land of too many people and too little food, thousands of cultivatable acres were sown with only bones and veneration.

During summers in Jiangsu, temperatures rose to 106 degrees and monsoon rains poured from the heavens until the Grand Canal rose from its bed like a watery beast and coiled over the earth, devouring the peasants' mud dwellings. Fields flowed together into lakes as the farmers fled in crude boats and rafts or climbed the few trees, clinging to branches like tattered birds. As brightly colored paper and pottery idols washed away with livelihoods, the people wondered what they had done to arouse the malevolent spirits.

When the land was dry, winds roared through the Gobi Desert and swept billowing sheets of yellow dust through Inner Mongolia, over the Great Wall, and fifteen hundred miles south into Jiangsu. Grit blotted out the sun and seeped under doors and through window frames and every other crevice. The people's gods turned furies, ranging the earth to unleash all manner of terrors. Hailstorms battered tender life to death. Droughts scorched, and black clouds of locusts ravaged grain fields and gardens like a billion demonic buzz saws.

It was during these times of tragedy that the Chinese turned to the missionaries and clung to them, seeking refuge in their compounds and begging food for their starving children. For a while, the people forgot prejudices and resentment and swallowed the foreigners' religion and medicines.

"God is not an idol," the Westerners explained to a people who had more gods than they could count. "There is only one true living God who loves you and sent His Son to die as a sacrifice for your sins," they'd say to the ragged prisoners as they brought bread and bandages to them in wretched prisons, where the whistling of the guards announcing an execution was as constant as the wind.

Some Chinese understood. They believed what the missionaries told them. Others did not, and wondered what this Jesus had done to anger His Father so.

The Chinese thought the foreigners a curious people, with hair and eyes the colors of wheat, sky, soil, and grass. Men had teeth like mules and women had feet as big as boats. They came from a cradle in the West where the sun, they said, rose while it set in China. The missionaries in North Jiangsu called themselves Southern Presbyterians, and the ones in the southern portion of the province called themselves Northern Presbyterians. The superstitious Chinese, who reckoned themselves one year old at birth, decided that these strange visitors must be at least one hundred years old when they were delivered from their mothers' wombs.

To many, the missionaries were *yang gui zi*, or foreign devils, who had been disgorged from East India Company ships along with the opium traders during Queen Victoria's reign. The people of God and traders of "foreign mud," as the drug was called, fell under the same anathema. The missionaries were no different from those who forced opium down China's throat. Many Chinese believed that the missionaries were ambassadors of a wicked imperialism and devoid of respect for Chinese government and culture.

The Bells could not have entered China at a more politically unstable time. The Manchu dynasty had become increasingly corrupt since the beginning of its rule in 1644, and in 1911 had been overthrown. The Chinese had turned to the West for hope, believing that they too could enjoy power, affluence, and advanced technology if China became a democracy. The Republic of China was born, founded by Western-educated Sun Yat-sen. His successor, Yüan Shih-kai, appointed chieftains or warlords to govern the eighteen provinces, believing that he could exercise central control over them and their armies.

"Official bandits," as the peasants called the soldiers, roved about raping, pillaging, and murdering while warlords fought among themselves for dominance. Wealthy landlords fled the countryside for the safety of city walls, leaving irrigation and flood control systems unattended. The fruits of democracy were marauding, flooding, and droughts. For the peasant once oppressed by the empress dowager, the new republic embodied a more formidable randomness and terror. For some intellectuals, it was time to study other foreign ideologies, such as Marxism.

What the official bandits left in their wake the local criminal element crept in like rodents to devour. The "dirt bandits," as they were called, were civilians who tilled the soil by day and, disguised, raided their neighbors by night. Dirt bandits were fond of kidnapping children and selling them into slavery or prostitution. If ransom was the objective, notes would arrive in small bundles containing a severed ear or finger. Another gory reminder would follow if payment was delayed. Though missionaries were not immune, they made it known that they would not pay ransoms under any circumstances.

Final disillusionment with the West came with the Treaty of Versailles in 1919, when the West gave Japan former German concessions in China's mountainous Shandong peninsula. It was a gift that was not the West's to make and symbolized to the Chinese that China was perceived as inferior, unworthy of the rights that other nations enjoyed. Less than a year later the Comintern sent three members of the Bolshevik party to China. Within months the official Chinese Communist Party had been organized.

In describing the political and economic scene in China, the missionaries used the word *chaotic* repeatedly in their letters and diaries. At night, rifles cracked in the countryside beyond the Bells' compound wall, shattering smooth silence like firecrackers. In the hospital, Dr. Bell did not always know whether he was treating a bandit or an innocent peasant. On one occasion, he recognized his bandages on a criminal's head impaled over the city gate. None could predict when Chinese sentiments would turn antiforeign, as they had in the 1900 Boxer Rebellion, when churches were burned and Christian missionaries and their Chinese converts were murdered. Life and death, the Bells believed, were as much a part of God's Providence as their traveling to China had been.

1. William Wilson became of interest to his descendants in 1912 when Staunton-born Woodrow Wilson became the twenty-fifth president of the United States. Family legend has it that he was a descendant of William Wilson, but intensive study of family pedigrees has never been able to verify this claim. Woodrow Wilson's biographer, Arthur S. Link of Princeton University, observes that when Woodrow Wilson was elected president of the United States, all of his relatives came out of the woodwork. William Wilson and kin were not among them.
2. Kenneth Scott Latourette, *A History of Christianity* (New York: Harper & Row, 1975), 2:1019.
3. Jimmy and Sophie Graham are not related to Billy Graham.

2

CHAPTER

A Second Little Nuisance

Courtesy of Ruth Bell Graham Personal Collection

RUTH

Ruth was a very normal child but above the average in spirituality. I'd say she was rather deep in her feelings. She was a very thoughtful little girl, and she was pretty, with curly hair and big hazel eyes.

—*Margaret Sells, former missionary to China*

In late spring 1920, wheat and barley fields in the North Jiangsu lowlands burgeoned with the most promise in forty years. Chinese peasants in shapeless gray-blue trousers worked silently as the earth warmed to imminent summer. The collectors of night soil wove through the crowded streets of Qingjiang, stinking buckets swinging from *bian dans* across their shoulders as they headed to replenish fields.

The Qingjiang General Hospital was filled with Chinese suffering from cholera, tuberculosis, and venereal disease. Doctors treated burns and knife and gunshot wounds inflicted by bandits who frequently tortured victims into revealing where the family money was hidden. Domestic beatings and shootings had dramatically increased since the fall of the last Chinese dynasty nine years earlier, when Chinese men had been cutting off their queues. It was speculated that squabbles once settled by the painful yanking of the long braids now found more violent expression.

There were the usual cases of attempted suicide, when Chinese lost face or hope and swallowed match heads or arsenic. Children carried into the hospital manifested scalps eaten to the bone from home treatments of arsenic for that "heavenly thing," as the Chinese called malaria. Doctors removed long needles from torsos and faces and battled other home remedies for meningitis and for *kala-azar*, or black fever.

Most Chinese did not trust the Western doctors. Healers from far away were monsters who made medicines from dead Chinese baby eyes and bones. The missionary physicians were alchemists who changed Chinese marrow and other bodily elements into gold. Often the superstitious Chinese did not visit the hospital until no hope was left, and tumors weighing ten, twenty, forty pounds and more were removed. A one-hundred-eighty-three-pound woman arrived at the hospital gate, pushing her tumescent belly ahead of her in a wheelbarrow. After Dr. Bell removed the tumor, she weighed ninety pounds. Untreated fractured bones healed at bizarre angles and were rebroken and set. A local peasant finally resorted to alchemy at the Western hospital when his broken ankle fused and his foot pointed backward.

By 1920 Dr. Bell was the superintendent of the growing hospital. He was known for his compassion, humor, and long hours. Often he performed as many as nine operations in the morning, leaning over a sea of white in the glow of a low, tin-hooded lamp while nurses with towels wiped sweat from his face. At meals he frequently teased Virginia and the children by describing that day's procedures in graphic, gory detail. A highly skilled surgeon, he was versatile enough to remove cataracts or fill a tooth. He could amputate a leg and fashion a prosthesis from a beam of wood. He made house calls fifty miles into the countryside, his black Harley-Davidson motorcycle with sidecar bumping over the rutted, six-foot-wide dirt roads. He sometimes gave his own blood to patients, because the Chinese would not donate theirs, not even for money.

Blood, the Chinese would explain, "is handed down from our ancestors. He who loses it in this world will not have it in the world to come. Who would willingly spill or waste a drop of it?"

What mattered most was souls, and Dr. Bell would later say that the hospital existed "primarily for the preaching of the Gospel." Ambulatory patients were required to attend daily chapel. There was a full-time evangelist on the hospital staff to work with the male patients and a Bible teacher to work with the women. To Dr. Bell, the spiritual gifts were more significant than athletic or surgical skills. On a slip of paper under the glass covering his rolltop desk, he had scribbled the fruits of the Spirit, a reminder of the *Love, Joy, Peace, Long-Suffering, Gentleness, Goodness, Faithfulness, Meekness,* and *Self-Control* that he aspired to manifest in his own life.

He was renowned for his courage. Once two hundred corrupt militiamen began looting the nearby home owned by the Grahams, then on furlough in the United States. When a houseboy rushed to the operating room to alert everyone, Dr. Bell raced to the scene. He kicked down the locked gate and chased off the thieves, then pursued them to their camp, where he retrieved a stolen bicycle.

On another occasion, while he was traveling by barge, a Chinese man who could not swim fell into the Grand Canal. Dr. Bell dove into the muddy water after him while other passengers watched in amazement, not understanding why this foreigner would risk his life for a coolie. In an environment where the most formidable mental enemy was the feeling of futility, Dr. Bell's colleagues knew him as a man who was never tormented by discouragement. To many Chinese, he was Chong Ai Hua, or "the Bell who is lover of the Chinese people."

On Thursday, June 10, 1920, Dr. Bell ran upstairs to his bedroom in the family's gray brick Chinese house on the compound. He rolled up his sleeves, scrubbed his hands, and filled a pan with steaming water. His heart thudded harder than it normally did when he delivered a baby. This was his own. No one recalls what time she arrived, but it was in the year of the monkey, which, according to Asian astrologers, spawned multitalented, adventuresome, and witty people. Ruth McCue Bell, named for her paternal grandmother, would fulfill those prophecies.

She began life rather unceremoniously. Her parents' Chinese friends did not pass out red-dyed eggs or ignite strands of firecrackers to celebrate the birth of a girl. Now, the Chinese thought, poor Chong Ai Hua had two little nuisances. Rosa Wertenbaker Bell had been born two years earlier. Ruth's birth certificate was registered in the Nanjing consulate, which would be destroyed in 1927, leaving no official proof of Ruth's arrival in this world.

In 1922 the Bells built a two-story gray brick house on the compound to accommodate their growing family. Their modest new home had a corrugated red tin roof, a two-level porch, and three dormer windows. It was less than a hundred yards from the hospital operating room where Dr. Bell began work at 8:30 each morning, after breakfast and family devotions. As was true of most missionaries, the Bells were determined to Westernize their children in preparation for their one day leaving for American colleges, husbands, and homes. Ruth's parents worked to make what could have been Spartan living conditions comfortable. After the hospital acquired a generator, Dr. Bell equipped his house with electric lights and a refrigerator. Later he installed a telephone system in missionary homes within a mile radius of his compound, more than a decade before lines would connect Shanghai to the smaller cities.

Perhaps the most troublesome inconvenience, and one that could not be remedied, was the absence of indoor plumbing. Bathrooms were nothing more than two cubbyholes, one off the upstairs porch and another off the kitchen.

Each featured a square wooden box with a hole in the middle and a five-gallon bucket underneath, which was emptied daily by a collector of night soil. Though there was a well on the compound, the water was too hard and contaminated for drinking or cooking. Each day, water was carried from the Grand Canal and emptied into the large earthen jars, or *gangs*, outside the kitchen door. Half a cup of crystal alum was stirred into the murky water with a long stick, until impurities settled.

Most canal water was used for cooking and was deemed suitable for drinking only after it was boiled in a large kettle in the kitchen and filtered twice through cotton in Dr. Bell's homemade galvanized tin water cooler in the pantry. What was left in the *gang* was heated each week and carried to an upstairs bedroom for bathing. In the winter, the water was poured into a tub set before a trash burner stoked with soybean stalks and bits of trash to thaw a narrow margin of air. Usually Rosa would take her bath first.

Young Ruth would follow, slipping gingerly into the tepid water and spending the next few minutes rotating in the tub as the fire scorched one side and icy air froze the other. After a brisk scrubbing, Ruth hurried into a flannel gown and crawled into bed with a hot water bottle. Trash burners were the only source of heat in the bedrooms. Downstairs, the fireplace and the kitchen stove were stoked with some of the fifteen tons of Shandong coal Dr. Bell purchased for forty-five dollars each winter.

Mrs. Bell began furnishing their new home with the half-dozen Empire maple, oak, and mahogany pieces her father had crafted for her not long before she married. Other items were made by a local Chinese carpenter. The living room was decorated in shades of blue with Mandarin rugs on polished hardwood floors. A coal grate was in one corner, an upright piano stood between two windows, and flowered paper covered the walls. The Bell children were schooled in the strictest of manners, with dress clothes required at dinner and no elbows on the table. Tardiness at morning devotions meant no sugar on porridge, and sassing was unthinkable. The Bells ate Chinese food, a cuisine that would always be Ruth's favorite. The family also enjoyed fried chicken, biscuits, apple pie, and other southern fare.

Tomatoes, lettuce, asparagus, and other vegetables were grown in the small garden behind the house, which Mrs. Bell shared with the other missionaries. Through constant attention, Mrs. Bell turned the family's bleak patch of earth into a lush space shaded by mulberries, Chinese elms, locusts, and fruit trees that rustled like starchy petticoats with each stir of air. Chrysanthemums, geraniums, lilacs, irises, and roses bordered the porch and the compound wall.

Like most missionaries, the Bells hired Chinese helpers and paid each of them two American dollars from their combined seventy-five-dollar monthly salary, an amount that tripled when converted to Chinese currency. Wages and working conditions in the Bell household were superior to those endured by other Chinese peasants. The cook was the head of the housekeeping staff, and without his prowess at bartering in the marketplace, Mrs. Bell would have had to contend with merchants tripling their prices the minute her foreign face appeared.

She taught the cook to prepare American dishes, though some of his early attempts at making biscuits, for example, were disastrous. She supervised him closely to ensure that he washed all vegetables in boiled water and practiced other sanitary measures. Other housekeepers did the laundry and cleaning. In the gatehouse lived Liu Er, an affable sentry who monitored all who entered and left the compound and carried water from the Grand Canal each day.

The family's most important helper and the one dearest to Ruth was her *amah*, or nanny, Wang Nai Nai, who lived in a small room in the Bells' house. She had been a procuress of "little flowers," or child prostitutes, before missionary Sophie Graham had converted her to Christianity.

Wang Nai Nai was barely five feet tall and weighed ninety-six pounds in her thickly padded winter clothes. Her face was broad and flat, with deep, cheerful wrinkles radiating from small dark eyes. Her thinning gray-streaked hair was always in a bun, and because she was of peasant stock, her feet had never been bound. Wang Nai Nai doted on Ruth and was sometimes less than affectionate with Rosa. To the superstitious Chinese, it was a shame for the first child to have been born a girl instead of a boy.

A housekeeping staff was not the luxury one might suppose. The help bickered among themselves and needed constant and close supervision. On two occasions, the *amah* forgot to wash Ruth's hands before bed and the child awoke screaming and bleeding after a rat bit her finger. Scorpions scuttled into laundry baskets, and bedbugs and lice stowed away on freshly laundered linen and clothing. The house would soon have been infested had Mrs. Bell not stood guard at the door to inspect each article the servants carried in from the hospital laundry.

Despite all precautions, illness was accepted as the norm. Scarcely a month passed without one of the Bells contracting flu, a cold, a viral infection, or unexplainable low fever. Mrs. Bell was plagued by daily headaches that ran through her temples like a white-hot iron and sent her blindly retreating t her bedroom, where she lay with the curtains drawn until the throbbing an ringing in her ears subsided. Home treatments of narcotics and soaking h feet in hot mustard water offered little relief. Though their cause would never be known, it was suspected that the headaches were malarial and triggered by stress.

The threat of death by disease was very real to missionaries, and foreign graves were plenteous. In December 1924, the Bells were given their first son. Nelson Jr. died ten months later of amoebic dysentery. His mother slipped his small body into a fresh white baby dress and lined his coffin with white linen. He was buried in the brick-walled foreign cemetery in Qingjiang where many other American children had been laid before him. Missionaries formed a dark knot beneath the bleak winter sky as they stood by the tiny raw grave and sang the Doxology.

"Praise God from Whom all blessings flow . . . ," little Ruth sang at hip level beside her parents, her round face swallowed by a coarse woolen cap.

Dying for Christ was part of the Christian tradition. Ruth was familiar with believers who had been persecuted and murdered during the Boxer Rebellion. She knew other stories of Christians who had suffered for the glory of God. The martyrs were Ruth's childhood heroes. To become a martyr was to weave one's story into the fabric of legend, the highest and most noble expression of faith.

To little Ruth, God was an all-powerful, heavenly Father. She so dearly loved Him for His loving her that at the end of each day, just before she sank into a heavy sleep, she would kneel beside her bed and pray that He would let her die for Him. Rosa, the pragmatist, countered her sister's prayer with one of her own: "Please, God, don't listen to her!" The difference between the sisters' requests was significant. Ruth was imaginative and tended to romanticize. To her, a death by bullet or long knife was appealing. Rosa was more grounded and fantasized about being kidnapped by a band of bandits. They would carry her off to the black hillside, where she would proceed to convert them around the campfire.

Ruth was an unusually spiritual child, but behind brown curls and innocent eyes crouched a mischief maker who chased Rosa around the yard with dead bugs and, on one occasion, a pair of scissors. Spats were small typhoons, the sisters' tiny bodies disappearing into a whirling cloud of flailing feet, fists, and tangled hair. Rosa and Ruth shrieked and pummeled with such ferocity that the household help gathered round and placed bets.

Fights in the Bell household, however, were the exception rather than the rule. Tense moments were usually defused by Dr. Bell's sense of humor. He wasn't the stereotyped Calvinist who disapproved of fun, but believed in working and playing equally hard. In the yard, he built a fifteen-by-twenty-foot brick swimming pool that held five thousand gallons of well water. A source of pleasure, the pool enabled the family to endure unbearably hot summers, when most missionaries fled to the cool mountains of Kuling or to Japan. The Bells did not take vacations, but stayed at the hospital compound, working as usual and taking frequent dips.

Dr. Bell and his missionary colleagues built a clay tennis court on the compound and made a golf course by sinking soup cans into the lawn. Perhaps Dr. Bell's most curious creation was a corn popper he built from a trench mortar. When the pressure reached one hundred and eighty pounds and he pulled the trigger, popped kernels exploded into a cheesecloth bag. Liu Er, the gateman, was placed in charge of this contraption, and the first time he tried it, the blast knocked his chair over backward.

Rosa and Ruth's playmates were Hampton and William Talbot, sons of missionaries living half a mile from the Bells, and Sandy Yates, whose missionary parents lived in nearby Huaian. During the school year, Sandy stayed with the Bells, and several afternoons each week the children convened in one of the yards, where they played kick-the-can, croquet, and tag. They capered in the sandpile, on the swing, on the monkey bars, and in the tree house Dr. Bell had built high in the arms of a mulberry tree. Ruth played with dolls and hung over the edge of the tree house until her brain swam in her head like an egg yolk. She balanced on the six-inch-wide top of the compound wall and often followed it to school.

Like most children, Ruth was curious. One afternoon she decided to investigate a large nest high in the tallest tree in the yard. Without a thought she shinnied up the trunk and discovered a brook of buzzard fledglings. Scarcely had she peered at their hungry maws when the parents returned and began dive-bombing her. Ruth walked along the top of the wall the next day and was smashed on the top of her head by one of the putrid, grudge-bearing birds.

Ruth's greatest indulgence was her pets. Her menagerie included canaries, pigeons, ducks, turtles, and a goat. But her favorite was Tar Baby, a black mongrel quite attached to Ruth but notorious for grabbing Chinese women by their bound feet and dragging them off the walk. Ruth was perpetually rescuing guinea pigs from the hospital laboratory, picking up lost baby ducks, and discovering another flea-infested kitten to carry home and bathe in Lysol. In an early diary entry she wrote, "I found a baby mouse today, but it bit me and died."

When one of these pitiful creatures, whether mouse or bird, died, she would assemble Hampton, William, Sandy, and Rosa and hold an elaborate funeral complete with hymns and eulogies. The deceased was buried in Ruth's animal cemetery near the sandpile. She was so tenderhearted that she had a habit of picking up any dead animal she stumbled upon whether it was a pet or not. Her mother put an end to this when she noticed a rank smell coming from a closet one day and discovered a dead bird Ruth had forgotten in a sweater pocket.

Two years after the Bells' arrival in China, the Communists and Kuomintang, or Nationalists, had formed the first united front since the fall of the last Chinese dynasty. Chiang Kai-shek succeeded in unifying China, bringing many of the warlords under control and establishing himself in Nanjing, the capital of the republic. But in the spring of 1927, he turned on the Communists and ordered the assassinations of party members and labor organizers, precipitating a bloody civil war which would last until the late thirties.

The inland missions lay in the path of marching troops, and the missionaries kept their ears to their radios, listening for instructions from the American consul in Shanghai. In late spring, the order crackled repeatedly, "S.P.M. missionaries in Taizhou, Qingjiang . . . be on the banks of the Yangtze River tomorrow morning. The USS . . . number 245 will pick you up." The Bells sailed to the United States and settled in Waynesboro for several months, where a third daughter, Virginia, was born. From Waynesboro they moved to Holden, West Virginia, where Dr. Bell headed the surgical department at a local hospital. A year later the family moved to Houston, Texas, where Dr. Bell served as a lay minister at First Presbyterian Church.

China reopened to missionaries the following year, 1928, and the Bell family set sail on the SS *President Cleveland.* They arrived in Qingjiang on December 15 to discover that soldiers had ransacked the hospital and smashed the X-ray machine and other expensive equipment. They had stolen doorknobs, locks, electrical fixtures, and blankets and had slashed window screens that kept flies and other insects out of wards. Groups of soldiers had occupied the Bells' home but found little to steal, since shortly after the evacuation Chinese friends had hidden the family's belongings in the attic and removed the staircase, plastering over the entrance. Soldiers were puzzled by this strange American-style home that appeared to have an attic but no way to get to it. They periodically questioned Liu Er.

"I have worked here many years," the gateman would blandly reply, "and never heard anything about an attic."

Other missionaries were not so fortunate. Addison and Katherine Talbot discovered that all of their belongings had either been stolen or destroyed. Soldiers uprooted rosebushes and shrubbery in search of buried valuables, until the once opulent yard looked as if a giant mole had gone on a burrowing spree.

After several weeks of repolishing floors and whitewashing walls, the Bells' home was restored. Once again it was filled with the smells of baking bread and bubbling molasses candy and the sounds of the family singing hymns, accompanied by Mrs. Bell on the piano. Dr. Bell continued his hospital duties, and his wife worked in the women's clinic, recording names and symptoms before patients saw the doctors. She taught her daughters to read and write, and when the occasional missionary barrel of secondhand clothing was shipped over from the United States, she rummaged through it with gusto and set about ripping and reshaping fusty old-fashioned garments into dresses and suits.

In this setting Ruth began to define her world. Family was a buffer, a refuge. Beyond it, on the other side of the compound wall, was nothing but suffering and death. In this setting she began to discover her tastes. She admired the delicate beauty of the Orientals with their almond eyes, ebony hair, and graceful manner. She felt awkward and unattractive by comparison. Beauty was the fresh flowers and ancient edifices that sprang from the earth, or seemed to.

Ruth admired rich red lacquers made of pig's blood, and leathers, silks, satins, and the ornate calligraphy that she one day would pen. Wood was rare and old, and worn smooth, and she would always prefer flooring that had known a crowd and furniture that could tell a story. Ruth Bell would have been content to remain happily safe in her imaginative, warm little world, but the realities beyond the wall began to intrude.

3
CHAPTER

The Year of the Horse

Courtesy of Ruth Bell Graham Personal Collection

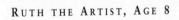

RUTH THE ARTIST, AGE 8

With children nestled close, parents warily eyed armed soldiers loitering on deck, "waiting for the first bullet to be shot."

—Dr. Nelson Bell, 1930

It was the summer of 1930, the year of the horse, which in Chinese mythology symbolizes wisdom. In the Qingjiang marketplace the pungent odor of ripe, raw meats and vegetables mingled with the savory smells of frying fish, cabbage, and garlic. Merchants hawked wares, and donkeys burdened with sacks of rice, pottery, and reeds clattered skittishly in the choked, narrow street. Peasants moved in a noisy throng, while beggars crusty with filth and disease watched slyly from the borders, like blackbirds along a fence, waiting for their next chance to extort a coin.

Nelson Bell had removed the isinglass flaps from his black Austin Healey before driving his family to town. The foreign car and its foreign devil driver crept ahead in a series of stops and starts, an ideal target for the wispy Chinese boy just yards from the driver's open window. The boy launched a mouthful of spit as the car lurched forward, and Ruth, perched innocently in the backseat, was splattered on her rosy right cheek. Horrified, she watched her father jam on the brake and spring from the car like a rabbit, the perpetrator darting through the crowd, his Western nemesis bounding after him. Snatched midflight, the boy was spanked soundly, in a rare moment when a missionary experienced justice, small though it was.

Misfortunes, injustices, and tragedies had struck the missionaries prior to 1930. But a flurry of shocks, seemingly random in their cruelty, would blow through the Bells' world as never before. Ruth, now ten, was old enough to understand each one in all its harsh detail.

The first shock was Gay and Ed Currie's second loss. Several years earlier their three-year-old daughter Lucy Calvin had died of botulism after wandering into the pantry and eating contaminated string beans. The Curries were missionaries in Haizhou, a hundred miles north of Qingjiang, and were the Bells' closest friends. Gay was a schoolteacher. Ed was a robust preacher, affectionately dubbed the "Wrestling Parson" during World War I, when he would challenge servicemen to the mat, stipulating that losers accompany him to the next church service.

The morning of November 24, 1930, household staff left the Curries' three-year-old son John Randolph unattended and he fell headlong into a caldron of boiling water. Moments later the scalded child died in his mother's arms. The Christians' response was again one of acceptance.

"So swiftly did his little spirit return unto God who gave it," missionary Jack Vinson wrote at the time, "it seems as tho' he were only running on eager, impetuous, hasty feet, at the Savior's call and springing into His waiting arms. . . . It's well with the lad. He is safe forever in Jesus' keeping."

In 1931 death would visit a young missionary couple in Qingjiang. He was a clergyman, attractive and gentle, his wife handsome, with porcelain skin, dark eyes, and long black hair. For ten years they lived on the compound with the Bells, spending many evenings together talking and reading aloud and playing Rook and Twenty Questions or listening to the grainy music of the Victrola. On the day of Ruth's birth the couple had held hands on the Bells' living room sofa, waiting until the first strangled cry rang through the house. In 1927, they were transferred a hundred miles south from Taizhou, where the dialect was different and they had no friends. The wife rationed her energy between four young children and the Chinese whose souls she longed to reach.

She sank deeper into the oblivion of exhaustion. There was no professional help for missionaries so far from home. Often, as she sat on her husband's lap, she spoke longingly of their furlough the following summer. It would be the first in seven years. One day, the Southern Presbyterian Executive Committee sent a cable that unjustly criticized missionary wives for not working hard enough. All field workers were informed that salaries were to be cut. Furloughs would have to be delayed another year due to the depression in America and a shortage of funds in the mission board's treasury. On October 26, at three o'clock in the morning, while her husband slept, the wife crept out to the frosty yard and cut her throat.

Missionaries did not publicize suicides. Silence and shame followed families through the years, children and grandchildren preferring names left unmentioned, as they have been here. To take one's own life was a senseless tragedy, not a martyrdom. Dr. Bell had another view and was unusually candid in discussing the tragedy with his family. He wrote the Executive Committee a blistering letter in response to their insensitive one.

Days later, bandits raided the town of Yang Jia Ji, and one of the field's most respected and popular missionaries, Jack Vinson, traveled there to check on his flock. The marauding band captured him and some three hundred Chinese. Still weak from a recent appendectomy, Vinson could not keep up with the other prisoners, and one of the bandits menacingly poked him with the barrel of a rifle.

"If you shoot me," Vinson simply said, "I'll go straight to heaven."

He was murdered, as were thirty-five Chinese. When Ed Currie retrieved his slain comrade, he found Vinson deposited on a makeshift bier inside a Buddhist temple. As Currie moved the body to wrap it in grass matting, the head rolled off. In America, wreaths might be hung on doors and periods of mourning observed, but life for the missionaries went on without pause no matter who died or how. God, they believed, took care of the dead. It was the missionaries' job to care for the living.

Ruth was shaken by the deaths but took her cue from her parents and accepted them as God's will. She would, however, have a more difficult time conceding to one of life's lesser intrusions. In 1930, Dr. Bell decided it was time to expose his daughters to more advanced schooling than they had been receiving in their mother's bedroom each morning. Prior to Ruth's tenth birthday, lessons in hygiene, spelling, arithmetic, reading, and geography had come from secondhand textbooks and dog-eared *National Geographic* magazines mailed from friends in the United States.

On June 8, the Bells set out for Shanghai to meet Lucy Fletcher, a young schoolteacher hired by the Foreign Mission Board in Nashville, Tennessee, to teach the missionary children. Ruth and her family sailed the hundred and twenty-five miles south to Zhenjiang on a launch infested with bedbugs, mosquitoes, fleas, and rats. With children nestled close, parents warily eyed armed soldiers loitering on deck, "waiting for the first bullet to be shot," Dr. Bell recounted in a letter to his mother.

From Zhenjiang they traveled by train to Shanghai, where Lucy Fletcher's steamer was berthed, and received word from the American consulate that the fall of the central government was imminent. All women and children were to evacuate North Jiangsu. Typically, Dr. Bell ignored the warning. He was well informed about the political situation in China but, like many of his colleagues, was not willing to admit that a Communist victory was possible.

"Communism," he acknowledged that summer, "is certainly growing and becoming more bold." But as for a takeover and the subsequent withdrawal of the missionaries, "Christ," he believed, "will surely return before that disaster."

Nor would he or many of his colleagues realize how menacing the Communists could be to Westerners until 1935, when Red soldiers on the Long March forced missionaries John and Betty Stam up a hill two hundred miles north of Qingjiang. The couple was stripped of padded clothing, their throats cut.

The threat of the government's impending fall passed quickly, and the Bells and their new teacher traveled back to Qingjiang. Lucy Fletcher was an attractive, dark-haired woman in her late twenties; she moved into a bedroom just below Ruth's, much to the child's dismay. Ruth resented this new source of authority and found Lucy's high-strung personality grating. Ruth would hate school. She just knew it. But her fears were soon dissolved by Lucy's warm, sisterly attentions. The new teacher became a confidante and mentor, and her students loved it when she read aloud *Borden of Yale, Huckleberry Finn*, and other classics. Lucy introduced the poetry of Edith Gilling Cherry and the works of Amy Carmichael, who would influence Ruth more than any other writer.

A skilled Bible teacher, Lucy inspired a love of and respect for the Scripture. Her methods were rigorous, the children required, for example, to summarize all fifty chapters of Genesis. Lucy offered five dollars to any student who could flawlessly recite from memory the Sermon on the Mount. After weeks of struggle, Ruth recited the three chapters, making only one error. She collected four dollars and fifty cents.

School filled Ruth's life with new adventure and took her beyond childhood boundaries. Each morning, shortly after eight o'clock, she, Rosa, Sandy Yates, and Lucy left the compound for the mile walk along the ancient twenty-foot-high mud wall. After centuries of erosion the wall was mounded and pitted by the wind, and battlements protruded like worn teeth in an old man's gums. The moat below was scattered with shallow puddles of scummy water, a popular spot for the disposing of dead infants.

Two pariah dogs the Bell children had named Gorgon and Mussolini ranged among grave mounds north of the wall, waiting for the small bodies occasionally seen facedown in the brackish moat water, not far from peasants rinsing rice and night-soil buckets. Local superstition dictated that if a child died before cutting his teeth he could not be buried lest evil spirits return to take a brother or sister. Bodies were shoved through small orifices in brick hutch-shaped baby tombs or were abandoned on grave mounds or in the moat. It was not unusual for sick or deformed infants to be left before they were dead.

As Ruth and Sandy walked with Lucy through the cold early morning air on October 17, 1932, they were halted midway on the wall by a peasant woman's cries of "Alive! Alive!" The woman motioned toward the moat where a baby boy lay in the mud at the edge of the water. Ruth recorded the event in a letter to Rosa, who was away at high school in Korea: "I scrambled down to where it lay and saw it breathe, then give a tiny cry, so I ran for Dr. Woods and then came back and Miss [Fletcher] went to hurry things up while I stood and fanned off the huge green flies that had settled on it. . . . Its eyes were opened and filled with pus so that all you could see was yellow. A few rags lying by were all it had and its tiny naked body was blue from cold."

The infant was bathed and fed in the mission hospital. Two days later, he died.

4

CHAPTER

Crumbling of the Wall

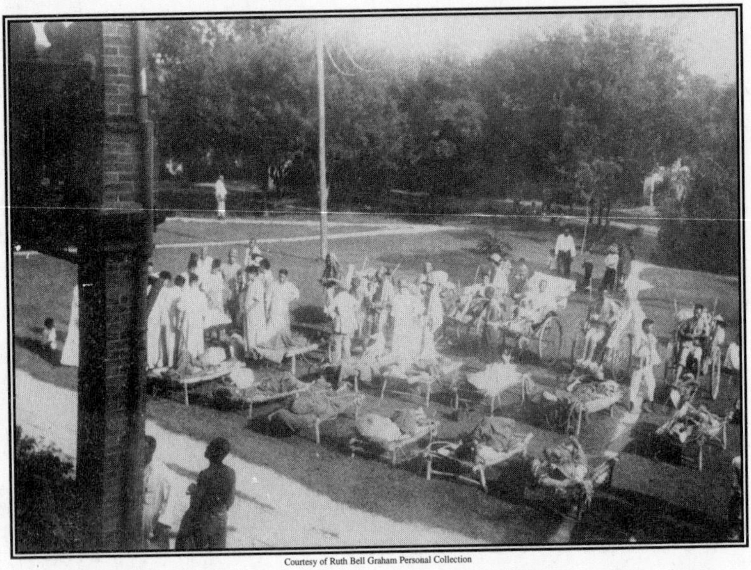

Courtesy of Ruth Bell Graham Personal Collection

War Wounded at Dr. Bell's Hospital

Ruth has real artistic talent. For a long time we knew she was clever with drawing but recently she shows remarkable talent. . . . But it has never been a talent I have especially desired for a child of mine.

—*Dr. Nelson Bell, 1930*

By age twelve, Ruth had ceased any coveting of martyrdom and dreamed of being a missionary. She admired the goodness and courage of those she knew and was moved by kindness. The missionaries were kind to all, especially to the poor, the sad, and the suffering. Ruth would become a spinster missionary to the nomads in Tibet, she decided. It was a rather bleak future to cast for a girl whose mind was filled with bright, imaginative particles just beginning to coalesce.

Each day at dusk, Ruth would slip away to her favorite nook in the house, her tiny attic bedroom, with its doorway so low that she had to stoop to enter. A small window facing west overlooked the city's worn earthen ramparts stretching across the earth like a scar. Grave mounds erupted from the fields like lesions, creating a barren vista broken infrequently by lone herdsmen grazing sheep and goats. As night fell, Ruth watched shadows roll in a giant wave over the wall, across the fields, and beyond the evergreen-bordered priests' graves. The setting sun ignited roofs of a distant village and turned the horizon crimson, as Ruth watched and imagined.

At a young age, she had begun to demonstrate an original artistic leaning strongly tinged with Gothic elements and absurd humor. She sketched cartoon figures and fantasy creatures and painted flowers, landscapes, and religious scenes. Nature took on special meaning, and life of all kinds became symbolic of greater truths. Her pragmatic father took a dim view of these budding abilities.

"Ruth," he wrote his mother, "has real artistic talent. For a long time we knew she was clever with drawing but recently she shows remarkable talent. . . . But it has never been a talent I have especially desired for a child of mine." He failed to see how his daughter's creativity would aid her in Christian service. Mrs. Bell, however, was more sympathetic to Ruth's romantic and sentimental nature. They were traits indigenous to Leftwich blood, and it was probably from Mrs. Bell's ancestors that Ruth also inherited her hypersensitivity. She was a cuddly, dependent child who at age thirteen had a morbid fear of leaving home for the first time.

Rosa had sailed away in 1932 for Pyeng Yang Foreign School, fifteen hundred miles from Qingjiang, in Pyongyang, in what would later become North Korea. It would have been far more convenient had the Bells sent their children to Shanghai American School, as many missionaries had. But the Bells preferred the curriculum of Pyeng Yang, a Christian school of a hundred and forty students, where academics were rigorous and the Bible was acknowledged as the authoritative word of God.

Ruth's dread of going away was made worse by a sudden awkward stage that could not begin to hint at her eventual physical splendor. At thirteen, she was plump and gap-toothed and wore glasses. She fastened her hair in a barrette, and the round, black frames hiding her eyes looked like something a prankster might have penciled in. Her dowdy appearance might have been ignored had she been a scholar. But she was no more a bookworm than was her German shepherd, Prinz, and she had not been from the first moment Mrs. Bell had begun tutoring her in the bedroom and accused her of being "somewhat scatter-brained."

In fact, Ruth was quite intelligent, though it was probably true that she had more marbles in her creative pocket than she had in her mathematical one, and they did tend to bounce about, clatter, and roll to all corners, as her voracious curiosity rapidly shifted from one topic to another. Her intelligence was more intuitive than analytical, and her lack of academic prowess didn't make the notion of leaving home for Pyeng Yang any more palatable. It probably wasn't coincidental that two weeks before she was to set sail from China she was stricken with a high, tenacious fever.

On September 2, the Bells and Lucy Fletcher accompanied Rosa, Ruth, Hampton and William Talbot, and missionary friend Sophie Montgomery to Shanghai, where they spent the night in the missionary home at 4 Quinsan Road. The Victorian brick building, in the city's International Settlement, was a boardinghouse run by Edith Spurling and her two English spinster assistants.

Missionaries often stayed here while traveling through the city. That hot, sticky night, Ruth lay awake on top of tangled sheets, tears flowing as she begged God to let her die before morning.

Early the next day the Bell sisters and friends boarded the *Nagasaki Maru*, and from the rail Ruth watched her parents diminish on the receding quay as the ship sailed down the Huangpu River to the East China Sea. Hours later they crossed into the Yellow Sea, where a typhoon swept up the steamer as though it were a toy, buffeting it with fifty-foot waves. From water-streaked portholes Ruth watched heaving waves crash over the lugsails of a junk a hundred yards away. Seasickness dulled her fear of the storm and the ache of separation. When the water once again was still, she retreated into silence, burying herself in sadness.

In Nagasaki the young travelers boarded a train. Merchants hawked outside their car, advertising *"Bento! Bento!"* Ruth and friends opened the window to exchange coins for wooden boxes containing chopsticks, white rice, and Japanese pickles. The moon was round and low like a ripe fruit, its luminance settling over the landscape like pollen. The train lumbered a hundred miles northeast where the Sea of Japan seeped inland to form misty bays flecked with shadowy fishing boats.

In Moji, boa constrictors coiled around half-naked men, musicians played, and laughing faces wavered in torchlight as the city celebrated its harvest festival. The young Americans boarded a ferry in Shimonoseki and sailed across the Strait of Korea to Pusan, to get on another train, their exotic and uneasy pilgrimage moving on. Muted, straw-roofed Korean villages and jagged mountains streamed past Ruth's window, and she drew the curtain around her sleeping shelf.

Each night that fall she covered her head with her pillow because she did not want her two roommates to hear her cry in the Spartan gray brick dormitory that seemed like hell. She wrote her parents three times a week, begging them to let her come home. Her long letters ranged from the pathetic to the desperate, including a six-foot-long Japanese scroll filled with her ornate script and morose pondering. Word of her unhappiness reached the school's administration. One day she was summoned to the office of headmaster R. O. "Pops" Reiner, who a decade later would be captured by the Japanese, strung up by his thumbs, and given the water treatment.

Reiner motioned for this rather awkward-looking and shy young lady to be seated. He wanted to know if it was true that she was homesick.

"Yes, sir," she replied sincerely. "And I've lost weight too."

"How much did you weigh when you arrived here?" he asked, studying her thoughtfully.

"One hundred and thirty-three pounds, sir."

"I see," he said. "And how much do you weigh now?"

"One hundred and twenty-nine pounds, sir."

"I see." His eyes sparkled behind his glasses, but he was too kind to laugh.

The unhappy letters home continued, and finally, on October 13, Dr. Bell wrote Mabel Axworthy, the young woman in charge of the primary grades:

> [Ruth's] letters have not been typical of a normal homesickness as much as a feeling aggravated by introspection and failure to get out with the other children properly.... We feel she has been staying in her room too much; not only has she written these long letters to us, but she has also written long letters to other members of the station. They are really exceptional in their descriptive character, but they take time she should be spending either in study, or in play.... We feel Ruth has a slight tendency to revel in the sad side of things, letting her religion (which is exceedingly real and precious to her) take a slightly morbid turn.

Ruth's concept of eternity was real and wonderful, and she tended to let her mind drift that way when she was homesick and tired or surrounded by unpleasantness in general. "Some people," her father frequently remarked, "are so heavenly minded that they're no earthly good." One day, Ruth and a friend were ironing, and Ruth exclaimed, "Oh, just think, the end of the world may come soon and then we will be so happy!" The friend, somewhat weary of Ruth's fantasizing about Heaven, blurted, "Oh, you Bell girls surely are stuck on the end of the world!"

When Miss Axworthy received Dr. Bell's letter, she asked Ruth to mother the eighth graders. Soon Ruth was so busy looking after them that she forgot herself. It was a remedy that would become habit, and one she would frequently prescribe to others in the future. Her homesickness subsided and her wish for the end of the world was, once again, tucked back into its mental cupboard. This did not mean that she wanted to stay in school. In December she opened her final offensive by announcing to her father that she had been praying and was convinced that it was God's will for her to come home.

"Well," he replied firmly, "your mother and I have been praying too and that's not the answer we got."

Finally, she surrendered to her fate and found, before long, that she was actually enjoying herself. One year she was elected class president. She became the cartoonist and poet for *The Kulsi*, the school yearbook. A prankster, she was not above stuffing a pair of hose and placing shoes on the feet, and leaving this hanging out from underneath the dorm mother's bed. Ruth was known to rub shoe polish on the back of doorknobs and model snakes of clay and coil them in shadowy corners.

After her junior year, the Bells were furloughed to the United States. They rented a stone house in Montreat, North Carolina, eighteen miles east of Asheville. Rosa, who had contracted tuberculosis the year before and dropped out of Pyeng Yang, began treatments at a nearby sanatorium. She and Ruth finished their senior year of high school at Montreat, graduating in the spring of 1936, and Rosa, the beloved older sister, left for Wheaton College, twenty-five miles west of Chicago. Ruth was barely sixteen when she returned to Korea for the year of study. Her parents believed she was too young for advanced American education.

5

CHAPTER

War

Courtesy of Ruth Bell Graham Personal Collection

RUTH AT 17

I pray constantly that God will help us bear the testimony and witness we should. A faith and confidence exhibited only in times of peace does not amount to much.

—Nelson Bell, 1937

Throughout the sweltering summer of 1937, Virginia Bell sewed six hours daily. Stacks of print skirts and dresses grew with the threat of war.

Since the late nineteenth century the Chinese had been embittered by Japan's expansion into Manchuria, the northeast region of China, with three provinces and more than half a million square miles of farmland, forests, and mountains rich in coal, iron ore, gold, lead, and copper. By the early thirties, Japan's incursions were rapidly escalating. In March 1932, the Kwantung Army completed the occupation of Manchuria, creating the puppet state of Manchukuo, which became an industrial and military base for Japan's expansion into Asia. The aggression would culminate in the bombing of Pearl Harbor.

On July 7, 1937, the Japanese attacked Chinese troops at the Marco Polo Bridge (Lu Gou Qiao) near Beijing, beginning the occupation of northern China. That same summer, Chinese Communists and Nationalists ended their own civil war and united against Japan in an attempt to end the violation of Chinese territory.

Fall arrived on August 8, according to the lunar calendar, and the cloud-spotted, deep blue sky shone like Ming porcelain. The sun was hot, but a steady breeze cooled the compound, rustling like rain through mulberry trees and weeping willows. Mrs. Bell was forty-five now. Her hair was graying, her figure matronly, and the strain of work and daily headaches had begun to show in her face. She had spent the summer working on a new wardrobe for Ruth, who was to board the *Empress of Asia* on August 19 and sail to Vancouver.

From there Ruth was to travel by train to Wheaton, Illinois, where she would begin her freshman year of college. Rosa was spending the summer in Waynesboro with her grandmother, reveling in being away from home. She had written cheery letters to her family about college life, and if these observations were supposed to encourage Ruth, they did not.

"Ruth," her mother wrote, "is a precious child and still a child and going home will be hard for her. It is certainly the one hard thing missionaries have to do, have their children so far away during these important years."

Missionaries could never be certain how their children would fare once they left compounds for America, where they would fall in love and choose careers. In the West, evil was more difficult to define than it was in the Orient, where the fruits of sin were the horrors of infanticide, spiritism, robbery, and murder. As the Bells had done when they chose a high school, they had picked a college where the Bible was respected as the authoritative word of God. Dancing, smoking, and drinking alcoholic beverages were forbidden at Wheaton.

Ruth was not interested in higher learning, for she had already planned her future. Ruth Bell would spend her life in the arid Himalaya mountains of Tibet, the Roof of the Globe. She would never marry. She would need a utilitarian knowledge of Tibetan and the Bible, and she certainly didn't need to sail halfway around the world for that. Her parents smiled at such talk.

At seventeen, Ruth had shed her adolescent awkwardness. The gap between her front teeth had disappeared, as had her chubbiness and her glasses. At five foot five, she was slender, shapely, and graceful. Her nose was chiseled, her forehead broad and high, and her hazel eyes changed depth and shade with every shadow and light. When she laughed, which was often, they were flecked with gold. In more somber moods they hinted of amber. Never much for premeditation or analyzing after the fact, she acted on impulse more often than reason. Ruth was unusually kind. She was prone to fill the voids in other people's lives, and not think about her own. She did not seem to notice the fawning attentions of young men and throughout her life would remain oddly unaware of a physical beauty that would rather startle people when she walked into a room.

While Ruth and her mother made the final preparations for college, Dr. Bell prepared for war. He stockpiled a six-month supply of kerosene, fuel oil, and gasoline. Sugar, flour, and vegetables were plentiful, but the family would have to do without butter. Thirteen-by-eighteen-foot American flags were painted on the roofs of the hospital and their home, and the Stars and Stripes waved from a flagpole. Ordinarily, the missionaries did not flaunt their foreignness, but Dr. Bell was determined that there would be no "accidental" bombings of the mission compound. The boxy RCA Victor radio became the family's focus, and throughout each day Dr. Bell slipped on the headphones and fidgeted with dials as he fished news from deep static.

On Friday, August 13, the day Ruth's baggage was to be sent ahead by launch to Zhenjiang, Chiang Kai-shek sent his best German-trained units to Shanghai where Japanese were garrisoned. The ensuing battle was savage. Chinese dignity and hostility were no match for Japanese weapons, and before the day was spent the city fell. Planes and pilots were assigned to the small airfield near the Qingjiang mission. Chinese began fleeing the larger cities by the thousands, seeking asylum in the less important ones or in the countryside. Launches hovered offshore where refugees could not overwhelm them.

Dr. Bell canceled Ruth's travel plans, made new ones, and then canceled again. "She is jubilant over the prospect of staying," her mother wrote the next day. "There is nothing left for *us* to *decide*. It is just impossible to go. We feel like we are on holiday. . . . We are pretty well blocked-in, but feel we are as safe here as anywhere."

While Chinese planes raided Japanese troops in Shanghai, a typhoon roared inland from the Yellow Sea. Bewildered Chinese huddled in doorways and alleys as nature and man ravaged them. Inland, the missionaries and their converts registered no fear. One Sunday morning the Bells sat in church as the bell outside began clanging madly, announcing an air raid. Three hundred and fifty members of the congregation remained seated, and the service continued. In villages where foreigners were fleeing, the missionaries took the fourth commandment literally and rested on the Sabbath.

On August 14, as Mrs. Bell sat in the living room monitoring the radio, the U.S. consul began urging all foreigners to leave the inland cities. More than two hundred Europeans and several Americans and missionaries had been killed days earlier when a Chinese plane accidentally bombed a Chinese settlement in Shanghai. On Monday, August 16, the Japanese raided Nanjing twice and bombed Yangzhou, a hundred miles south of Qingjiang. The local Chinese panicked. In anticipation of air raids, they dug deep trenches. On foot with low-caliber rifles, they attacked planes.

The fighting drew closer, and on Tuesday, August 17, as the Bells were eating supper, three Japanese planes attacked the Qingjiang airfield. Two bombs landed near the runway but did little damage. A third landed in an open field and killed a cow; and a fourth bomb did not explode. The Chinese were terrified. Dozens of them pitched belongings over the compound wall and begged for sanctuary inside the hospital and other mission buildings.

"Every time we leave the compound," Mrs. Bell wrote, "they think we're evacuating. Just our being here means a lot to their peace of mind."

On August 19, white ensigns fluttered from tugs pulling crowded barges down the Huangpu River to awaiting steamers. It was the day Ruth was to have sailed from China, had it been a different world. Nine hundred refugees jammed the *Empress of Asia*, and it left Shanghai without her. "Prospects for college that fall," she wrote, "faded gloriously out of sight." Her relief would not last long.

September 1, the American ambassador urged the Bells and colleagues Jimmy and Sophie Graham to leave immediately for the United States. The Grahams had been in the China mission field for forty-three years, and a recent stroke had left Sophie partly paralyzed. But neither sickness nor danger would provoke them to heed the ambassador's warning. The Bells were of the same mind. "We don't feel any urge from the Lord," Mrs. Bell wrote at the time. Five days later, the American consul general wired the Bells: "Urgent: Americans advised make plans proceed Haizhou from where evacuation about September 20 will be by Naval vessel probably to Shanghai telegraph immediately Consulate Shanghai or Embassy."

The next day, Dr. Bell wired back: "Message received please wire whether later evacuation possible. Auto roads Haizhou under water [Sophie] Graham invalid travel difficult, local conditions normal. Can you assure us that in complying with your telegram we will proceed either Shanghai Qingdao? Some have financial and mission responsibilities which make this imperative. How much baggage permitted each individual?"

On September 8, a voice crackled over the radio, addressing the "stubborn missionaries and leader," warning the foreigners that they had been invited for the last time to leave. The Bells began packing their belongings and storing boxes in the attic. On September 17, at dawn, they piled baggage on the porch and Ruth stood sentry, eyeing the dozen rickshaw coolies milling in the yard. Inside the bare house, the Bells and their domestic help sang "God Be with You till We Meet Again," waiting for Jimmy and Sophie Graham to arrive.

The small group would travel north on the Grand Canal by launch, then transfer to a houseboat in Suqian, and take a train to Haizhou, where an American destroyer would be waiting. From there the Bells and Grahams were to sail to Qingdao, a hundred and ten miles north of Shanghai. Japan had too many commercial and industrial interests in Qingdao to bomb it, and many missionaries already had sought refuge there.

Coolies loaded rickshaws. They picked up poles and trotted along the narrow street to the canal, powerful calf muscles knotting like fists with each slap of bare feet. Houseboats, barges, and sampans crowded the muddy water, and women washed clothing as children bathed with ducks and geese. Chinese friends had gathered on the shore to say good-bye and help the missionaries board. Ruth stared out of her open cabin window at coolies passing through the small water gate in the ancient city wall. They dipped buckets into the canal and left with dripping loads swinging perilously on *bian dans*. High above the city's tiled roofs, buzzards glided in a clear sky, and with a sharp blast of a whistle, the barge eased forward. A warm breeze washed through the cabin as friends on the shore disappeared around a bend.

At two o'clock the next morning, the Bells and Grahams transferred to a houseboat, owned and piloted by a Chinese family who lived on the aft deck. The bow was cluttered with spare oars, pots, shoes, and other belongings wedged into the thatch of the passengers' shelter or fastened to the boat. A low-burning oil lantern gently bobbed from a post. Ruth unrolled her blanket and settled on the dusty wooden floor between her sister Virginia and Sophie Graham's servant girl Gwei Yin. A soft wind puffed the boat upriver while Ruth lay half asleep, listening to groaning wood and water lipping. Hours later, at dawn, the sun rose through willows lining the shore.

Saturday afternoon, September 18, the group docked one mile from the Longhai Railroad, ten minutes after the departure of the 2:20 train they were scheduled to board. From a mud hut telegraph office in the tiny village of Yuin Ho, Dr. Bell sent a wire and was instructed to spend another night in the houseboat and take the next morning's train to Haizhou, where another band of withdrawing missionaries would wait for them. The next morning, the Bells and Grahams reached the station by 8:30, but this time it was the train that was late, owing to an air raid.

They boarded at 10:30, and less than ten miles from Haizhou were again delayed when a warning sounded. Twelve Japanese bombers returning for a raid in Xuzhou-fu were fast approaching. Passengers dove from cars and hid in fields as the ominous droning sounded on the horizon. The missionaries sat quietly in train cars, heads bowed, as a gray sea of clouds high above them slowly and heavily settled over the rails, shrouding the creaking locomotive and those cringing in the fields. Bombers roared blindly overhead and were gone. "The Lord," Mrs. Bell recorded, "is not unmindful of His own."

American consular authorities had alerted the Japanese of the missionaries' evacuation and had been assured of cooperation. Obviously, Japan's idea of what this meant wasn't exactly what the Americans had in mind. The Bells and Grahams when they reached Haizhou crouched in a dugout, wondering where the train was, as the city was being shaken by the most severe bombings of the war. Dr. Bell did not believe that the attacks were coincidental.

"That demonstration in Haizhou Sunday," he wrote soon after, "was evidently put on for our benefit. . . . Lovely cooperation, wasn't it?"

The train arrived in Haizhou late that afternoon and at 8:00 P.M. Ruth and her fellow travelers boarded a tugboat in the Haizhou harbor for the four-mile sail to the destroyer. The sky was clear, and a full moon followed them out to sea. Ruth stood on deck watching the lit-up American ship get bigger as the tug got closer. Invisible Chinese eyes spied from military posts in black crags on either side of the bay. The tug's pilot cut the engines and steered alongside the destroyer, and a narrow wooden footway was secured with rope.

Cresting waves jerked the two vessels in and out like a berserk accordionist. The gangplank slammed against the tug as the ships rolled together and apart, opening a maw of black churning water between them. Chinese lifted Sophie Graham and perilously made their way across the straining plank while American sailors reached for her. Faces were tense, garments drenched with spray, as men braced beneath the dead weight of a woman almost crippled. Fear was palpable, when, quite suddenly, the sea got quiet, "as if an immense hand had stilled the water and held the ropes," Ruth wrote at the time. Sophie Graham was passed from one set of strong hands to another. The instant she was safely aboard, water and wind unleashed their fury again.

The destroyer had traveled less than a mile when nine Japanese warships, with external lights extinguished, materialized in the night. The dark, silent vessels circled, and slowly went on their way again, without explanation, it seemed. The Yellow Sea was as smooth as a millpond, and the American ship plowed ahead at thirty knots, reaching Qingdao at 1:30 A.M. Women and children were not allowed to spend the night on board, and naval boats intercepted the small party and carried them ashore. By 3:00 A.M. the Bells had settled into friends' cottages on the Jiaozhou Bay. They had arrived with their radio, bedding, summer clothing, and table silver.

From Qingdao, travel to the United States was possible. Dr. Bell booked Ruth on the USS *Chaumont* to sail October 22 to Kobe, Japan. "My, but it is hard to see her leave," her mother wrote. "She is timid and would far rather stay here." The Friday morning of Ruth's departure, she and a missionary friend traveling with her were awake by 5:30 and on the quay by 7:00. Ruth paid a steward five dollars for embarkation and hugged her family good-bye. It would take six days to cross the Yellow Sea and sweep around the southern tip of Korea toward Kobe.

Though Ruth did not want to leave, she was at least comforted that her family was safe in Qingdao. She could not know that in less than three weeks, while she was yet aboard ship, they would return to Qingjiang, unable to stay away from friends and responsibilities any longer. The Bells found conditions in Qingjiang much worse than they had left them. Emboldened Japanese pilots had begun firing machine guns at the hospital to frighten the staff, and bombings had become closer and more frequent. It seemed the brief evacuation had served no purpose beyond getting Ruth out of China. As cold sea waters tumbled together, covering a swath left by her ship, the connection between Ruth and her birthplace vanished, and she drew up a rather peculiar list for a confirmed spinster:

If I marry:

He must be so tall when he is on his knees, as one has said, he reaches all the way to Heaven.

His shoulders must be broad enough to bear the burden of a family.

His lips must be strong enough to smile, firm enough to say no, and tender enough to kiss.

Love must be so deep that it takes its stand in Christ and so wide that it takes the whole lost world in.

He must be active enough to save souls.

He must be big enough to be gentle and great enough to be thoughtful.

His arms must be strong enough to carry a little child.

In Japan, Ruth boarded the SS *President McKinley* for Seattle. She settled into steerage, directly behind a massive propeller where the ship's metal hull was the only buffer between her and what seemed a fathomless sea. During her nineteen-day passage, two people would jump overboard. The first suicide occurred early in the voyage, on a cold evening shortly before midnight, and deeply affected Ruth.

By her account, a young American wrapped in a heavy overcoat, and in the throes of clinical depression, sat on deck smoking. He got up to crush the cigarette butt beneath his heel, and before his medical attendant could intervene, his patient hurled himself over the rail, disappearing into tumbling waves. Minutes later, the ship's engines abruptly died, and the sudden silence awakened Ruth. She sat up and peered through the porthole, shivering in the raw air seeping around it. Beyond, the dark sea and starless sky were one, and a long needle of light probed the water's surface as a lifeboat filled with twelve sailors searched for the man who had jumped minutes earlier. A sense of foreboding settled over Ruth as she watched their progress. The atmosphere became sinister.

Fifteen feet below her "lay a long rope curling and twisting in the water like some phantom snake," she recorded at the time. "A chill crept down my spine." She slipped her coat over her gown and hurried to the deck, where a small group of passengers had gathered along the rail. They watched the lifeboat rise and fall while "a wind laughed through the mast tops," Ruth wrote. "Laughed to see man battle with the elements over one small human body. Laughed at his helplessness." Her aroused imagination teased her eyes.

Several times she thought she saw a body or parts of a body bobbing in the wake. She thought she heard muffled human cries of distress rising above the wind and the wash. After a fruitless search, the lifeboat was hoisted aboard, and Ruth, cold in the dank, salty air, returned to her bunk.

When she viewed events through her faith, nature became symbolic of eternal truths. It was a tool used by God to reveal glory and love. The blanket of clouds had shielded the train from the vision of the Japanese pilots. The sea had become still when the sailors carried Sophie Graham over the gangplank. Ruth's description of the suicide, in contrast, portrayed a savageness in nature that reduced people to faceless pawns in a random universe.

To her, that was the world without spirituality, without the meaning implied by God's existence and subsequent participation in human lives. Separation from God was the heathenism outside the compound wall. It was the hell of being alone in the universe with oneself. Without a Creator, all creation was heartless. The world was formless, a void, with darkness upon the face of the deep.

6

CHAPTER

An Innocent Abroad

Courtesy of Ruth Bell Graham Personal Collection

RUTH, SENIOR YEAR AT WHEATON

There was a certain other-worldliness about her.

—*Harold Lindsell*

Ruth's life in America began in the Chicago train station, where she was a solitary stillness amid shuffling shoe leather, and hissing decompressed air, and clanking steel. Bundled in a black wool coat, she was surrounded by battered bags and trunks. Her worldly goods included hand-me-downs reshaped by her mother, three scarves Ruth had made herself (one pink, one blue, and one white), a small collection of favorite books, and a dog-eared King James Bible. She arrived on the Wheaton College campus in size seven saddle shoes that bled chalky white polish whenever it rained, her dignity slightly wounded by the freshman orange and green "dink" planted on her head. She had been in this strange new world no more than a month when she almost got kicked out.

Several male upperclassmen had vied for Ruth Bell's attention since the day they spotted the young beauty. Twice they whisked her into Chicago for dinners and ice shows. She was the only freshman on these double dates, and on both occasions her escorts chose to ignore her tiresome 10:30 curfew. Both times, it was after midnight when she was deposited in front of the tightly locked Williston Hall, a peculiar pile of red brick Gothic Revivalism that towered over the sloping lawn and served as the student cafeteria and women's dormitory. Ruth's first-floor room was the last one on the west end, just close enough to the ground for her to rustle behind boxwoods and, with a boost from her date, crawl over the sill.

On her second Friday night of crime, one of Ruth's friends dropped by her room for a visit and found she wasn't there, or anywhere, it seemed. A search of the sign-out book in the lobby revealed that Ruth had left no clue as to her whereabouts. A verbal alarm rang through the corridors, finally reaching the ears of the elderly dorm mother, who weeks earlier had portentously advised one of Ruth's dates, "She's so heavenly looking she won't last long on this earth." The dorm mother scowled through pince-nez, periodically scanning the floors. Sometime after midnight, Ruth appeared in the hallway, toothbrush in hand, heading toward the bathroom. She was quickly intercepted.

"Where have you been and how did you get in?" the dorm mother demanded.

"I've been on a date and I climbed through my window," Ruth innocently said.

She was expeditiously given an appointment with the dean of students.

Ruth lived by a strict but simple moral code. During her childhood she had never been handed a book of regulations containing dozens of petty sins. The original Big Ten were enough. She had just come from a world of air raid bells, Japanese bombers, and bandits. This new threat called curfew failed to impress her. She had never given the Wheaton College handbook a glance. She was not inclined to burden people with her concerns, and was less inclined to like it when people wished to be burdened with them. Ruth maneuvered in her own way, and along her own routes, and this wasn't always appreciated, as she was soon to find out from Dr. Wallace Emerson, a psychology professor and the rather stern dean.

His office was in Blanchard Hall, an imposing fortress of towers and battlements built of limestone covered with ivy. In his chambers, next to the president's office on the second floor, Emerson sat behind a sturdy oak desk facing a wall of books. Wire spectacles perched on his nose, and a thin mustache and goatee framed an unsmiling mouth. Ruth demurely seated herself at a prudent distance.

"Anybody has the right to think anything he wants of you," he coldly announced.

Ruth's gaze never wavered during his avalanche of harsh words, her throat tight with tears she did not cry. She would not break, and he assumed she did not care, so he admonished her for what seemed an eternity. Finally, he was silent, his face impassive as he looked at this young woman whose demeanor baffled him.

"You have disgraced the school," he said without emotion. "You have disgraced your parents. You have disgraced yourself. You can choose between expulsion for a semester or an indefinite campusing."

Returning to China was impossible and Ruth had no intention of moving to Waynesboro. What would she say to Grandmother Bell? How would she explain?

"I prefer to be campused, sir," Ruth remarked in a steady voice.

He nodded and released her. Hurrying to the infirmary where Rosa was in bed with pleurisy, Ruth shut the door and began to sob. Terribly upset, she related the story until a visitor's knocks sent her into the closet because she did not want anyone to see her cry. Ruth, who had never let a young man hold her hand, much less kiss her, had never imagined before this incident that she might appear to be something she wasn't. She felt dirty. She perceived herself the victim of injustice. The men responsible for returning her to campus after curfew had gone unpunished. The thought that she had disgraced her parents filled her with despair, for that was something she "would rather die than do," she wrote at the time.

Ruth was not allowed to date or to leave the school grounds, restrictions that were perhaps more troublesome for Harold Lindsell than they were for her. The twenty-four-year-old senior was a lanky, brown-eyed blond with a fondness for dapper pinstripe and double-breasted suits. He was considered the campus gentleman-scholar and was, by chance, well acquainted with Rosa, who had told him all about her younger sister. Since September, Lindsell had eagerly awaited Ruth's arrival. On the November afternoon when he first spotted her in the cafeteria, there had been no doubt who she was. Without delay he headed for the infirmary, deducing that if he visited Rosa long enough, he was bound to meet her sister.

More than an hour passed before Ruth appeared. Lindsell had not taken off his camel's hair coat, as if to imply he could stay only a minute. Days later, he telephoned to ask if she would accompany him to the Friday night Literary Society meeting. She seemed a bit flustered. He was seven years her senior, and she already had a date. She did not want to say no and hurt Lindsell's feelings, and, to her horror, she heard herself accept. On a brisk Friday night in November he escorted her to the meeting.

"I thought she acted a little strange," Lindsell later recalled. "It turned out I'd sat her next to the boy who'd asked her out to the same thing."

Lindsell began escorting Ruth to classes and enrolled in one of her sketching courses, though he wasn't remotely artistic. He became her confidant, and his attention flattered her and rebuilt her recently shattered self-esteem. He became her mentor, and this was most helpful, for Ruth was unabashedly ignorant of American innuendo and double meanings. Her parents had never discussed sex with her, and she later claimed to have "learned the facts of life from the Bible." Her speech rivaled Mrs. Malaprop's, her naiveté as pure as distilled water.

On one occasion, Lindsell asked what the Bells ate for Thanksgiving dinner in China. "Bastards," Ruth replied, meaning bustards. When she attended her first American wedding, Lindsell was an usher and offered her his arm at the door. "Oh, Harold!" she laughed as she shoved it away.

By the spring of 1938 the Wheaton faculty realized that Ruth's infractions were committed out of ignorance, not wickedness. They lifted her sentence, much to the relief of the Bells, who had remained steadfast in their trust of her. By this time, communication between them and their daughters in America was erratic. The Japanese were censoring mail in Shanghai, and letters sometimes took more than two months to reach the mission station.

Throughout northern and central China the land was rent with zigzagged trenches. Soldiers had seized railroads, burned villages, and smashed bridges. Tanks lumbered over rutted roads, white smoke puffing from machine guns as ill-equipped Chinese infantrymen were slaughtered. The Bells' son Clayton and daughter Virginia were virtually the only American missionary children left in the interior. Their parents firmly believed that nothing would happen to them without God's sanction.

Flags with the Rising Sun floated over cities around Qingjiang. Japanese bombers sheared the hospital's red tin roof, snapping the American flag to attention in their wake. Waiting areas, outpatient clinics, and some three hundred and fifty beds overflowed with Chinese who had been torn by bullets and shrapnel and crushed by falling roofs. Many people had lost limbs and were charred and punctured by rocks and wooden splinters, as Japanese anti-American sentiments became overt.

In the past, Nelson Bell had placated local platoon leaders by inviting them on personal tours of the hospital facilities. The American surgeon had served them tea and sweets, as he indicated with an almost Oriental deference that inside the compound he, not the military, was in command. Such courtesies, he knew, could work but so long. Many of his colleagues were receiving the treatment that he felt sure was soon to come his way.

"The destruction of life and property [is] sweeping over us," he wrote. "The list of Americans who have had their faces jabbed and slapped by the Japanese is a long one and getting longer. The homes, schools, and hospitals of American missions which have been looted and destroyed by Japanese already run into the hundreds."

While conditions in China worsened, Ruth began fighting a battle of her own. In the spring of 1938 she was visited by a young man who had attended high school in Korea with her. Now a student at the University of Chicago, he had abandoned the Christian faith of his childhood and challenged her to do likewise. It could be the best thing that ever happened to you, he suggested. It would be her liberation, he urged, and doubts began to sift and shape.

Ruth gave much thought to all she had been taught. After much debate, she decided she had no trouble accepting the existence of a Supreme Creator, a Universal Truth, a supernatural unifying force. The earth was too ordered, she thought. But what about the Bible? How could she be so sure its words were true? What if Jesus Christ was nothing more than a brilliant philosopher, a Socrates of sorts?

"He was either God or a liar or crazy," Ruth announced to Lindsell one day.

He suggested that she accompany him to the home of a certain seasoned Bible professor. "Perhaps he could pray with you," he added hopefully.

"I don't want prayers," Ruth replied. "I want proof."

She and Lindsell argued for weeks.

"How do you account for the sin and sickness in the world?" she challenged him. "How do you know that what the Bible says is true? Is there any proof?"

She argued with her friends, or with anyone who would let her, until classmates wanted to flee when they saw Ruth Bell headed their way.

"I can't be sure that God loves me, for who am I amongst so many?" she dejectedly said to Lindsell one afternoon, toward the end of the summer of 1938. "I don't feel loved or cherished. I'm not even sure He's aware of my existence."

Again, Lindsell patiently and systematically presented what he believed, adding simply, "But Ruth, there is still the leap of faith."

This made sense, she decided, and throughout her life she would often explain that if God could be measured, He would be too small. If He could be proven, He would be too simple. She did not have all the answers, but she no longer felt she needed them. The Presence she had sensed since birth was there, like warmth she couldn't see, like music she couldn't touch.

Before school began that fall, she visited her grandmother and invited Lindsell for a weekend. He wanted to marry her. She had just turned eighteen and was too young, she gently explained to her crushed suitor. Ruth remained convinced that she wouldn't marry anyone now or ever. It did not occur to her that she had yet to meet someone as independent and stubborn, someone as baffling and physically compelling as herself. Far away, in the rural South, such a person did exist.

7

CHAPTER

Billy Frank

Courtesy of Ruth Bell Graham Personal Collection

YOUNG BILLY FRANK

My love has long been yours . . .
since on that day
when we first met;
I will never quite forget
how you just paused
and smiled a bit,
then calmly helped yourself to it.

—Ruth Bell Graham[1]

It was early fall 1940, and maples flamed in red and gold on the Wheaton College campus. The October sun burned obliquely from a clean blue sky, and the air was tart. Billy Graham was slouched in an orange pickup truck, hot light spilling through the windshield and over his trousers. His sleeves were pushed to his elbows, and long slender legs ended sharply in a pair of scuffed brogans.

Beside him, Johnny Streater squinted in the white glare, fingers loosely curled around the wheel, head slightly tilted, as the two young men chatted. Streater, a senior, was a twenty-five-year-old Floridian with short-cropped curly brown hair and dark mischievous eyes. Four years earlier he had bought the truck and built up the metal flatbed with wooden plank siding. He had painted WHEATON COLLEGE STUDENT TRUCKING SERVICE in large blue letters on the doors.

Billy was a twenty-one-year-old North Carolinian with a distinctive voice and a passion to save souls. Already an ordained Baptist minister, he had graduated from Florida Bible Institute in Tampa, where he had practiced preaching to cypress stumps, working hard to sand southern cadences smooth like rough old wood. By now, it was a challenge to guess where he was from. He had arrived at Wheaton the month before, chagrined to find he was once again a lowly freshman.

There was a poignant boyishness about young Billy Graham, a well-mannered decency that drew people, and before Streater had thought twice about it, he offered him a whopping fifty cents an hour to help haul furniture, luggage, and other belongings for the students and local residents. Billy was six feet two inches of raw-boned scaffolding topped by a mane of wavy, dark blond hair. He had perpetually dark circles under his eyes, his face a striking concentration of strong features that seemed to have been forged or chiseled. His brow was high and intelligent, nose and jaw strong. His deep-set eyes were remarkably piercing and as blue as a Siamese cat's. Wheaton classmates called him "Preacher," for he'd already had plenty of experience holding revival services and proclaiming the Good News from street corners and barroom doorways.

Billy had forsaken his Presbyterian heritage, not in response to urges of heart but to deacons who threatened to cancel revival services he was holding at a small Baptist church in Florida unless he agreed to be immersed. Without struggle or fanfare, he was baptized in a nearby lake. Though he sometimes doubted his call to the ministry and his effectiveness, he never questioned his insatiable desire to reach lost souls. It was an obsession, and time after time he would find himself pacing in front of a crowd, preaching from the supple black leather Bible gripped in his left hand.

William Franklin Graham Jr. was born November 7, 1918, on a dairy farm outside Charlotte, North Carolina. False news reports declared that World War I had ended at eleven o'clock that morning. Four days later the war did indeed end, and Billy Frank, as his family called him, began his boyhood on a two-hundred-acre tract in the piedmont where days began hours before dawn and ended soon after dark. His world was earthy and unchanging, punctuated by the pleasant sounds of warm milk drumming pails and bottles thick with cream clattering in the delivery truck bumping along loamy red dirt roads.

Nature was cyclical, moving from life to death, from death to life, stirring in the thaw of March and waning in October. By late June, the lemony perfume of magnolias and the fragrance of apple blossoms were gone, and jaded nature got hot and slow. Fat sunflowers and orange day lilies swayed from spindly stems along roadsides, and steamy and monotonous summers droned on like lethargic beetles by day and rude cicadas at night. Winters were endless raw hours rarely culminating in the enchantment of snow, and trees were dead silhouettes against bleak fields.

Perennially, there was the rapacious kudzu that transformed majestic oaks and pines into leafy dinosaurs reared on massive hindquarters, waiting to devour little boys who wandered too far from their fragrant kitchens or fusty barns. The cadence of Billy Frank's world was constant. Men were born on the land and died there, just as their fathers before them. There seemed to be no question that Billy Frank would maintain the rhythm and become a farmer like the five generations of Graham men before him.

It is believed that Billy Graham came from a brave, hearty stock. His early forebears include "Sir John with the Bright Sword" Graham of Kilbride, Scotland, noted for his courage, and John Graham of Claverhouse, Viscount Dundee, notorious for his persecution of the Scottish Covenanters during the reign of Charles II. With more certainty it can be said that Billy Graham's direct ancestors emigrated from Ireland in 1772 and settled on a thousand acres along the Catawba River at the North and South Carolina line.

His grandfather William Crook Graham, born in the fall of 1840, was an opinionated Democrat with a temper and a fierce loyalty to the Confederacy. After he died in his armchair in 1910, he was lauded as the "bravest Confederate in Mecklenburg," a suspect accolade in light of his company muster roll, which indicated that he was absent without leave on at least two occasions. Inspired by patriotism or bounty bonds, Private Graham served for the duration of the Civil War in the Sixth Regiment of the South Carolina volunteers. He suffered typhoid fever and a grievous leg wound and was eventually taken captive by an enemy troop. Like his ancestors, he was devoted to the land, and after the war he returned to his farm in the Sharon township. In 1870 he married Mollie McCall and they raised eleven children in a log house on the center of their property. Their ninth child, born in June 1888, was named William Franklin.

As a young man Frank Graham was a solid six foot two and handsome. He was fond of fat cigars and fine clothing, and was a raconteur known throughout the county for jokes and colorful yarns. Though he lacked formal education, he was considered one of the shrewdest horse traders in the piedmont, his handshake as binding as a signed contract. He was kind, dutiful, and frugal, his religion rooted in works rather than grace until 1906, when he attended a revival at a local Methodist church. For nine evenings he attended services and spent the late-night rides home in his horse-drawn wagon unraveling what the evangelist had woven into his brain. On the tenth night, no amount of tugging or picking would eradicate the message. As the steadily clopping hooves carried him back to the farm, Frank realized he had been converted.

Four years later, when he was twenty-two, he drove his sporty buggy to Lakewood Park, west of Charlotte, where couples drifted in rowboats and took languid strolls on Saturday nights and Sunday afternoons. Not long after he'd tethered his horse he noticed a slender young woman with fine strong features and pinned-up dark blond hair. Her name was Morrow Coffey and she was eighteen. She eyed him obliquely, and not for the first time. She had seen him riding through the county and had wanted to meet him for quite a while. Before the Saturday evening ended, the two had been introduced. The gentleman who had accompanied Morrow to the park found himself alone, and Frank treated Morrow to her first roller-coaster ride and drove her home.

Morrow had grown up just outside Charlotte, her forebears having settled in the Carolinas at the end of the eighteenth century. Her father was Benjamin Morrow Coffey, a dark, sharp-featured man who in his youth, as Morrow recalled the legend, had penetrating brown eyes that could look right through a person. When he was nineteen, he enlisted in the Eleventh Regiment of the Confederate Army, and on an early March morning he left home. Slipping him a New Testament and kissing him farewell, his mother stood at the edge of the yard, watching his easy stride as he receded into the horizon.

Throughout the war Benjamin carried the small leather-bound book in his breast pocket, and his last vision of his mother watching him leave home for war hung in his mind like an icon. On July 1, 1863, the opening day of the Battle of Gettysburg, he fell near a rill along Seminary Ridge, a bullet lodged below his left knee. As he lay upon the blood-soaked earth, smoke and flames around him, a shell burst nearby and blinded his right eye. After a four-hour wait, he was carried from the field, loaded into a dray with other wounded, and carried to a hospital. He woke up later from a whiskey-induced sleep and discovered his sawed-off leg in a tub beside his bed. In early 1864 Benjamin Morrow Coffey returned to his home and married his childhood sweetheart, Lucinda Robinson. He began farming with a wooden leg and a mule.

When his third daughter was born, he abandoned his hope of having a son and named the girl Morrow, after himself. She grew up in the thousand-member Steele Creek Presbyterian Church, and by the time she met Frank Graham, she was a conservative, no-nonsense believer. She set the tone for their lives together on their wedding night in 1916 when she unpacked her Bible before all else and began what would become their family tradition of daily devotions. It was her mission to cure her card-playing, cigar-smoking husband of his worldliness.

The Grahams lived in a two-story, white clapboard house, with a sloping porch, on a patch of dirt where an IBM building now stands in one of Charlotte's prime business districts. Their first child, a daughter, died shortly after birth. Billy Frank was born a year later, followed by two sisters and a brother. Morrow was determined to raise her children in a Christian atmosphere, but in the early years the Graham home, like the Coffeys', was more church-oriented than it was spiritual. The Graham faith, like their affections, was inhibited. Young Billy Frank's faith was a ritual of moral regulations, blessings at mealtimes, and church on Sunday morning.

As a boy, he crackled with nervous energy like a long, thin wire. He chewed his fingernails and had a mild stutter. Billy Frank was impetuously magnanimous, with a proclivity for exaggeration and lavishing both friend and foe with kind words and generous favors. The athletic arena was the one place where he could vent the electrical storm within, and each day he unleashed it on the basketball court or baseball field.

"When we were teenagers, we didn't know what 'hyper' meant," his brother, Melvin, recalled. "When I think back, he was probably hyper."

Billy Frank's mother often said in exasperation that she wanted the doctor to give him something to calm him down.

When Billy Frank was ten, his family moved into a sturdy brick house on a barren rise not far from the place of his birth. By age twelve, he was head and shoulders taller than other boys and thin as a reed at a hundred and sixty pounds. He had corn-colored hair and wide blue eyes, and an intensity that often caused people to think there was something unusual, if not important, about him. When he wasn't working on the farm or playing baseball, he was riding with pretty girls around the county in a friend's convertible.

Depending on whom Billy was interested in—and he dated a different girl "about every week," claimed his sister Catherine—it was common to see him holding a young lady's hand in the sunshine, her hair whipping in the wind. In fact, he was rather much the local heartbreaker. As Catherine later recalled, "He was just so good-looking, and the girls were just crazy about him."

Young Billy Frank was not spiritual in the least. God was like a flower pressed between the pages of a book, to be briefly sentimentalized when chanced upon in the A.R.P. Presbyterian church he attended each Sunday. Academics, like his religion, were largely ignored, and conveniently there was little time to study. Each morning he and Melvin rose at 2:30 to begin chores, a schedule so habitual that Melvin would momentarily blink awake at that hour for the rest of his days. Tumbling out of the house into an indistinct world of shadows and silence, the two brothers would amble along a narrow path, cutting through the alfalfa field and finally reaching the barn. The boys delivered their quota of milk to Uncle Clyde Graham, who lived across the road and owned a bottling machine. Milk was poured into glass bottles, fitted with cardboard stoppers, and stamped GRAHAM BROTHERS DAIRY.

After a rigorous scrubbing and a hearty breakfast, Billy Frank went to school. He was not an exemplary student and one of his teachers visited his mother to tell her so. Perhaps in an effort to frighten Morrow Graham into motion, the teacher paused on her way out to declare, "Billy Frank will never amount to a thing."

In the spring of 1934, when Billy Frank was fifteen, a revival was held seven miles from his house. Lawyers, doctors, farmers, the wealthy and the poor, turned out in droves. They bumped along rutted roads in trucks and glided from fine city dwellings in shiny sedans, while Billy stayed in the cool solitude of his red brick home, ignoring what he judged to be a raw-lumber tabernacle full of emotionalism.

Mordecai Ham had been preaching at the revival for three weeks, having been brought to Charlotte by Albert Sidney Johnson, the prominent minister of the First Presbyterian Church. The fiery Baptist minister had gotten such a drubbing in the newspapers that Billy Frank's own church had refused to acknowledge Ham's existence. One afternoon one of Frank Graham's assistants, Albert McMakin, announced he would attend that evening's service and urged Billy Frank to go along. To please him, Billy Frank agreed. Bathed and already perspiring in the warm night air, they climbed into McMakin's car and roared to the tabernacle.

It was jammed. Wives wearing dark linen and voile and straw hats sat beside dapper businessmen, while women in blousy cotton dresses sat primly next to farmer husbands stiff in shiny Sunday suits. Faces were tanned like belting leather, white in a band across the brow from the shade of hats, and flesh glowed from soapy scrubs that could not reach slivered moons of dirt beneath broad, furrowed nails. The airless atmosphere was heavy with moist heat and toilet water, and young Billy Frank shrank into the back and peered over slicked-down hair and hats. Ham was intelligent and articulate, and unabashed in his hatred of sin. Billy listened with fascination, and from that moment on he couldn't stay away.

Night after night Mordecai Ham warned about hell, fornication, and liquor, his eyes snapping, bone-white hair falling across his wet brow. Unnerved and convicted, Billy ducked and dodged whenever the preacher's accusing finger seemed pointed his way. Then one night the fear slid from him and the minister's voice became strange, distant, as though the voice of God were speaking directly to Billy Frank Graham. A yearning stirred deep within, filling him irresistibly, and in a way he did not completely understand. Sawdust shifted beneath his shoes as he walked forward to surrender himself.

Revivals came and went like the seasons. For some of the local folk, equilibrium was restored a week after the tent had been folded and the evangelist had moved on to another town. For others, their walk to the altar changed them. Though superficially Billy Frank was the same young man his friends had always known, inside his soul was embattled, waged in a struggle he could not ignore. To him, God was a force to be tangled with. How much simpler had God been that-great-something-out-there looking down on him. Instead, God was a powerful and persistent presence. For the next eighteen months, Billy Frank was torn between Christ and worldliness. When the weather was warm, he would lope through the woods behind his house, jumping over two deep gullies, headed for a creek. He would sit on a boulder in the sun, spending uninterrupted hours reading the Bible and praying, as he mulled over what to do with his newfound faith.

In the fall of 1936, he left home for the mountains of Cleveland, Tennessee, where his parents had enrolled him in the recently founded Bob Jones College. Billy would last one semester. After the open, sunny world of the farm, Bob Jones College impressed him as a windowless, dark room where the emphasis was on sin, on "thou shalt nots," and on the eradication of worldliness. Griping was forbidden. Signs posted in the barrack-style dormitories warned students they had better mind their attitudes as well as their tongues. Athletic competitions with other colleges were nonexistent. Holding hands and kissing were felonious. Billy's spirit withered, and a tenacious bout with the flu robbed him of his strength.

In early January, Billy sat in Dr. Bob Jones's office, nervously informing the formidable man that he was leaving. Jones flayed the young man for his lack of Christian integrity, for his blighted character. With the urgency Jones so often employed when promising the faceless unbelievers an eternal scorching hell, he promised Billy a lifetime of failure. Billy had sidestepped the aura of God's will because he had darted from the shadow of Bob Jones. At the tender age of eighteen, Billy was lost.

The following February, Billy transferred to the Florida Bible Institute, and, buoyed by the sunshine and cheery atmosphere, he thrived. He began preaching in empty buildings or in a nearby swamp where no one could hear him attempt to banish the remnants of his southern accent and a nervous stutter. He preached anywhere he was invited, practicing each sermon as many as twenty-five times before feeling confident enough to deliver it. He condemned sin and warned of damnation, possessing a power that from the beginning was mesmerizing. Local reporters strayed into his services, making such observations as "Young Graham does not mince words when he tells church members that they are headed for the same hell as the bootlegger and racketeer unless they get right and live right."[2]

Posted around Tampa were his homemade handbills: "Have you heard the young man with a burning message?"[3]

His first year at Florida Bible Institute, he fell in love with an attractive, dark-haired young woman whose name, many years later, was rarely mentioned.[4] In 1938, Billy asked the woman to marry him. She accepted, only to reject him the following year because she was in love with someone else. It was a sharp blow, and Billy begged God to change what had happened, to somehow reverse the inclinations of her heart or of his. But prayer, he discovered, was not a wish book filled with slick promises of happiness and plenty. He supposed it might be possible that God did not always give him what he wanted because He'd rather give him what he should have. In his greatest hour of dejection, Billy gave what was left of himself to all that he conceived of God.

He graduated in 1940 and left Tampa with a new earnestness about his Christian call. He promised himself he would never kiss a woman again until he knew she was the one, as he put it, who was to be his wife. He would ignore women in general, as much as he could, and focus his energy on his work and on his preaching. His resolution lasted about as long as it took for Johnny Streater to tell Billy all about a striking young woman named Ruth Bell.

"She's beautiful," Johnny Streater said one afternoon as the truck bounced through the Wheaton streets. "She's the second nicest girl on campus, the nicest being my girl, of course."

Streater and his fiancée, Carol Lane, were studying Chinese and planned to go to China as missionaries after graduation. He was an eager matchmaker, and often as he and Billy made their rounds in the truck, Streater would vividly describe Ruth's physical and spiritual merits. One day this mounted to the hyperbolic clincher: "She's so spiritual that she gets up at four o'clock each morning to read her Bible and pray." Though Ruth did have devotions first thing in the morning, in truth she was usually staggering out of bed that early to study Greek, a course she would later describe as her academic Waterloo.

"I want you to meet her," Streater concluded.

"Well then," Billy said, "let's go!"

His opportunity came in November of 1940 when he and Streater strolled from the library to Williston Hall for lunch and discovered Ruth in the hallway chatting with friends. Streater introduced them. Ruth smiled, slightly startled by Billy's intense blue eyes. He acknowledged her with a courteous reserve that masked his sudden rush of interest.

"I fell in love right that minute," he later claimed.

At the time, he managed to hide his feelings so well that it would be a while before Ruth was aware of them. Indeed, in later years she would never quite recall the first time she met Billy, but she thought it might have been when he and Streater were playing chess on a table beside a window.

Billy wrote his mother right away and told her he had found the woman he would one day marry. He loved Ruth because she looked just like her, he ardently said in his letter. Morrow, knowing blarney when she saw it, burned the letter years later for fear that Ruth might discover it and be insulted. Nothing happened until early December, when Billy, Streater, and several friends were studying in Frost Library and noticed Ruth sitting at an empty table on the other side of the room.

"Go ask her! Go ask her!" the men urged, as they jogged Billy to his feet.

Quietly, he walked across the painfully silent library and slipped into the chair beside her as the librarian scowled her warning against socializing. He waved off her disapproval and invited Ruth to accompany him to the school's presentation of Handel's *Messiah*. She accepted and watched his retreating back with interest.

The day of the concert a steady snow fluttered against the windowpanes of the beige frame house at 304 North Main Street, four blocks off campus. Ruth and seven other coeds lived upstairs in tidy rooms furnished with honey maple desks, dressers, and beds covered with firm new mattresses. Her room was directly to the right after climbing the stairs. Its two windows overlooked a Baptist church, and the boyhood home of Harold "Red" Grange, the acclaimed Chicago Bears running back. Downstairs lived the elderly maiden sisters Julia and Cornelia Scott, who had become more than a bit fond of Ruth after learning that she was the mysterious do-gooder who had been sneaking out before daylight on snowy mornings to shovel the walks cornering the house. Ruth Bell filled the women's world with unexpected pleasures. At Christmas, she left stockings bulging with nuts, sweets, and trinkets, and throughout the year circulated humor through the house.

It was a minor matter for Ruth to pick just the right dress to wear on her first date with Billy Graham. She had only one good dress, a plain black wool sheath that she had made herself.

"Which dress shall I wear?" she asked her roommate with mock seriousness, "my black one or my black one?"

"Neither," she replied. "For a change, why don't you wear your black one?"

Ruth pinned up her hair, slid into her one pair of pumps, and looped a strand of dime-store pearls around her neck. Billy arrived at the front door, spruced up in a blue tweed suit he had bought for fifteen dollars at a Maxwell Street bazaar in Chicago.

Billy was unlike anyone Ruth had ever met. Weeks earlier she had overheard him praying with a group of students and had marveled. He wasn't unctuous or pious, nor did his words emerge in the smooth reverential tone of a Christian elder statesman. He was earnest, quietly confident, and personal. Clearly, he spoke as one who knew God, and knew Him well, she decided. He was a man who seemed to comprehend the amplitude of God's might and authority. He seemed to comprehend it so thoroughly, in fact, that it had become part of him. Ruth wrote at the time:

> Bill is a real inspiration—because, I suppose, he is a man of one purpose & that one purpose controls his whole heart & life. He is dead in earnest yet richly endowed with the fruit of the Spirit. . . . Humble, thoughtful, unpretentious, courteous.

As Billy escorted her through the milky, snowy air, leading her over the frosted walk to the concert, he seemed completely unaware of his uniqueness, his poignancy, his gift. This intrigued her. In his mind he was an uncertain freshman who longed to win souls for Christ and win Ruth Bell for himself. He felt inadequate to do either. To Ruth, he was the cool, self-assured gentleman who, much to her fascination, was neither obsequious nor flirtatious. Indeed, because he kept his emotions tightly cloaked, he politely ignored her. She pondered this as they sat side by side in the triumphant flow of Handel's music, never imagining that at that moment he was, as he recalled years later, "a bundle of nerves" inside a bargain-basement suit.

Afterward, she entered her room, and the windowpanes were cold and clear. Beyond the arborvitae-covered porch, the lawn and the elm-bordered street were round with snow, the night blanked out and noiseless. Ruth knelt on the carpet beside her bed and prayed, "God, if You let me serve You with that man, I'd consider it the greatest privilege in my life."

For the next month Ruth and Billy's relationship went nowhere. Ruth began 1941 by flunking Greek and ancient history. "How will you hold up your head around school?" she lamented in her journal the last day in January. She wanted to tell Billy and ask him what to do, and instead acted silly to cover up. She spent time alone in her room, shedding tears and scanning the Psalms for comfort, her lifelong way of dealing with disappointments and depression.

Johnny Streater was convinced that his friend Billy was hopelessly in love, and warned him, "Whoa boy, you'd better slow down!" Billy listened, much against his will, and avoided Ruth altogether until the first of February, when she wrote him, inviting him to her house party, one week before the event and two months after her friends had gotten their dates. He accepted and invited her to go to church with him on that Friday night, February 7. He preached, and in her journal she wrote of "the authority with which he spoke—The humility, the fearlessness." When the service ended, "The star, seen and admired from afar, became a human, personal thing—within reach."

Afterward, he drove her home and parked his 1937 green Plymouth at the curb. Unable to sleep, she sat up until the early hours of Saturday, writing:

> I watched his profile as he guided us thru the Chicago traffic (tho he didn't know it). Noted the steel of it marked the glint in his eyes where the streetlights flashed past. Felt the masterful firmness of his hand beneath my arm as he guided me thru the crowd at the church. Was impressed by his unaffected thoughtfulness.... Something big has happened.

When Billy walked her to the door that night, he had hesitated. "There's something I'd like you to make a matter of definite prayer," he began as they stood on the porch, their breath vaporizing in the cold, brittle air. "I have been taking you out because I am more than interested in you and have been since the day Johnny Streater introduced us last fall. But I know you have been called to the mission field and I'm not definite."

Billy had been surrounded by would-be missionaries ever since his arrival at Wheaton. He had never felt pulled in that direction, until recently. He went on to explain, "And not all because of you either, though I have wondered if the Lord has been speaking to me through you." Many years later he would admit that he had been so in love with her that he was tempted to consider spending his life in the arid mountains of Tibet if that was the only way he could be with her.

Ruth, however, had no idea what he was thinking or why he was standing on her porch on a bitterly cold night talking about the mission field. Baffled, she watched his car disappear in a swirl of exhaust. She didn't see him again for several days, and she filled the pages of her journal with ruminations of love and what marriage was all about. When she and Billy finally passed each other, he seemed preoccupied, almost indifferent. Ruth could only assume that he was reacting to her. "The strange creature waits 'till I begin wondering if he's changed his mind," she complained in a letter to her parents, "then he asks me out."

On March 3, after studying in the library and attending a student council meeting, he walked her home in a snowstorm. Late that night, she wrote:

> How wildly it blew the snow into swirls and sheets and drifts! It was slippery too, and I would have fallen but for the strong hand beneath my arm where it was needed. (I think I'm just stalling for time.) He asked me if I had been praying and if I was thinking seriously about what he had said. . . . He hasn't mentioned caring for me yet.

Ruth's security was further weakened when the wife of Professor Mortimer B. Lane dropped by to issue her a warning. Ruth was in bed, miserable with a cold, when Mummy Lane, as the students affectionately called her, appeared with a quart of freshly squeezed orange juice and a list of the young ladies Billy had dated and dropped over the years. "Ruth," she concluded, "I don't want to see you hurt." Opening her *Daily Light* that night, Ruth read, "Meddle not with them given to change." She and her roommate collapsed in a spasm of laughter.

That winter she began describing Billy in letters to her parents: "He must be six-three or -four. Has blond wavy hair. Is very slender. All of which is quite immaterial. His great earnestness is what most deeply impresses those who know him. . . . More about that later. I know if I went on it would begin to sound allegorical. And why all the detail anyway?"

A pattern began. She would describe Billy, then drop the subject only to reintroduce it, sometimes in the next paragraph. It seemed two voices were speaking. Her reason claimed that he was just another date, and her emotions could not let him go.

"Despite Bill's fearlessness and sometimes sternness," she wrote, "he is just as thoughtful and gentle as one would want a man to be. Maybe it's the South in him. . . . At any rate, he really makes you feel perfectly natural and looked-after without being showy or obnoxious. Sounds like I'm in love, doesn't it? Don't get worried. I'm not."

She changed the subject, only to resume telling her parents all about him in the next sentence, reminiscing about a date on a recent snowy evening:

> You know—funny how the little things pop up in the memory. His way of going about things, his self-control . . . the way he put both hands on the wheel and squared his shoulders when we began, the strength and keenness of his profile when the streetlight fell thru the snow sifting on the windshield and lit up his face. I wasn't watching him directly, but one sees a lot out of the corner of one's eye. Oh, I shouldn't be writing all this. You'll think me a romantic nitwit.

Ruth's college career was briefly interrupted in March of 1941, after doctors performed what they thought was a routine appendectomy on Rosa and discovered that she had tubercular peritonitis. Rosa began convalescing in the private home in Wheaton where she had been living. Ruth dropped out of school, eager for the chance to look after the sister who for so many years had looked after her. Ever since Ruth had left home for Korea, Rosa had demonstrated an almost motherly concern for her. During Ruth's first winter in Wheaton, Rosa had noticed her sister shivering in her thin cloth overcoat and had promptly taken her to Marshall Field's in Chicago. Using her own meager savings, she had bought Ruth a heavy beige wool coat, one that was much warmer, much more handsome than anything Rosa would ever have bought for herself.

Though weak from her illness, Rosa was still hearty enough to employ her matchmaking skills. She urged Ruth to fall in love with Billy. The local consensus was the same. He and Ruth were suited for each other, and half the campus, it seemed, was "praying for the relationship." Ruth was praying for it too, but sometimes she wasn't sure whether she should petition for a win or a loss. In his enigmatic manner, Billy expended considerable energy ignoring her.

Then he would materialize from the vacuum and ask a question like "Do you think I'm asking you out too much? Because I don't want to embarrass you by taking you out too frequently."

Ruth suspected Billy was being overcautious, but would never have dared to broadside him with her suspicion. So the game played on, reaching its culmination later that spring when he said to her, "I haven't tried to win you, Ruth. I haven't asked you to fall in love with me. I haven't sent you candy and flowers and lovely gifts. I have asked the Lord, if you are the one, to win you for me. If not, to keep you from falling in love with me."

After that remark, Ruth decided to start dating other men. The ensuing flurry of dates had predictable results.

"Either you date just me or you can date everybody but me!" Billy announced.

He became domineering, quizzing her about how much sleep she had gotten and whether she had exercised and had eaten properly. She was known to be whimsical about meals, and if he discovered she hadn't eaten lunch, he'd march her downtown to buy her hot chocolate and a sandwich. Chin propped on folded hands, he'd grin at her from across the table while he forced her to swallow every crumb. On double dates he had the annoying habit of changing her order from iced tea to milk. As he watched after his woman in the manner of his ancestors, he harbored the notion that she had surrendered her career plans. This was a grave miscalculation, and it almost cost him the war.

"I think being an old maid missionary," Ruth informed him one day, "is the highest call there is."

"Woman was created to be a wife and mother," he countered.

"There are exceptions," she said matter-of-factly, "and I believe I'm one of them."

"If that's the case," he announced, "we will just call a halt, during which time you should search the Scriptures and pray until you find out just what is God's place for woman in this life. And when you find out and are willing to accept God's place, you can let me know."

As Ruth would recall some fifty-five years later, "Billy was brought up in a house where the women did not question the men, while in the Bell house, that's all we did." In the rural world of Billy's youth, the woman's life revolved around her husband's. Suppressed, the woman developed the facility of asserting herself invisibly. Morrow Graham was gentle and submissive, living eighty-nine years without ever owning a driver's license because her husband did not think women should drive. Yet it was she who kept the books for the dairy farm and ran the household.

Ruth, in contrast, was accustomed to strong-willed, outspoken women like her mother. Billy's authoritativeness was galling and became the couple's most volatile point. On April 23, 1941, Ruth and Billy got in their worst fight yet over this very notion, and he threatened to end the relationship. The degree of Ruth's hurt surprised even her, and she wrote:

> I felt almost as if I were beating my fists against a wall. There was nothing to do but call it all off, he said, if I couldn't see it that way. When he said that, I felt as though the bottom had dropped out

> of everything. Life lost its meaning. I crumpled under it. . . . For a moment, I lay my head against him—but that has little to do with it all. I recall the grip of his hands, the way the stars looked—so distant and so bright, the way the night wind blew thru his hair—the look on his face as he looked over me and far away. "What shall we do?" he asked. So until I understand more clearly what the Lord would have me do, and until I am in the center of His will, Billy won't see any more of me. And he left.

Five days of insomnia and misery passed, and on April 28, Ruth tried to call Billy, only to learn he was out of town. She had yet to admit she was in love, but certainly what she wrote at the time would lead one to believe exactly that:

> Night fell. A new moon hung in the west. Thru the branches of the trees it gleamed like thin silver. The woods were quiet. Somewhere within there came a terrible sense of loneliness. I wanted him. I needed him. He should be coming to me thru the woods and I would run to meet him and I would tell him I knew now, and I would yield—everything. And he would hold me close—but he would be very quiet. And it would be over with—all this struggling and thinking and reasoning—this feverish tossing to and fro in my mind.

Ruth sent for him, and the next evening, Tuesday, she recorded hearing a car drive up, and firm, quick steps on the walk out front. He was tall and straight in a light tweed suit, and she went to him.

"I think I know now, Bill. That's why I sent for you" was all she could think to say.

"When did you decide, Ruth?"

They began to walk toward their favorite spot in the woods, his hand firm beneath her arm.

"I don't know . . ." Her voice dropped off. "But I thought it only fair, Bill, to tell you that . . ."

She stood staring off, at a loss, and for an instant it seemed that the rustling trees, the frogs and crickets and the distant sounds of a train all waited in breathless anticipation of what else she might say. "I looked up at him," she wrote in her journal, "and I wasn't afraid." Billy was standing still, looking down at her, waiting, his face stern.

"That—I loved you," Ruth finally finished.

For a moment Billy stared at her in quiet disbelief.

"Darling!" he exclaimed, and he crushed her to him.

At last, she wrote, it was over:

> Only the terrific pounding of his heart told me he had not known what to expect. . . . It was such a perfect evening. We rode. The night wind blew past us. He reached for my hand. Whose hand do you wish it was now? I demanded impishly. I was just trying to decide which it felt the most like, he returned unabashed. I snatched my hand away and withdrew myself to the far corner of the seat. . . . We were under the pines by Old Lawson. The town clock struck eleven. Before we started for home . . . I looked up. He was looking toward the south. His face, clean and strong—had the look of one who knows where he is going and who he is to meet at the end of the way. It was the old strength of purpose which has awed me before. I waited. Looking down he smiled and gathered me to him a moment. I would like to kiss you, he said. But I think that should wait.

By June, the interminable winter had finally moved on, leaving the earth fresh and emerald. Gone with the cold was the routine of daily walks to class, faces nettled by snowy blasts, minds dull from long nights of study. Summer vacation was upon them. Students hauled battered trunks and suitcases, straggling from dormitories to waiting cars, joyous at reprieve and pained at good-byes.

Billy's Plymouth was packed for Florida, where he was to hold youth revival services for several weeks. Before leaving, he asked Ruth to marry him. She paused, then said she could not answer him. She could not stop crying, and he would not leave without knowing what was wrong. She reminded him again of her lifelong belief that she was meant to be a missionary. She wasn't sure she should give this up. Worse, she had a terrible sense of foreboding about being Mrs. Billy Graham. She was terrified of losing her identity.

"Ruth," he remarked, "I think it would be a very good idea if you would forget your girlhood ideals, your crazy ideas, and the advice of your friends. Forget it all. And just be Ruth Bell for a while."

He headed south with a heavy heart.

1. Ruth Bell Graham, *Sitting by My Laughing Fire* (Waco, Tex.: Word Books, 1977), 54.
2. Untitled personal scrapbook, Collection 15, Archives of the Billy Graham Center, Wheaton, Illinois.
3. Untitled personal scrapbook, Collection 15, Archives of the Billy Graham Center, Wheaton, Illinois.
4. Ruth also had a practice of placing a white sticker over faces in photographs of people out of favor with her.

8
CHAPTER

The Ring

Courtesy of Ruth Bell Graham Personal Collection

THE RING, 1941

It was so very good of God
to let my dreams come true,
to note a young girl's cherished hopes
then lead her right to you.

—*Ruth Bell Graham*

From the war-torn cities of China came the cries for mercy: *"Ko lien! Ko lien!"* Starving peasants wandered aimlessly amid collapsed buildings and rubble-covered streets, their eyes vacant, the stench of death clinging to the earth like fog. They pummeled tree bark and skimmed slime off ponds for food, and there were rumors of cannibalism. The climate was restive and ready for propagandizing and organizing in the name of change, as the Communists continued to undermine the Nationalist regime.

In Qingjiang, the missionaries were imperiled, and their work was overwhelming. Occupying Japanese soldiers were becoming overtly resentful of what they conceived of as the Americans' influence over the local Chinese. The Japanese were embittered by the United States government's willingness to sell fighter planes to China. It didn't surprise Nelson Bell when the American consul entreated him to flee. At first, Dr. Bell refused. He could not abandon the people when they needed him most. He soon reconsidered when he learned that his wife was suffering from malaria and a kidney infection and that Rosa had been admitted to Zace Sanatorium in Winfield, Illinois, with both lungs tubercular.

In May 1941, the Bells set sail for home. A month later Germany would attack Russia, scotching Soviet military aid to China and speeding the economy's downward spiral. In August, Japanese would capture the remaining Qingjiang missionaries and, without explanation, imprison them in the attic of the Bells' house for a month. Many of the Bells' colleagues had already been sent to concentration camps to face starvation, torture, disease, and death.

Ruth was elated over her parents' return. At last they were safe and would meet Billy Graham. She wrote them June 2 while they were yet aboard ship, failing to mention that he had asked her to marry him. During the summer, her letters and diaries were a tangle of emotions as she and Billy continued their clash of wills. Putting it in perspective more than half a century later, she said, "When Bill was young he wanted to play professional baseball, and I wanted to go to Tibet. In truth, neither of us had any business doing either, and physically could not have."

The Bells arrived at Wheaton July 4 for a brief visit with Ruth and Rosa. Then they traveled to the Mayo Clinic in Rochester, Minnesota, for thorough medical examinations. Dr. Bell purchased a car and drove his wife, daughter Virginia, and son Clayton to Waynesboro, where they would live with his mother for a month. Ruth remained at Wheaton with her ailing older sister. Billy meanwhile was preaching in Tampa and checking daily for a letter from Ruth. One morning, a thick envelope postmarked July 6 arrived. It bore her familiar unique script, and he sequestered himself in his manse bedroom before eagerly ripping it open. He felt a rush of joy as he read her words. God, she believed, would have her say yes to his proposal of marriage.

Though Ruth's ambivalence had not disappeared, she believed the relationship was "of the Lord," she explained to her parents in a letter July 7, after telling them what she had done. "I almost stand in awe of him and yet I'm not afraid of him," she wrote. "To be with Bill in this type work won't be easy. There will be little financial backing, lots of obstacles and criticism, and no earthly glory whatsoever. But somehow I need Bill. I don't know what I'd do if, for some reason, he should suddenly go out of my life."

Around this same time, she wrote in her journal, casting an eerily accurate future:

> If I marry Bill I must marry him with my eyes open. He will be increasingly burdened for lost souls and increasingly active in the Lord's work. After the joy and satisfaction of knowing that I am his by rights—and his forever, I will slip into the background. . . . In short, be a lost life. Lost in Bill's.

In late July, Ruth rode the train to Waynesboro and Billy, thinner and drawn, drove northwest in his Plymouth, prepared to meet his future in-laws for the first time.

"When you see me," he wrote Ruth, "don't expect too much. Although I may be thin, remember, I lost the weight pointing souls to the way of salvation."

The Blue Ridge rolled like a hazy frozen ocean to Billy's left, wrapping closer with each mile before setting him down in the Shenandoah Valley. Old gnarled apple trees with hard green fruit flanked whitewashed fences on the roadsides. Beyond, velvety pasture land was freckled with white-faced cows. On July 30, a hot, cloudless Wednesday afternoon, he nosed through Waynesboro and parked at Grandmother Bell's house, discovering that there was no room for him there.

Dreading the unexpected drain on his already thin wallet, he registered at the nearby Hotel Wayne. At sunset, he and Ruth went for a spin along the Skyline Drive, and "thru the dusk lay blue mist and a tiny light or two—and far above, the young moon," Ruth wrote. "All was ours that night—The mountains, the wind, and the moon.—All was ours and now, I am his."

At dinner Billy found to his delight that the reception was warmer than he had even hoped. He thawed in the steady flow of the Bells' humor. By dessert, the two men had struck up a friendship that would lead to Dr. Bell's being Billy's closest adviser for the next thirty-three years. The next morning, Thursday, Billy checked out of his hotel and discovered that his future father-in-law had paid the three-dollar room charge. Billy, Ruth, and her family left for Washington, D.C., where Dr. Bell had an appointment with Far Eastern officials at the State Department, whom he planned to warn that the Japanese intended to attack the United States. Friday morning the medical missionary braved the capital and was politely ignored.

Saturday, Billy left for Charlotte, relaxed of mind and soul, for the Bells had accepted him. Ruth would join him in several weeks to meet his family, which by now was more than a little curious about Ruth. For months, Morrow Graham had urged her son to bring home a snapshot of this young woman who was alleged to look like her. Melvin, not privy to that description and knowing only that she was from China, expected her to have straight black hair and Asian features. Billy's sisters didn't strenuously exercise their imaginations over the matter because they assumed she "was probably just another one of Billy Frank's girlfriends," as Jeannie later explained.

At the brink of summer Billy had finally coerced Ruth into relinquishing a photograph, something she never did gracefully, or honestly, for that matter. There were few things in life she disliked more than having a lens leering in her face and its owner coaxing her in a cloying voice to "say cheese." It wasn't unusual for her to enlist her sense of humor just before the shutter clicked, resulting in any number of comical contortions. Nor was it out of the ordinary for her to surgically remove her likeness with scissors, leaving gaping holes in yearbooks and group portraits.

Having no idea what he was up against, Billy patiently waited while she rummaged through her belongings to fill his request. Explaining innocently that it was "all I could find," she handed him a snapshot taken when she was a thirteen-year-old frump, with long hair pulled back and fastened in a barrette. Demurely holding a hollyhock at her waist, she looked like a parody of a cemetery monument. His first morning home his family passed the picture around the table in silence.

"Well," Morrow Graham said, clearing her throat, "she doesn't look like that now, does she?"

On a Saturday afternoon in August, Billy ushered Ruth into his home. Dressed smartly in a navy suit, a flower in her lapel, she entered the sunroom where Mrs. Graham sat regally beside a crystal bowl of white petunias. "Oh," Billy's mother recalled thinking with pleasure, "she's beautiful."

During the week that followed, ten-year-old Jeannie roared Ruth around the countryside in a black pickup truck, instructing her in the art of driving, which culminated in Ruth's backing through a hedge in front of the house. Evenings were spent on a hard pew inside Sharon Presbyterian Church where Billy was preaching each night that week. What Ruth witnessed was the opening scene of her life with him, the reel of film snapping into place and beginning to spin.

On Saturday night after the service they retreated to the fishpond behind the house, where the air was warm and fragrant with the smell of new-mown grass. Their romantic moment was abruptly ended when a man named Herbert began pounding on the front door, pleading to see Billy. An alcoholic who had known Billy since childhood, Herbert had attended that night's service and resisted the altar call. After downing several stiff drinks, he found himself staggering to the Graham farm, unable to stand his misery a moment longer.

He was weeping when Billy led him into the parlor and gently shut the door. He had tried to stop drinking in the past, but each time he stayed away from the bottle for several days, one of his friends would hand him a glass and off he'd go on another binge. His wife and children feared him. Throughout his angry, drunken years, something beyond him—he figured it was God—had followed him quietly and relentlessly like the moon over a traveler's shoulder. Herbert was tired of running.

Ruth and Billy's mother sat in the family room, pretending not to notice the man's loud sobbing and wild talk. Then Billy invited them to pray with him and Herbert. Quietly, Ruth listened to the cascade of self-mortification pouring from the man. "I had never heard a broken-down sinner pleading for forgiveness," she wrote at the time.

On Sunday, after dinner, Billy led Ruth through woods and pasture to the red-banked Sugar Creek where he had spent so many hours in his youth basking in the warmth and peace he craved. It was his sanctuary, the place for his most private self, and he was sharing it with her. They sat on a boulder, the shallow water running sluggishly below their feet, the sun working highlights into their hair. They entreated God to save his childhood friends, to redeem people like Herbert. "As I listened while he prayed," Ruth recorded, "I realized a little bit the burden weighing on his heart." They lingered until the sun burned obliquely through trees and the shadows were long.

That night's service was somewhat disconcerting. Billy's delivery was too fast, his gestures so exaggerated that he looked like a caricature of himself. It was a bit much for a staunch Presbyterian whose idea of worship was a dignified delivery and a quiet reverence in the congregation. As the organist began playing the familiar hymns for the altar call, Ruth closed her eyes and, almost apologetically, asked God to overlook the frailties of man and touch the hearts of at least one or two people around her.

A quiet creaking fluttered down rows as more than forty stood. In a steady stream they moved forward, eyes fixed on the bare wood beneath their feet, tissues dabbing tears. Ruth watched in disbelief, filled with awe as she stared at Billy standing at the end of the aisle, head bowed, hands folded beneath his chin. He did not wear the pious face of a spiritual salesman who had just delivered a slick pitch. His power was in the message he had faithfully presented. He was the instrument, not the musician. She saw that then.

On their way home, he was quiet, disappointed that the high school friend he had prayed for most had remained firmly planted in his seat during the altar call. She too was silent, knowing that there were and always would be times when he was silent, absorbed, almost unaware of her existence. This would never get any easier, really. The distance she felt may not have been intended, but it bit and she would struggle with it always.

Monday Ruth rode the bus to Montreat, where her parents were buying a house. Then the first week in September, the Bells drove to Waynesboro, leaving Ruth to stay in a rustic summer cabin in Black Mountain with her friend Gay Currie, who had grown up with her in China. They invited Billy to spend the day. On September 5, while he was making the two-hour drive, Gay blacked out Ruth's front teeth, unfastened her long hair, and helped her select a homemade, flower-print dress that was at least two sizes too big. Kicking off her shoes, Ruth set out to meet her beau, her bare feet patting along the country road winding downtown.

She didn't know that Billy was dressed in white from collar to shoes and had a surprise for her too. Tucked inside a pocket was a yellow-gold engagement ring, purchased with every penny of the sixty-five-dollar love offering he had received from Sharon Presbyterian Church. Thick red dust billowed from his car's back tires as it lumbered up the grade, driving right past the "snaggle-toothed" mountain girl, as he later described her, staring at him from the roadside. Suddenly recognizing the quizzical face in his rearview mirror, he crunched to a halt and backed up. A bit unsettled by this unexpected scene in his romantic drama, he silently opened the car door for her. Then he began to laugh.

The unpainted pine-board cabin was located in an isolated mountainous tract, wild with huckleberry bushes, mountain laurels, and rhododendrons. A slender stream whispered through the side yard, and a thick rope swing dangled from a tree. Ruth and Billy sat on the porch in bright sunshine, staring sleepily at the vista as they talked. The Black Mountains slumbered in the distance, their contours taking on human shapes as shadows moved across them during the waning afternoon. Blighted chestnut trees jutted from slopes and ridges like broken feathers, as though a tribe of giant Cherokee had reclined in various positions around the Swannanoa Valley a millennium before.

Near dusk, the couple drove fifteen miles west to the top of Sunset Mountain, famous for its panoramic view of Asheville and for Beaucatcher Tunnel, which had been blasted through years earlier. As the molten sun set on one side of the ridge and the pale moon rose on the other, he gave her the ring,[1] and they kissed.

Ruth's exuberance would quickly fade when her life was temporarily interrupted that fall, and her health began a slow spiral toward exhaustion. Listless and fatigued, she often slept until noon in the house her parents were renting in Montreat while their new home on Assembly Drive was being renovated. Fearing that Ruth had a touch of malaria, they forbade her to return to Wheaton the first semester. They decided to send her with Rosa to a sanatorium in Albuquerque, New Mexico. On November 6, the Bells tucked her into a train bound for Wheaton to meet Rosa at Zace Sanatorium. Together the sisters boarded a train for Albuquerque.

The Southwestern Presbyterian Sanatorium was a cluster of gray stucco buildings with red slate roofs. It was located on sparkling green grounds, interwoven with tidy gravel drives and stately Lombardy poplars. Rosa was restricted to the infirmary, and her sister moved into a building nearby. There Ruth spent the days in her glassed-in sun porch, absorbing clean hot light and the majestic view. To the east, the Sandia and Manzano Mountains rose eleven thousand feet, and extinct volcanoes puckered to the north. She luxuriated in it all, curing like fruit in the sun until she felt weightless and absolved of all responsibility.

"It rained yesterday and a cold wind was blasting," she wrote her parents.

"It blew all the clouds away last night and morning found us in a crisp cold world of dazzling sunshine and snow-capped mountains. The air is so clean and fresh like on board ship. I am feeling on top of the world. Such a respite," she added, "is a blessing. It makes people stop rushing around and gives them time to stop and begin really enjoying life."

It's not surprising that she would, at this moment of detachment, entertain second thoughts about the engagement. Doubts settled in with tenacity and Billy was not there to chase them away. She wrote him a crushing letter, saying she did not think she was in love with him and that marriage was, perhaps, unwise. Miserable, he could do nothing but wait until Ruth returned to Wheaton.

In December, she returned to Montreat, believing that she was leaving her sister to die. Doctors had already performed a phrenicectomy on one lung, permanently collapsing it, and were giving Rosa weekly treatments to induce pneumothorax, or a temporary collapse, of the other to rest it. But in February, she announced that she would refuse further treatment. God would heal her, she decided. As a physician, her father realized that the consequences of Rosa's actions might be death, but as her father and a man of great faith, he did not want to interfere with her act of Christian commitment.

"Make sure you're being led by God," he told her, "and use your own head."

Despite her doctors' emphatic warnings that Rosa would hemorrhage to death, Dr. Bell instructed them to comply with his daughter's wishes. All treatments were stopped. Struggling out of bed each day, Rosa began visiting and helping other patients until her strength was spent. With each attempt, her determination and energy increased. Eventually she was walking a mile into town daily, where she would force down an ice cream soda at the drugstore before returning to the sanatorium. By the fall of 1942, her lungs had expanded, and X-rays confirmed that she had been completely cured.

"Only God could have done this," one of her physicians marveled to Dr. Bell.

Ruth returned to Wheaton in January of 1942, and Billy asked if she wished to give him back the ring. She hesitated, depressed by the finality of the gesture and unsettled by the image of him vanishing from her life. No, she answered, her words edged in frustration. The problem, she explained, was that she still believed she was meant to be a missionary.

"Listen," he said, "do you or do you not think the Lord brought us together?"

"Yes," she had to confess.

"Then," he said firmly, "I'll do the leading and you'll do the following."

As Ruth would later remark, with mischief in her eyes, "I've been following him ever since."

Ruth could live with this condition as long as she wasn't tethered like a nanny goat, which was sometimes how she felt. She almost slapped his ring back into his palm one afternoon during a disagreement over church affiliations. Already an ordained Baptist minister, Billy had no interest in returning to the Presbyterian Church, a change that would involve three years of seminary after college if he wished to become a Presbyterian minister. Since he had left the Presbyterian Church, he assumed that Ruth should do the same, and as they were riding in the car one afternoon, he commented that "Dr. Bell couldn't possibly be a man of God and remain in the Southern Presbyterian Church."

Ruth and Billy disagreed about other matters, too, such as her health habits, which had never been good and now were worse. By March, she had lost ten pounds and was suffering from insomnia. Having never felt the slightest impulse to do anything more rigorous than walking, she marveled at Billy's daily regimen of wrestling, jogging, and calisthenics. Billy did his best to help her mend her ways.

"Saturday night," Ruth wrote at the time, "he presented me with a bag of grapefruit and oranges and a box of [vitamin] pills . . . and the order to go upstairs and clothe myself warmly. Then he marched me up to the end of Howard St. where houses are nil and he started in. And I mean he started in. Sixty times he made me jump, feet apart & clap my hands over my head & sixty times he made me hold my arms out and touch first right hand to left foot, then left hand to right foot. Plus other of his pet calisthenics. There was no pleading for mercy and no teasing him out of the notion."

In the main, Billy's lectures on the merits of good diet, sufficient sleep, and exercise went in one ear and out the other, as Ruth described it.

Billy worried about her because it was his nature to worry about most things, a trait indigenous to Graham blood and one that would always amuse his family. His pessimism would prompt his own children to nickname him "Puddleglum," after the valorous though pessimistic Marsh-wiggle in C. S. Lewis's fairy tale *The Silver Chair.*

The Monday after Ruth's strenuous and unprecedented exercise session, she felt ninety years old and crippled.

"It's good for you!" Billy said cheerfully when she complained.

"Well, you needn't have started the exercising off with such ferocity," she retorted.

"If you'd been exercising all along like you were supposed to," he said, "you wouldn't have gotten sore."

In the fall of their senior year Billy opened a savings account and began tucking away dollars for their future. They would be married, Ruth decided, on Friday, August 13, 1943,[2] and Billy didn't yet know how he would support a wife. He had applied for an army chaplaincy after the Japanese had bombed Pearl Harbor but had been told to wait until he graduated from college. Then he would need either a seminary degree or one year as a pastor followed by a preparation course for the chaplaincy offered at Harvard University. He had also considered enrolling at the University of Chicago to earn his master's degree in anthropology, his college major. Meanwhile, numerous churches were offering him jobs.

One morning in chapel in the fall of 1942, Providence intervened. A Christian businessman named Robert Van Kampen gave his testimony and afterward noticed the lank blond who happened to be sitting in the front row. On a whim Van Kampen wandered over to chat.

"What do you want to be when you finish school?" Van Kampen asked.

"A preacher of the Gospel," Billy replied.

Van Kampen booked him for the following Sunday at the small Western Springs Baptist Church, located in a middle-class suburb fifteen miles from Wheaton. It had one hundred members and no minister. Each Sunday a different layman would meet with the congregation in the basement of the unfinished building. Pews were rows of flap-bottomed seats purchased from a defunct movie theater. Walls were brick, the floor cement, and a coal furnace grumbled from a corner. Billy accepted the invitation, began preaching there regularly, and was offered the job of pastor.

If he accepted, he would begin after graduation and his salary would be forty-five dollars a week, one-third of which would pay the rent of a small, furnished apartment in nearby Hinsdale. In early January 1943, he decided that this was what he would do, stipulating that if the army accepted him he would be released from the church immediately. He sealed the deal with a handshake without ever having consulted Ruth. She was incredulous that he had not even asked her opinion. She was also very concerned, for she believed his call was to evangelism, not to the parish.

The spring of their senior year Ruth saw previews of what was to come. President of the Student Christian Council and a respected speaker, Billy was chosen by Dr. V. Raymond Edman to replace him as the preacher at the Wheaton Tabernacle, which was attended by both faculty and students. Billy was also in demand at churches throughout the state, while Ruth spent most of her weekends, even the senior grand finales, alone.

"I'm a rotten sport about his leaving," she wrote home. "It's no fun. I never thought about this side of it. What is it going to be like after we're married? I probably won't see as much of him then as I do now."

1. Several days later, Ruth's ten-year-old brother Clayton eyed the ring and innocently asked, "Is it a diamond or a grindstone?"

2. Coincidentally, on Friday, August 13, 1937, Shanghai had fallen to the Japanese, thus delaying Ruth's departure for college; and on August 13, 1910, Nelson Bell had asked Virginia Leftwich to marry him.

9

CHAPTER

Wartime Wedding

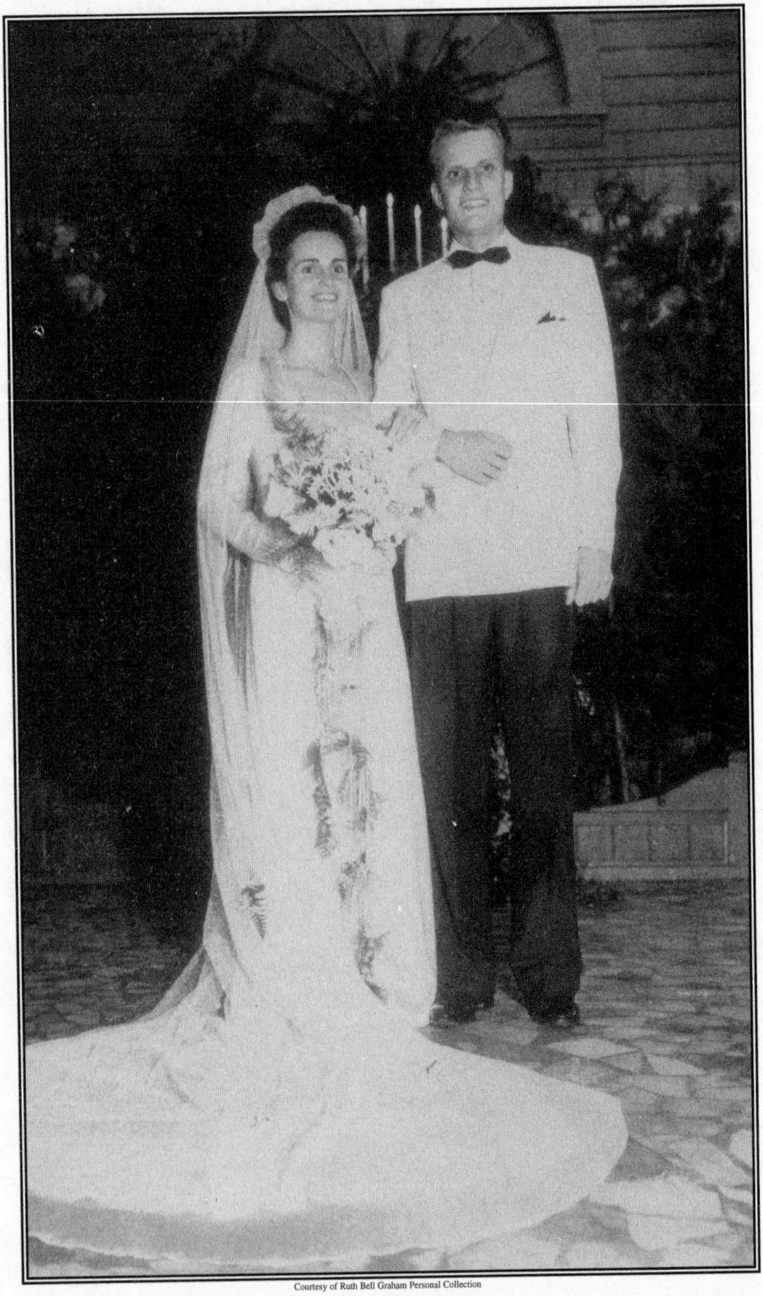

Courtesy of Ruth Bell Graham Personal Collection

WEDDING PORTRAIT, 1943

Now that I love you
and see with eyes
by love enlightened
and made wise,
I wonder how
men look at you
who do not see you
as I do?
They see (they must)
the fire and steel,
the driving force
I also feel.
But
do they ever,
ever see
that gentler side
revealed to me?

—Ruth Bell Graham

Shortly before 8:00 P.M. on Friday, August 13, 1943, the setting sun was a dying ember and long shadows crossed the stone walkway leading to the arched door of the Montreat Presbyterian Church. Inside, clematis draped from windowsills and the altar, mountain laurel banked the stone platform, and white candles sputtered quietly. Two hundred and fifty guests, mainly missionary friends, sat in hard wooden pews.

Ruth waited just outside the sanctuary, elegant in a homemade gown of white satin and a long veil of point d'esprit. Her white satin cap was shaped like a dogwood blossom and quilted in pearls. She carried a bouquet of painted daisies and tuberoses, and moved slowly down the aisle toward the tall young man in white jacket and black trousers who was to be her husband.

Repeating the vows they had written themselves and memorized, they were married by the Reverend John Minder, a friend from Billy's Florida Bible Institute days, and the Reverend Kerr Taylor, a former missionary in China. Sophie Graham's daughter played the organ and Chinese friend Andrew Yang sang a solo. Rosa was the maid of honor. Ruth's sister Virginia and childhood friend Sandy Yates were bridesmaids. Billy's sister Jeannie, who would later marry Billy's future associate evangelist Leighton Ford, was the junior bridesmaid.

This was a wartime wedding, and those in it made up in imagination what they lacked in funds. Ruth's childhood missionary friend Gay Currie had decorated the sanctuary, scouring the coves for foliage. The bridesmaids' dresses were second-hand, and Mrs. Bell had made the bouquets.

Billy and his brother, Melvin, had always been close, and Billy had asked him to be the best man. The groomsmen were Wheaton classmate Jimmy Johnson, and Grady Wilson and Roy Gustafson, who would one day be important members of the Billy Graham Evangelistic Association. Ruth's brother, Clayton, was the junior groomsman; he would one day be a prominent Presbyterian minister. This was more than a marriage of two people. It was the union of two entirely different backgrounds, as symbolized by the men who performed the ceremony and the people who participated in it. It was a partnership of permanence, its vows so sacred that Ruth would never remove, for even a moment, the thin gold band that Billy slipped on her finger.

After the ceremony and a late reception, the Grahams drove northeast toward Blowing Rock for the honeymoon. As is often the case with a honeymoon and the beginning of a marriage, not all was perfect. By Thursday, the seventy-five dollars Billy had saved for the trip was gone. The couple returned to Charlotte and Montreat to visit their parents before starting on the seven-hundred-fifty-mile drive to Hinsdale, Illinois. A cold front rushed in and Ruth caught a chill. By the time they parked in front of their apartment at 214 South Clay Street, she had a high fever.

Billy was scheduled to preach in Elmira, Ohio, that weekend and did not think he should cancel. Uneasy about leaving a sick wife, he checked her into the best local hospital he could find before he left. His telegram and box of candy did not mollify her. He was aptly though inadvertently punished when the collection was taken and he pulled out one of the two bills in his wallet. To his dismay, he realized he had dropped the twenty instead of the five into the plate. Since his intention had been to tithe the smaller amount, Ruth let him know when he returned home, "that's all God gave you credit for."

This slot of second priority would take some getting used to, and Ruth soon enough learned that Billy would rarely cancel a preaching engagement regardless of how ill either one of them might be. Years later, he slipped in the bathtub and cracked three ribs hours before he was to address students at Oxford University, but he mounted the podium as usual, without benefit of pain medication.

Frequently victimized by pneumonia, he would spend much of his life standing bareheaded in rain-swept stadiums. In the fall of 1995, with Parkinson's disease, more fractured ribs, and a broken back, he would show up to say a few kind words at a friend's retirement dinner. He would do interviews, submit to photo shoots, make television appearances, and preach at two major crusades. Ruth would not have changed him. "I'd rather have a little of Bill," she was known to say throughout it all, "than a lot of any other man."

As a young minister, Billy received numerous invitations to preach throughout the Midwest. Rarely was it financially possible for Ruth to go with him, and the separations were wretched.

"Before I was married," she wrote her mother in March of 1944, "I worried because I didn't miss him more. Now I worry because I can't miss him less."

Unknown to him, many times after he had walked out the door, she would crawl into bed with a severe headache or an upset stomach. When the pain had passed, she would tend again to household chores, cleaning the white wicker furniture, the small kitchen, and throw rugs. She spent hours studying her Bible and thumbing through magazines and newspapers in search of sermon ideas, an avocation she would enjoy from then on. Many of Billy's better book and sermon illustrations can be attributed to her perusals. It was at this time that she discovered the authors who were to become her favorites, such as George MacDonald, G. K. Chesterton, Alexander Whyte, and Frank W. Boreham.

It became habit for Ruth to scour secondhand bookstores, and tucked in her billfold was a list of coveted out-of-print books. In later years her bookshelves would be full of her finds, including numerous first editions signed by the authors. Reluctant to let her husband outgrow her intellectually, she developed the habit of reading biographies, histories, novels, and books about art and foreign countries. Billy's appreciation of her intelligence and learning was something he often proudly mentioned to friends and family.

It was during times of aloneness in a small house in a strange town that she began to gather her energies and talents into a core of independence. The result was not a reclusiveness insensitive to others, but a strengthening by degrees. Her own profound faith and relationship with God carried her through the most trying times, and from them she derived her ability to survive and rescue. But in some subtle ways, the old injuries never stopped smarting.

Her avoidance of them simply became a matter of routine. This was observed in the spring of 1996 when she was due to see an out-of-town friend, and then was not to be found. Ruth had gone out to run errands. As the truth unraveled, Billy had just left for Minneapolis. Typically, Ruth could not sit alone in the house after the door shut, but diverted herself. The never-ending separations were and would always be, perhaps, her greatest sacrifice to him and the world.

The first phase of their marriage was peppered with the usual adjustments and oversights. He draped his wet towels over the top of the bathroom door. She depended on serendipity instead of recipes for cooking, and the results, like a yellowish batch of pickled peach Jell-O, were not always palatable. Nor did he appreciate her quick tongue.

"I have never taken your advice," he told her bluntly one day, "and I don't intend to begin now."

"*I'd* be ashamed to admit," she replied, "that I had married a woman whose advice I couldn't take."

Billy wasn't always a paragon of sensitivity. One day several of his bachelor friends visited unannounced and suggested that they all go into Chicago.

"That would be fine," said Ruth, who was eager to escape the monotony of the apartment. "I have some shopping I can do. I'll go get my coat."

"No," Billy said. "We guys just want to be alone. No women today."

No amount of begging would change his mind. Through tears she watched the car drive away, and she prayed, "God, if You'll forgive me for marrying him, I'll never do it again."

Billy did not intend to be unkind. He was simply inexperienced in making a new partner happy and secure. When he realized how much he had hurt Ruth, he was full of tender apologies. She did not like to nag, but quietly let him know her feelings. Indeed, from the beginning, she understood him better than his deacons did.

Billy's travels irritated certain pillars of the church who wanted the minister at their beck and call around the clock. At first, no one dared utter a syllable against him, for he was doing the church far too much good. By early 1944, attendance had doubled and tithing had increased so dramatically that the church leaders had redeemed their mortgaged sanctuary and ceremoniously burned the contract in a pie pan.

Then a well-known radio broadcaster named Torrey Johnson invited Billy to take over "Songs in the Night," a forty-five-minute program of preaching and singing. It was broadcast live from the church each Sunday night at 10:15. Billy persuaded gospel singer George Beverly Shea to assist, and immediately the show was a hit. Ruth's job was to sit near her husband during the broadcasts, beyond the eerie glow of the colored lightbulbs around his table, and pass him notes during the hymns, offering suggestions for his next remark.

"All she'd have to do," Shea recalled, "was write a sentence down and he could keep on going."

Soon the show was being broadcast twice each Sunday. Billy became a celebrity, and the town of Western Springs dubbed him "That Hustling Baptist Preacher." The speaking invitations multiplied and some of the deacons began to grumble. One finally suggested that if Billy did not discontinue his travels, the church should cut his salary.

He had received numerous job offers from churches and radio stations, and though he did not intend to accept any of them, "he enjoys hanging that over the deacons' heads once in a while when they get out of hand," Ruth wrote her parents. "If they think they can run Bill, they've got another think coming." He was also plagued by several parishioners who were the resident troublemakers. Like magpies, they formed a black knot in the congregation, generating a cackle of criticism about the minister and his non-Baptist wife. The nuisances swooped in to snatch up the slightest glitter of gossip, and in keeping with good Calvinist tradition, Billy offended them mightily.

"Some of you need to confess the sin of troublemaking," he announced during an evening service as he stared unabashedly at the guilty flock. "A person tries to build a testimony for God in this town and all you do is tear it down. You had better confess before God has to remove some people. As for me, I'm here to [do] this job for God and with His help, I'll get it done regardless."

Despite the problems, Ruth recorded at the time, "God is blessing and when a man gets saved it makes everything seem worthwhile."

Billy had twice applied for an army chaplaincy and had both times been refused because he was underweight. But in August 1944 he was accepted. Had he followed this course he likely would have been assigned to a base where he would have spent the remainder of the war behind a desk. Still three pounds underweight, he would not have been sent overseas. This question became moot when illness intervened and changed the course of his life. First, he began experiencing stress-related paralysis of the throat, and in early October contracted a dangerous strain of mumps in both sides of his neck.

A doctor visited him daily, but there were no antibiotics available. Ruth camped at his bedside, feeding him strained baby foods and liquids. Several times his temperature climbed so high he became delirious. One night, burning up, he began describing angels on the ceiling. "Can't you see them?" he asked. Ruth, desperate with the fear that he was dying, knelt beside the bed. Her prayers were tears. When he finally emerged from his sickbed six weeks later, he was as pale as death and weighed a mere one hundred and thirty pounds.

Soon after, a hundred-dollar check arrived from a woman who had heard Billy on the radio. "Please go down to Florida and take a vacation," her note read. The money could not have come at a better time, and he and Ruth drove to Miami. They rented a small room on Seventy-ninth Street, several miles from the ocean, not knowing that Torrey Johnson was vacationing in a hotel three blocks away. When Johnson discovered that Billy was staying nearby, he invited him to go fishing. While reeling in "at least a score of big fish," as Billy recalled, Johnson asked him to become a full-time evangelist for Youth for Christ.

Should Billy accept the offer, he would be responsible for organizing rallies, or crusades as they were later called, and new Youth for Christ chapters throughout the United States and Canada. After discussing it with Ruth, he accepted the offer. He resigned his position at Western Springs and his army commission, believing he could reach more servicemen through his rallies than from behind a desk. The members of his congregation were not surprised by his decision. They had sensed that it was only a matter of time before he would leave. Neither their church nor any church could contain this man who paced about like a caged tiger.

"I don't think Billy would ever have made a very good pastor," observed Myrna White, a former parishioner. "I don't think he's the type who would be happy settling down in one place." Robert Van Kampen realized that it was time for his protégé to pack when he found fourteen preaching invitations in the church mailbox one morning. "Our church is too small," Van Kampen recalled thinking. "God has given him a special gift. He is going to be another Billy Sunday or Dwight L. Moody."

Married to an evangelist, Ruth knew that the separations could only become more frequent, and she reasoned that if she couldn't be with him, she should at least be allowed to live where she would be happiest. Early in 1945, the Grahams packed the car, drove south to Montreat, and moved into an upstairs bedroom in her parents' house. For the next year Billy would travel to virtually every large city in the United States, thanks to a wealthy man from Kenosha, Wisconsin, who had given him and Johnson airline credit cards. There was not enough money to buy Ruth plane tickets. Unless Billy drove to his rallies, she stayed in Montreat.

In the summer of 1945, Ruth prepared for the birth of their first child. Finding a plain straw bassinet, she painted it blue and lined it with quilted blue satin. She trimmed it with yards of her wedding veil. On September 21, while Billy was away, Ruth gave birth. She named her Virginia Leftwich, after her mother, but called her "GiGi," which is Chinese for "sister." Ruth became her mother's friend and apprentice. They cooked, gardened, sewed, and cleaned house together. Secure now in her parents' home with her new child, she found the separations tolerable. For the first time since Ruth had left Qingjiang for Korea in 1933, she felt she had really come home.

In 1946, Billy and his new exuberant and handsome song leader, Cliff Barrows, held rallies in twenty-six cities in the British Isles. Later that year Youth for Christ enjoyed a larger budget, and Billy was told that Ruth could travel with him from time to time. Her early trips abroad were educational, if not humorous, for she was more naive than he was. Her first trip was in December.

She was to travel to New York and fly to London, where she would meet her husband. By the time the taxi drivers and waiters had collected their tips, and the airline agents had penalized her for overweight baggage, she boarded the DC-4 with two cents in her billfold. She lost her first dinner somewhere over the Atlantic and changed into her homemade red wool robe late that night in the men's restroom. She discovered the mistake the next morning when she retrieved her dress, which was hanging on the wrong door.

When the plane landed, she spotted Billy behind a fence just off the runway and, like a homing pigeon, headed toward him. A flight attendant in hot pursuit informed her, "You have to go through customs first." Her husband, enormously amused, added to her discomfort by moving into the lobby while the agent was slashing her bags with yellow chalk. "They're going to throw you in jail!" Billy announced repeatedly. The agent, long-faced and grim, as though he had been checking bags since the Norman Conquest, asked Ruth if she had any gifts to declare.

She thought a moment and whispered, "Just one. But don't let *him* see it." She nodded toward her husband. Fishing into her handbag, she discreetly slipped out a photograph of GiGi that she planned to give Billy for Christmas. It may have been the first time the agent had smiled in months.

That night, the Grahams checked into the exclusive Grosvenor House, financed by a friend who had instructed them to have a second honeymoon. Ruth marveled at the mysterious contraptions in the room, such as the bidet. "Why on earth couldn't you put your feet in the basin or use the tub?" she asked. And the tub? Why, she'd never seen one so big and declared that the wire soap dish looked like a bicycle basket.

After a month of bitter cold, foggy weather and a bland postwar diet of powdered eggs, potatoes, and bready sausages, an incident occurred which demonstrated that being married to an evangelist had its trying, if not absurd, moments. En route to Belfast, Billy and Cliff Barrows warned their wives that the Irish Christians considered cosmetics to be the paint of sinners. They urged Ruth and Billie Barrows to wipe off their modest makeup. The women dutifully obeyed. Powderless and minus eyebrows, Billie played the organ during the service while her husband led the singing, the couple mistakenly advertised as the "Barrows Brothers." Ruth sat in the audience, certain that the very people they needed to reach were the ones who now would be least attracted to these pale, frumpy Christians.

With thoughts such as those in mind, she appeared at a service several nights later with a dab of Tangee Natural shining on her lips. After the service, two Irish women confronted the Grahams.

"We received a tremendous blessing from your message," one woman said to Billy, while she looked pointedly at Ruth. "But we lost it when we saw that your wife was wearing makeup."

Surprised, Billy studied his wife's face, unable to detect the virtually transparent lipstick. "I'm sorry," he said, "she has no makeup on."

Ruth smiled.

This incident was not to be forgotten, it seems. Years later when Dr. Edwin Orr, president of the Oxford Association for Research in Revival, was addressing a group of men in Belfast, a gentleman raised his hand to ask a question.

"Is it true that Mrs. Billy Graham wears makeup?" the man asked.

Surprised, Orr evaded the question and again the arm shot up.

"What do you think of makeup?" the man asked.

"I don't know," Orr replied, "I've never tried it."

When the laughter subsided, the man's hand shot up again, and a neighbor jabbed an elbow into his ribs, exclaiming, "I say! Leave Billy Graham out of this, can't you? Don't you remember, John Wesley had a bad wife too?"[1]

In the fall of 1947, the Grahams were thrilled that Ruth was again pregnant, and they bought a two-story, partly furnished summer house across the street from her parents. It was built of white clapboard and fieldstone flecked with mica, the eaves curling low over large windows like a worn felt hat pulled over an old man's ears. With the forty-five hundred dollars they borrowed from the local bank they began making the forty-five-dollar monthly payments.

Ruth and her mother searched mountain junk shops for antiques and secondhand furniture. Virginia, home from nursing school at Johns Hopkins, helped them sand the drab green paint off the Victorian furniture sold with the house, refinishing the wood until it glowed like honey. Lamps evolved from adhesive tape canisters, old bottles, a small wooden bucket, and an ironware sugar bowl.

In May, Billy began to wonder if he was losing his authority at home. The first of what would be many hints came when Ruth was in the hospital with their newborn second daughter, Anne, and he decided on a whim to chop down the rhododendron thicket enclosing the yard. He gave the order and the workmen hemmed and hawed, staring sheepishly at their dirt-caked boots, before one of them finally replied in his mountain drawl, "Don't you think we'd best ask Miz Graham first?" They knew she would be horrified if she returned home and found the house visible to every driver and pedestrian on Assembly Drive, Montreat's main thoroughfare.

That summer, William Bell Riley, the president of Northwestern Schools in Minneapolis, summoned Billy to visit him in Golden Valley, Minnesota. Riley, a devout man and longtime admirer of Billy, was eighty-six years old and dying. A thunderstorm shook windowpanes as Riley jabbed a gnarled finger at the young evangelist and declared that Billy was to succeed him as president of the interdenominational institution, comprising a liberal arts program and a seminary. Billy's impulse was to say no, but he was intimidated by Riley's proclamation.

Ruth was opposed. Billy was an evangelist, not a scholar, she told him. Against his wife's wishes and his own good sense, he replied in September that should Riley die within the next ten months, he would accept the position until a new person could be chosen. On December 6, 1947, the man died, and at the age of twenty-nine, Billy found himself the president of a school with more than seven hundred and fifty students and no money. He gave the school the motto "Knowledge on Fire" and began forging the place into another Wheaton. His frustration mounted as his desire to preach and his new academic responsibilities yanked him hard two ways.

Ruth had no intention of going along for the ride and did not embrace the role of first lady. One day, a Northwestern Schools administrator telephoned her and cheerfully asked when she was moving to Minneapolis to occupy the president's mansion.

"Never," she let him know.

In the fall of 1949, Billy launched a crusade that would capture the country's attention. His fourth that year, it was held in a tent virtually the size of a city block in downtown Los Angeles. Eye-catching signs and newspaper advertisements proclaimed, "Dynamic Preaching, Heavenly Music, 6,000 Free Seats." Ruth joined her husband for what she thought would be the third and final week, leaving four-year-old GiGi with the Bells and fifteen-month-old Anne with Aunt Rosa in Los Alamos, New Mexico.

The 1949 Los Angeles crusade is legendary in Billy Graham history. Books, magazines, and newspaper articles hail it as his starting block. The myth, which was passed by word of mouth and in print, claimed that newspaper mogul William Randolph Hearst sent a memorandum to his reporters which read, "Puff Graham." Hordes of photographers and journalists descended on the meetings and Billy's name and face were circulated around the country. As is true of most legends, a portion of its fabric is woven of exaggeration.

It is a fact that William Randolph Hearst endorsed the young evangelist, and this was partially due to the thousands of Americans, English, Irish, and Scottish who had noticed Billy first. According to Hearst's son William Randolph Hearst Jr., his father was interested in what attracted the attention of the greatest number of people: In the past, senior Hearst had endorsed both Billy Sunday and Mary Baker Eddy. Billy Graham was not an obscure farmboy preacher who by the grace of Hearst became a star. The memo "Puff Graham" never existed, claimed Hearst Jr.

"Pop would have never sent a memorandum to an editor of his papers with the words 'Puff Graham.' He was not given to talking or writing in such cryptic style, and I never heard him use the word 'puff,' " William Hearst said many years later. "It was not a word used in the journalism profession except by press agents." Hearst, said his son, "was committed intellectually to help spread the Christian Gospel, and he highly approved of Billy's influence on America's youth."

What William Randolph Hearst did do, recalled Don Goodenow, picture editor of the old *Los Angeles Examiner* in 1949, was send teletype messages to his managing editors, urging them to "give attention to Billy Graham's meetings." Reporters and photographers from the *Examiner* and other Hearst newspapers were dispatched to the services. Each Friday night, Goodenow arranged a full page of photographs of Billy preaching, which ran in the Saturday morning paper and were picked up by the wire services. Favorable letters from readers piled up in the *Examiner*'s editorial department, and journalists began referring to Billy Graham's "charisma." He was eloquent and powerful, they wrote, and he had a commanding baritone voice.

"He did have an appeal for young people, no doubt about it," Goodenow recalled. "And even in the atmosphere of the newsroom, which can be callous at times, he was taken seriously."

Masses of people appeared at the tent, their interest generating more press, which in turn generated more public interest. Billy's image was elevated to a new high. "Churchmen say he's started the greatest religious revival in the history of Southern California," read the *Indianapolis Star* on November 2. "Old style religion is sweeping the city of angels with an evangelistic show overshadowing even Billy Sunday," said the Associated Press on November 4.

Three hundred and fifty thousand people filled the tent at the corner of Washington Boulevard and Hill Street as the three-week crusade stretched into eight. Billy was dumfounded and exhausted. He ran out of sermons and in desperation mounted the pulpit one night and read, word for word, half of Jonathan Edwards' "Sinners in the Hands of an Angry God." He ended with a few words of his own. It was a disaster. What may have precipitated a great awakening in the eighteenth century passed over the heads of his audience. He learned an important lesson then, Ruth recalled. Never again did he replace the Bible with another text.

Three thousand men, women, and children responded to the altar calls, but statistics can never tell the whole story. There were those who came in private, such as a man who wandered into the tent long after crowds had gone and lights were turned off. Johnny, the night watchman, was sleeping under the platform when the man stumbled through chairs in the sawdust-scented darkness.

"Who's there?" called Johnny, startled into consciousness.

"I just came back to find Jesus," came the reply.

Ruth witnessed the power filling that tent night after night. She realized "that this was without a doubt what God had called Bill to do." In a poignant scene that boded what fame would do to their personal lives, Rosa returned Anne to Ruth and the child didn't recognize her mother. And Anne ambled over to her father while he was talking on the telephone. He swiveled around and stared at her blankly, thinking she was a lost little girl who had wandered into the wrong room.

Billy believed that his path had been clearly set for him and began persuading the trustees of Northwestern Schools to relieve him of his presidency. In 1950, during a crusade in Portland, Oregon, he was offered a contract that would put him on the radio throughout the United States. In mid-August, he telephoned George Wilson, business manager of Northwestern Schools, asking him if he would handle any mail resulting from the broadcasts. Wilson agreed and suggested that they should set up a nonprofit corporation so that all incoming funds might be tax-deductible.

A lawyer in Minneapolis drew up the articles and bylaws, and the Billy Graham Evangelistic Association (BGEA) was born. At first, Billy would run the organization, conferring daily by telephone with George Wilson and associates in Minneapolis. Later a board was appointed to oversee the running of the organization and Wilson was appointed executive vice president. That November Billy began a radio program that Ruth christened the "Hour of Decision." It was initially transmitted by two hundred and twenty-three American Broadcasting Company stations in the country, and by 1960 the number would exceed one thousand, not including countless shortwave stations throughout the world.

In the late fall of 1950, Ruth prepared for Christmas early. She wrapped presents and decorated the house, trimming the tree with colorful lights. She trimmed another bassinet with her wedding veil, and on December 19 the

Grahams' third daughter was born. They named her Ruth Bell, but her mother nicknamed her "Bunny" because "she looked like a rabbit." Mother and daughter came home December 22, and with three children to manage, it was becoming increasingly difficult for Ruth to travel with her husband. His absences were more keenly felt, and, longing to be with him, she was increasingly isolated and torn when she would hear about him in the news. Days were lonely, and sometimes there seemed no escape.

On a rainy day in March 1950, while Billy was holding a crusade in Columbia, South Carolina, she wrote:

> The clouds were hanging low on the surrounding mountains. The whole outdoors was sodden and gray and gloomy. Then in the middle of it all I looked up from my kitchen sink and thru the window up on the side of the mountain was a bright patch of sunlight where the clouds had broken. The only patch of brightness in all that dismal scene. I thought how if I were free I'd love to climb up and sit in that patch of sunlight awhile . . . I shall have a little revival of my own.

In 1952, Billy, helped by Ruth, wrote his first book, *Peace with God.* On July 14, Ruth gave birth to their fourth child, a husky first son they named William Franklin Graham III. Billy could not hide his joy as he proudly carried him into the house for the first time. "I'd have loved another girl. But every man needs a son," he proclaimed of this feisty child who in 1996 would take over his father's organization and ministry and appear on the cover of *Time* magazine with him.

In 1953, Billy spoke at Church House, Westminster, in London. The English clergy and laity were impressed and invited him to hold a major campaign in their city the following year. The result would be the twelve-week Greater London crusade and Ruth's longest separation from her children.

1. Years later, during the Greater London crusade, the controversy over makeup again resurfaced. With great amusement, Ruth noted aloud to her husband that the mark of streetwalkers in a certain section of the city was that they wore no makeup.

10

CHAPTER

That Hustling Baptist Preacher

Courtesy of Ruth Bell Graham Personal Collection

PREACHING, 1950

I used to worry about Billy. When he started out, there was all that adulation. I was worried he might be tilted off balance by it. But then I met Ruth. Then I relaxed, knowing he had that strength on which to lean.

—*Paul Harvey*

The SS *United States* cut a wide, frothy furrow through the North Atlantic, and red and black stacks smudged gray across the light blue sky as the ship progressed northeast at thirty-five knots.

Midship in a handsome stateroom of soft rose, beige, and brown sat the "Revival Widow," as Ruth had been dubbed by the press. In front of her, three portholes gently bobbed as she sat on her bed writing a letter home while Billy conferred with team members. "Dearest Folks," she penned, "Here we are . . . already halfway to England. What a ship this is. . . . You should see our quarters! I'm sure John Wesley never had it so good." Her cheerfulness was a façade. Leaving her children would always be a wounding sadness she almost could not bear.

It was early afternoon aboard ship on February 20, 1954. The rising sun would be simmering behind the mountains in Montreat. When her mind drifted there, she could see mist wafting over her cloistered world, and shadows shyly creeping out from under thickets around the yard. She imagined rhododendron leaves tightly whorled in the brittle, wintry air, and twigs and branches wearing thick sleeves of ice along the rich black banks of the stream east of the patio.

> I'm so glad Bill has these few days of quiet and rest and wonderful food. . . . The menus are fabulous. And they urge you to ask for anything you can think of whether on the menu or not. For hors d'oeuvres I ordered pâté de foie gras one day as I'd read of it but didn't know what it was. I still don't. . . . Also had kangaroo tail soup. It was as nasty as it sounds. All I can think of that I'd really love, now that the voyage is drawing to a close, is corn bread and turnip greens.

She wrote with a fountain pen, waiting for shimmering black ink to dry as she kept one ear to the door. She had come to dread the quick step and staccato knock of Rob, their officious English cabin boy whose brisk and unannounced arrivals kept her busy darting into closets. The first evening aboard, she was standing in their hallway in her "sheer nightie" when he appeared in all his crisp efficiency. Dashing into the baggage room, she barely managed to snatch a robe out of her suitcase before another cabin boy opened the rear entrance in search of a passenger's luggage.

"Ah! Ah! Ah!" Rob wheeled around the corner, flailing after him like a crazed windmill. "*Madame* is in there!"

"All said," Ruth concluded, before folding the ship's creamy stationery, "I've been wishing for a little less service and a little more privacy."

In three days the Grahams would arrive at Southampton for the beginning of the twelve-week Greater London crusade at Harringay Arena in the north end of the city. Owned by the Greyhound Racing Association, the arena could hold some twelve thousand people. The London crusade committee had leased it for thirty-three thousand pounds at a time when money was scarce and preachers didn't draw crowds in England.

Billy's ministry was not yet well established outside the United States, and he was tense. He had insisted that Ruth accompany him. Uneasy about leaving her four children for such a long time, she told him that she would go only if she could sail home after the first month and return for the last. A friend had offered her a round-trip ticket to do this, and Billy reluctantly agreed. She carefully packed just enough to get her through four weeks. Her plans, however, were to disintegrate when he decided he absolutely could not do without her. Accompanying him, she would learn, also did not necessarily ensure quality time alone. During her three-month stay, they would find time for but a few meals together each week.

Ruth had hoped that when they reached Southampton, they would disembark relatively unnoticed. But on Monday morning, February 22, shortly before breakfast, the chief steward arrived at the Grahams' door holding a three-page radiogram. He explained that his copy of the morning news included an item which the captain, in an attempt to spare the Grahams any embarrassment, had ordered struck from the ship's newsletter. The chief steward handed Billy the original report. At the bottom of the first page, directly above an announcement of Queen Elizabeth's travel plans and below news that Senator Paul Douglas was appealing to President Eisenhower to recommend more tax cuts, was the following:

> London: A Labour Member of Parliament announced today he would challenge in Commons the admission of Billy Graham to England on the grounds the American evangelist was interfering in British politics under the guise of religion.

Billy discovered that the sudden uproar stemmed from a mistake in the calendars that the BGEA had mass-mailed to generate prayer and financial assistance for the crusade. The caption beneath one of the photographs read, "What Hitler's bombs could not do, Socialism with its accompanying evils shortly accomplished."[1] When Billy's director of Crusade Planning and Organization, Jerry Beavan, had written the phrase, he had not realized that Socialism, with a capital *S*, was synonymous with the Labour Party. Intentional or not, it was an unfortunate choice of words in a country still raw from the wounds of World War II. It seemed to some in Great Britain that Billy Graham was meddling in politics.

The mistake had been caught earlier, before most of the calendars had been mailed. A few, however, had slipped out. One found its way to Fleet Street and landed on the desk of Hannen Swaffer, the acid-tongued columnist for the left-wing *Daily Herald*. The furor began, culminating in Labour Party member Geoffrey de Freitass issuing the statement that Billy had read in the radiogram. "For a while there," Ruth wrote, "the wireless was kept buzzing with accusations, explanations, and apologies. And it kept us busy praying too, that the Lord would overrule this inadvertent mistake to his glory."

The crusade's chairman, General D. J. Wilson-Haffendon, sent Billy a telegram graciously offering advice and his hope that the blunder might indeed prove beneficial. "It's most unfortunate that while you were at sea this flare blew up," he wrote. "And it has made certain that a very much greater number of people will know about your ministry. But, I think it is vitally important that you should be extremely circumspect on the whole question of politics over here because the very people whom we hope to reach through the crusade are the people who are most offended at the unfortunate use of the word 'Socialism.'"[2]

The Grahams were warned that as a result of the controversy, the press would be on them like a pack of wild dogs. Sure enough, as the ship drew near Southampton the next afternoon, Ruth stared out a porthole and watched a tug pull alongside them. Twenty-five reporters and eleven photographers shoved their way aboard the SS *United States*. The Grahams already had abandoned their room, warned that it would be the reporters' first destination. The media and the public would always have a voyeuristic curiosity about how much the Grahams spent on food, shelter, transportation, overcoats, shoes. It was not uncommon for a passerby to make rude remarks beginning with "If Jesus were here today" and ending with any number of things: "Would He wear a hundred-dollar suit, eat steak, fly in a jet, own a swimming pool, drive an Oldsmobile, or stay in the Holiday Inn?"

Once a reporter, watching Billy disembark from the SS *Queen Mary*, sarcastically remarked to Grady Wilson, "When Jesus was on earth He rode a lowly donkey. I cannot imagine Jesus arriving in England aboard the *Queen Mary*."

"Listen," Wilson replied dryly, "if you can find me a donkey that can swim the Atlantic, I'll buy it."

The horde of reporters pushed noisily aboard the SS *United States*, crowded into the salon, and confronted Ruth and Billy. "I knew they were after Bill's scalp," Ruth wrote that night, "and there was nothing we could do but pray for wisdom and be as courteous and gracious as we could."

"We see you still wear makeup," a reporter said to Ruth.

"Is it true that your husband carries about his own special jug of water for baptisms?" another asked.

"What kind of hat are you wearing?"

"It's just a lid," Ruth replied dryly.

The next day the British press reported that Mrs. Billy Graham had been wearing a round white hat that she called a lid. Billy, wearing gray flannels and a black and gray tie, was smiling on the front page. "No Clerical Collar But My! What a Lovely Tie!" the caption read.

The reporters streamed off as the ship docked, shouting final questions and repartee as they passed. "Mrs. Graham," called one, "we're disappointed in your husband. We expected bright, hand-painted ties, flashy socks, and a sort of mass hysteria. And we find he's quite an ordinary chap."

Greeted by one of the largest press receptions ever held in Southampton, the Grahams disembarked quietly, not quite believing that the scores of newsmen, the cameras mounted on trucks, the gawkers, were there to see them. As soon as Billy set foot on the quay, microphones were shoved into his startled face.

"Who invited you over here anyway?"

"Do you think you can save Britain?"

"Don't you think your higher crime rate indicates you're more needed in your own country?"

"What will you do about Russia?"

One cynical question followed another, and all of it resulted in publicity that neither the London crusade committee nor the BGEA could afford. At the edge of the crowd, burly stevedores stared in annoyance at the hubbub, and Ruth, empathizing with them, moved in their direction, away from the mob. The SS *United States* towered above the crowd, gently rocked in the harbor as passengers and members of the crew poked their heads out of portholes and hung over rails and gateways, "their faces," Ruth recorded, "a curious mixture of amazement and a sort of what-on-earth-have-we-had-on-board look."

In Southampton, as Billy and Ruth passed through customs, they were greeted with encouragement.

"God bless you, sir," said a customs agent. "We need you here."

"I'll be praying for you, sir," a soldier promised.

The Grahams boarded a third-class car and rode to London's Waterloo Station, where they were again greeted by a record-breaking crowd. Above shouting porters and the noise of trains, thousands of voices rose in majestic hymns. People surged to welcome the American couple and to present Ruth with flowers, and in the confusion she became separated from Billy.

They moved into rooms 501 and 502 of the Stratford Court, a modest brick hotel with a small but friendly staff just off Oxford Street. Situated on the sixth floor of a wedge-shaped building, it was directly above a Dolcis shoe store. Across the street was a pub, and patrons erupted from it in the dark early morning hours, laughing and talking boisterously. Ruth's bedroom was adjoined by a sitting room, and Billy had a duplicate arrangement next door, so he could come and go without disturbing her. Their rooms were dreary, colorless, and bare, and wind howled around eaves and seeped beneath window frames in an eerie, icy wail.

The evening of the first meeting, March 1, did not bode well. Stars shone through charcoal clouds, the moist air portending snow. The Grahams nervously waited in one of the sitting rooms at the hotel. He was quiet and concerned. She was writing in her red leather journal. Bad weather would surely turn people away from the service, they feared. The anxiety culminated in the urgent ring of the telephone.

"It's begun to snow." Jerry Beavan's discouraged confirmation came over the line. "There's nothing the newspapers won't do to ruin the meeting," he added with heavy irony.

Billy fell silent as Beavan went on to tell him that thus far only two thousand people had trickled into Harringay Arena. A tenth of these were reporters and photographers confident of the American evangelist's opening night bust. Billy thought of the thousands of British Christians who were depending on him. He wondered what failure would do to their faith. Beavan added that Senators Stuart Symington and Styles Bridges had just arrived in London following an official business trip on the Continent. The politicians had announced to the press that they would not be attending the service because they had a dinner engagement.

The news that they had backed out was unsettling. Months earlier Billy had addressed the Senate prayer group in Washington and had been promised that two of their members would be on hand to introduce him to the crowd at the crusade's opening service. The Grahams wondered if the dinner engagement was a trumped-up excuse. The senators did not want to endorse Billy because of the scandal precipitated by the BGEA calendars.

"Bill looked sort of stunned when he told me," Ruth wrote as they waited for their ride to the arena. "And I thought I heard him praying in the other room just now. . . . The Lord has a purpose in this."

A dark green sedan and a driver, compliments of the Ford Motor Company, waited outside the hotel. "There are butterflies in my stomach," Ruth hurriedly scribbled on her way out.

Bundled in hats and coats, she and Billy rode in silence from central London to the North End, lulled by the thrumming of the engine, hand in hand as snow began a feathery downward spiral. In less than forty-five minutes, Harringay loomed a monstrous, windowless brick barn with virtually no cars in the parking lot. A shadowy stream of people filed beyond the milky aura of naked bulbs below the roof, heading nearby to an evening at the dog races. It was a sad spectacle, Ruth mused. The arena was virtually empty, while the racetrack thrived, filled with people sitting in witless wonder watching animals run in circles.

At a side entrance of the arena, team member Willis Haymaker intercepted Billy and Ruth and told a different story. "The building is filled to capacity!" he whispered in excitement, adding that the two American senators were there, waiting in Billy's office. All were astounded. When Beavan had telephoned an hour earlier, there had been only two thousand people in the arena. But thousands more had been en route by Underground, and they had converged at Harringay at once, moments before the Grahams had arrived. It was true that Symington and Bridges had a dinner engagement at 10 Downing Street with Winston Churchill but that wasn't for an hour yet. Though the American ambassador to the Court of St. James's had advised them to steer clear of Billy Graham, the two senators had never intended to renege on their promise.

Alone, Ruth ascended the large wooden platform and sat in her chair next to Billy's, behind the podium. Beyond were tiers of wooden bleachers, and below, twenty-five hundred additional flap-bottomed wooden seats had been set up; for the next three months they would snap shut when the crowd rose, cracking in succession like a string of firecrackers. Ruth hated sitting on the platform and always would.

"You long with them to worship the Lord," she confided to her journal. "And being stared at seems so out of place. But what can we do?"

During the next seventy-one nights, she would escape the spotlight whenever possible, worming through the masses to the far end of the oval arena, climbing to the highest tier, below the exposed steel girders. From this perch, Billy was a familiar sound, his blue eyes and keen features extinguished by distance. Around his wife, people were moved by the message of salvation, responding to the amplified voice, compelled and convicted by something stirring within as they sang the familiar lyrics "Just As I Am, without One Plea."

The singing at Harringay would, in Ruth's mind, remain unrivaled. One night in March, more than a thousand Welshmen made the four-hour train ride from Cardiff to Harringay. Cliff Barrows asked them to sing. Turning off the house microphones, he led them a capella in "Guide Me, O Thou Great Jehovah" and "I Will Sing of My Redeemer." Moved almost to tears, Ruth recalled, "I couldn't sing, only listen." Indeed, the singing at Harringay was so beautiful that the press began to suggest that it was what moved people to answer the altar call. Subsequently, Barrows eliminated the choir's singing of "Just As I Am, without One Plea." The people still came. The press began claiming that the silence was responsible.

Occasionally, Ruth would leave behind a clue of her presence. One night a kindly Englishman, big and old in thick spectacles, noticed that the woman beside him did not have a hymnbook, and he gave his to her. Had he perused it after the service he would have found scribbled inside, "Thanks for sharing your hymnbook with me. God bless you. Ruth Graham."

Night after night people filed into the arena until it could hold no more. Bobbies and team members firmly shut the doors, and faces pressed against the glass. Billy began preaching twice, sometimes three times daily to accommodate the crowds. "Not since the Dwight L. Moody revival in the late 19th Century has Great Britain been as deeply stirred," a journalist wrote, reiterating what was becoming increasingly familiar in the press. The crusade made the headlines almost daily, and in an attempt to learn more about this "Hot Gospeller," as the British called him, the journalists began to hound his wife.

"What is it like to be married to him?"

"Is he hard to live with?"

"Are you jealous of all the attention he gets?"

She was gracious, even humorous from time to time. But Ruth disliked being followed and quizzed. She was not keen on the elegant teas and black-tie dinners of London society, or of the special tours of English museums and landmarks. The couple was presented formally and privately to royalty, and on March 10 they lunched at St. James's Palace with the colonel and officers of the Coldstream Guards.

No matter how interesting, the social engagements were demanding and taxing. Suddenly, because Billy was a famous evangelist, he and Ruth were supposed to know how to dress and which fork to use when in the company of dukes and duchesses, earls and countesses. A week after their visit with the guards at St. James's Palace, an aristocratic couple invited Ruth to tour the Wallace Collection at Hertford House, Manchester Square. As she studied the objets d'art she made the mistake of asking the prickly curator what Richard Wallace had done "for a living."

"What do you mean, what did he do?" he coolly asked her.

"Well," Ruth explained uneasily, "I was taken to Kenwood and they claimed it was the home of the Guinness Beer people . . ."

"No, Madame," he interrupted, "Mr. Wallace did not have to work. He was a landed gentleman."

There were other adjustments to make. Entertainment was beginning to infiltrate religion, and it would take some getting used to on Ruth's part. One of the highlights of the Greater London crusade was to be the guest appearance of Roy Rogers and Dale Evans. Ruth was happy enough to have the legendary cowboy couple come until she learned that they were also bringing Trigger. "I think it *wrong* to have a horse in a religious service," she wrote in her diary in early March.

Ruth was accustomed to simplicity in worship. Horses and rhinestones grated on her sensibilities, and she was repelled by the presence of television cameras in the faces of people responding to altar calls. She understood the need for publicity, much of which was generated by the crusade committee in the form of billboards and banners, but she shrank from it. Accustomed to the quiet, unassuming tactics she had seen in the mission field, it never would be her modus operandi to entertain people to Christ. She would also learn soon enough that because a certain method was jolting to her did not mean it was intrinsically bad.

She had to apologize silently to Trigger, for example. On March 20, the cloudy Saturday that Roy, Dale, and Trigger performed, forty thousand children filled the dog track next door to Harringay Arena. Trigger danced and pranced and captured the youngsters' attention. Then Roy and Dale gave moving testimonies. The movie star couple was recognizable everywhere they went, and as Ruth observed what this had done to their personal lives, it made her more unsure. On Sunday, March 21, Roy and Dale invited the Grahams to dine with them at the Savoy Hotel and because of privacy problems had to have the meal sent to their room.

They ate on a pink damask-covered table as a spring breeze gently swayed curtains in the luxurious suite. Beyond the open window, Cleopatra's Needle pierced the sky above the Embankment. Roy told them he had just quit smoking, because of his health and because he knew he was constantly watched and emulated. He opined with a smile and crinkled eyes that he did not wish to set a bad example. For their entire week in London, they would have to hide when they weren't onstage. "Poor Roy and Dale are literally prisoners of fame," Ruth wrote at the time. "I wouldn't trade places with them for one billion dollars. I said *billion.* One little bit of fame is bad enough."

Hillary was a middle-aged nurse, a Christian who sang in the Salvation Army Songsters. Her husband was a good man, honest and industrious at his blue-collar job and kindly and faithful at home. They lived amid gardens and dunes in Southport, on the Irish Sea.

They had heard about the Greater London crusade for months and had tucked away shillings that they might attend. It was to be a welcome vacation of shops in the morning and services at night. They purchased their train tickets, made hotel reservations, and the days passed in quiet, happy excitement. One week before they were to leave, the husband became suddenly and violently ill. Hillary held him as he died.

With him went her will to go on. All religion and logic were devoured by a grief that daily sucked her mind away. With bags and ticket she boarded the train, lumbering two hundred miles southeast to London, her empty stare fixed to a window. She visited shops. She attended services. In a mechanical ritual she lived out the last scene that she and her husband had written together. Hillary intended, when it was over, to die.

But something nudged her during the service on her last night at Harringay. When the evangelist invited people to come forward, she rose heavily to her feet. Slowly, she followed hundreds of unfamiliar backs, watching the drab wool shapes bob and wind in front of her, vaguely, through the isolation of depression. She was led under the bleachers to the left of the platform and down a cold, narrow corridor. Midway to a tent called the Inquiry Room, where new converts were to be counseled, she could go no farther.

This was where Ruth found her, pressed against the wall, a woman with a slack, empty face. Twice Ruth asked if she could help and was greeted with silence.

"I should so love to help," Ruth gently coaxed again.

Hillary looked at her, then away. Finally, in a monotone, she told her story. When she had finished, she bitterly demanded, "Why are so many horrible creatures allowed to pollute the earth years without end when a virtual saint is snatched away without warning, without explanation?"

"What could I say?" Ruth wrote in her journal that night. "I with a husband, so happy and content. My words came like dust."

She prayed with the woman and copied her address. She would write to her, she thought, for in person she had failed. Ruth feared that she had failed ever since she had arrived in London almost a month earlier. Each night she joined the six hundred counselors and the dozen interpreters in the Inquiry Room, waiting to be used, secretly hoping she would be ignored. It wasn't that she didn't want to help. It was simply that she felt she couldn't.

Such a strange assortment of men and women converged upon that place each night. Dancers, actors, countesses, miners, people who had made profound wrecks of their lives came and were desperate to talk. An undertaker moved by Billy's sermon on Lazarus appeared. An escaped prisoner wandered back to turn himself in to God and the police. A Russian nobleman who spoke no English wandered back, and when he was asked by an interpreter how he could have understood the message well enough to respond to it, he replied, "When I entered this place I was overwhelmed by the presence of God. How can I find Him?" A towheaded little boy came after running to Billy and asking him breathlessly, "Mr. Graham, could you tell me where they are finding God?"[3]

Some, however, treated the Inquiry Room like the personnel window of a department store. It was the place to register complaints. On March 23, a smartly dressed woman approached Ruth, not realizing that this woman wearing the white silk ribbon with "Advisor" printed on it was Billy Graham's wife.

"Can I be of help?" Ruth asked.

"Well, not really," the woman replied tartly. "But you could answer one question for me. Why do Billy Graham and his team stay in such an expensive hotel?" She was a beauty consultant in a fashion shop and all of her clerks had been talking about it. "A room costs ten pounds a night," she added smugly.

Ruth patiently explained that the rooms actually cost two pounds ten, and she hoped the woman would walk away without asking how she knew. But the woman asked, and the blood rushed to her face when Ruth reluctantly told her.

As Ruth's first month in England drew to a close, two miseries nagged at the back of her mind. "I don't know where one single contact I have made over here has resulted in one single conversion to Christ," she wrote. "Not one; and I get so lonesome for the children I can hardly stand it." Her depression was acute at night. She didn't dare look at photographs of the children or conjure up their faces in her mind. She would turn out the lights and quickly pray, "Please take care of each one," before she climbed into bed and pulled covers up to her ears.

On March 27, she instructed a team member to purchase her a return ticket. The first month had passed and she was going home at last. When she told Billy her plans, he canceled them.

It wasn't completely in jest when he warned team members, "If you get her the ticket, you're fired."

He needed her. She was his most trusted confidante. He was emotionally dependent on her. A year after Harringay when he was in Glasgow alone, he wrote her:

> I don't have to tell you that you are in my mind every moment and that I love you with all my heart, and miss you so much that it hurts. . . . Naturally I think of you a thousand times a day and each little experience I wish I could share with you. Last night I told Lorne Sandy and Charlie Riggs to gather all the stories for me daily. I said, Last year every evening Ruth would bring me a number of stories of conversions of people who had come to Christ. I don't have her this year to report to me every night; therefore I am depending on you fellows. You see what an important place you had on the team. Your letters have been a balm in Gilead. They have given me inspiration, quieted my nerves. They bring me so close to you. Be assured that my love grows for you every day and I miss you more than I ever thought I could miss any person.

The thought of staying in London another two months was awful. Ruth was certain she was more needed at home. "If I've got to stay," she wrote March 30, "I wish I could be used. I've told the Lord I want nothing to be in His way of making use of me if He can." On April 1, Billy wavered and told her that she could leave. Overjoyed, she telephoned her children and told them that she would be home in a week. She packed her bags and immersed herself in various activities, trying to push away a lingering uneasiness that irritated her like a pebble in a shoe.

The next few days were raw, the sky solid with clouds. On April 4, she left her hotel alone and walked to Hyde Park, where she found a small crowd assembled at the Speakers' Corner, listening to Donald Soper (now Lord Soper), a Socialist Methodist preacher and well-known orator. He was notorious for his skill at making fools of those who dared to challenge him.

"This person says he believes the Bible from cover to cover!" he roared, pointing an accusing finger at a young man. "He looks like the type that would believe the Bible from cover to cover!"

Ruth worked her way through the laughing mob, moving closer to Soper just in time to hear him fire at her husband. She wasn't surprised. Billy Graham's face watched traffic from billboards and rode by on the sides of city buses. He was a target in political and religious circles and the butt of jokes in nightclubs.

"I have no patience with those who preach sudden conversion," Soper shouted. "To think an entire life can be changed in a half hour's time is a diversion of Christian truth!"

Ruth found his diatribe more depressing than annoying. "One had the feeling he was siding with the laughing unbelievers in his ridicule of simple-hearted Christians," she wrote. "It was time to close and just then I felt some drops of rain. A great black cloud had piled up overhead and it was as if Heaven wept to see a man of God (supposedly) stand and sow doubts in the hearts already full of bewilderment."

Dressed in a black-and-white-checked wool coat, bareheaded and without an umbrella, she hurried toward a nearby hotel for shelter. As she walked briskly along the rain-spattered pavement, she realized that a young man had fallen into step with her. As she turned a corner, he turned with her. Then he mumbled something.

"Pardon?" Ruth asked.

"A pity the rain had to break it up," he said. "Where are you going?"

"Back to my hotel," she replied in a clipped tone, quickening her pace.

He tenaciously followed her as she crossed a wide, busy street, darting perilously in front of cars.

"An American, huh?" he asked cheerfully, ignoring her obvious discouragement.

"That's right."

"Would you have time for a cup of coffee?"

"No thank you," she said. "I'd better get back to my hotel."

"What about tomorrow night? Are you busy?"

"Yes. I'll be going to Harringay," she said, and suddenly filled with mischief, she asked, "Couldn't you come?"

"I suppose I could," the man said with uncertainty. "And how about Tuesday night?"

"I'll be going to Harringay again."

"Again?" he asked, incredulous. "You won't be going to Harringay every night next week, will you?"

"Every night."

After a long, uncertain silence, he asked, "You wouldn't be connected with Billy Graham, would you?"

"His wife," she said as the man fled.

The response was typical when men tried to pick her up. They would do their best to strike up a conversation with this handsome woman wearing a wedding ring. The instant her identity became known, the gentlemen ran.

Though Billy had given Ruth permission to return to their home in North Carolina, she knew he did not want her to go. For the next few days she packed and unpacked, unable to decide what to do, and on April 5 she received a letter from a retired missionary:

Dear Mrs. Graham,

Have just heard of your problem to stay with your husband or go to the four children and am praying.

In case God says Stay, I feel constrained to send you a quotation from a friend's letter to me many years ago when we had to let the last of our five leave us and we had to stay in China. She wrote, You have the right to ask the Mighty One to do more for them than He could if you were with them. Open thy mouth wide.

He has been faithful to the promises and kept and used all five. I am writing this at the request of our youngest, who says she can testify to the fact that the Lord didn't let them down!

If the Lord says, Go, He will care for your husband better than you can, and as your choice is His, He surely will make that will clear.

That night the answer came to Ruth as she sat in the arena, the din of voices rising and falling at the dog track next door, a distant roar of idiocy in a weary, wounded world. Less than a decade ago England had lost one-fourth of its wealth and sixty thousand civilians in the blitz. London had suffered a coal shortage and was still in a brownout. Bombed-out buildings yawned from the cityscape like open sores. Only the wealthy wore bright clothing, most Englishmen drab and tattered like sparrows. The House of Commons demanded Winston Churchill's resignation and debated whether Britain should manufacture the hydrogen bomb. Voices rose and fell in rhythm with the orbits of dogs.

It wasn't an epiphany exactly, but as Ruth sat high in the gallery, thoughts and feelings sifted through and finally focused. It spoke for itself, she wrote. "The average man does not realize his peril. He fiddles gaily on while Rome burns about his ears. It's the gravity of the whole situation that gives me pause. If Bill feels he needs me if I can in any way be of help over here perhaps I should stay."

She canceled her reservation. Her problem wasn't her effectiveness. It was looking for visible results. Her husband could see the fruits of his ministry immediately in the crowds that gathered below his podium. For Ruth, there would rarely be instant satisfaction. It wasn't the nature of her mission. Yet there were those priceless, wondrous moments when she got her reward. Twelve years later, again in London, a creamy envelope was delivered to her hotel room. It was postmarked Southport, and a modest script flowed in lines straight and centered as though someone had taken great pains to be neat:

Dear Mrs. Graham!

I'm so happy to know you are in England. You won't remember me but in your big London Campaign I came down to hear Dr.

Graham. My husband had died suddenly the week before and I came to London to end everything. But in the meeting as I listened to the message God spoke to me. You were so kind and understanding it helped me so much to know, even in your busy life, you could think and pray for me!

My life is busy am still singing in the Salvation Army Songsters and trying to love and serve my Lord.

Hillary

On April 11, the Grahams drove eighty miles south for a weekend near Beachy Head in East Sussex. It was a rare moment of pause in their frenetic lives. The next morning, while the clock ticked steadily beyond church time, they ate breakfast and strolled along the white chalk cliffs. The thick turf ended suddenly and the sheer rock cascaded six hundred feet into the English Channel, its placid waters heaving lethargically, twinkling like a multifaceted crystal. Behind them rolled the Sussex Downs where William the Conqueror had invaded England some nine centuries before.

"We lay on our stomachs and peered over the edge, giddy from the dizzying height, and watched the sea gulls wheeling and preening themselves in the sun and nesting in the jagged rocks below. The water lapped gently on the rocky beach," Ruth wrote. The peaceful rhythms of the English Channel and the soft buffeting of the sun beckoned them to linger, but they had to leave for an evening church service to hear an Irish evangelist. The peaceful mood quickly dissolved when Billy reminded her of the Irish Christians' disapproval of makeup. Reluctantly, she removed what little she had on. That night she ventilated her feelings in her journal, defining a philosophy that she would later pass on to her own children.

> I'll just pray God will open Bill's eyes and heart to realize what a stumbling block a Christian's appearance can be to the unconverted, and not be too concerned with offending the saints. How difficult it is for a girl to see anything attractive in Christianity when Christians look so unattractive. It has become a matter of deep conviction with me. We Christians, through frowning upon relatively harmless playthings like makeup, bleached hair, nail polish, etc., make the Christian life a bugbear to young converts instead of a joy. I think it is especially easy for [people] to mistake their prejudices for their convictions.

On April 16, Good Friday, Billy preached in Hyde Park to more than forty thousand people. Ruth avoided the platform that had been built for the event, and wandered through the crowd, pausing every few dozen steps to listen to the orators spontaneously spawned during such services.

"Billy Graham wouldn't be over here if he weren't making money," pontificated a young man with a crew cut and thick glasses. "You know he wouldn't."

"It's all a form of mass hysteria," asserted his companion, a handsome, smooth-skinned Indian who punctuated each soft-spoken remark with delicate flutters of his poetic hands. "Six months after Mr. Graham's gone it's the same thing with Danny Kaye and the rest they'll get over it."

By this time, dozens had gravitated toward the two men like aimless beads of water, forming a curious puddle at their feet. Ruth craned her neck, peeking through ears, shoulders, and collars.

"Did you all see Mrs. Graham leave the platform?" the Indian asked the crowd.

Heads nodded in unison. They had indeed seen someone vacate the platform, a former movie star named Colleen Townsend Evans, who had given her Christian testimony and then left for an appointment.

"Did you notice how everyone was looking at her?" the Indian asked, his voice rising. "People aren't looking at her husband, they aren't interested in him. Everyone was trying to get pictures of *her*. They like to look at her just like they would a Hollywood movie star."

Ruth almost choked on laughter.

Suddenly a woman standing directly in front of her launched into a defense, claiming that Mrs. Billy Graham wasn't the one who had been sitting on the platform at all. On she chattered, turning and nodding here and there to address the crowd, her eyes finally resting on the amused woman behind her. "Why here's Mrs. Graham now!" she exclaimed.

The Indian smiled vacuously as Ruth stepped forward and shook his hand.

On Monday evening, April 19, she would indeed find herself on the platform, thanks to her husband, who had announced, without collaborating, that she would deliver a brief message that night. He clued her in that morning, and the rest of the day she was miserable with anxiety, her hands trembling. Billy, meanwhile, paced the room, offering what he thought were helpful suggestions in an effort to soothe her.

"Tell them about your childhood," he suggested. "Didn't you ever have any narrow escapes?"

She thought a minute and then replied that once in Qingjiang she and the Talbot boys found a grenade and, thinking it was a metal pineapple or scale weight, hung it by its ring from a branch in the mulberry tree over the pet cemetery. The gateman recognized their new toy and alerted Dr. Bell, who wrapped the grenade in a paper sack and dropped in into a lake.

"Listen," Billy said, obviously unimpressed, "your audience went through the blitz, remember? Why don't you just practice projecting yourself like Colleen Evans?"

"Oh, joy!" Ruth exclaimed. "That's a help. The closest I ever got to a Hollywood contract was a high school play in which I played the part of an old maid missionary."

That night, she moved to the podium, turned to her husband, her mouth strategically close to the microphone. "I could kill you," she said. Her few words were overwhelmed by the huge swell of laughter.

She was not at her best when shoved onto the stage. "Somehow," she recorded later that night, "God helped me through without my throwing up on the platform or falling up the steps."

The third month of the Greater London crusade unreeled at the same frenetic pace as the previous two. Billy had lost fourteen pounds, and both he and Ruth were exhausted. The press had reversed their original cynical opinion of him. Several reporters had gone forward at altar calls. In part, the media's change in attitude was due to his refusal to respond to criticism and insults. "I do not intend to get . . . into endless arguments and discussions with them," he explained in a letter to Ruth the following year. "I am going to take the position of Nehemiah when he refused to go down and have a conference with his enemies. He said, 'I'm too busy building the wall.' We are too busy winning souls to Christ and helping build the church to go down and argue."

The final two services of the Greater London crusade were on May 22, a rainy Saturday. The first was in White City Stadium and seventy thousand people crowded the stands and playing field, with umbrellas and newspapers held over their heads. The second was at Wembley, where people had camped overnight in the raw weather, hoping to get in. American and British flags tossed in sharp winds high above Empire Stadium. At entrances, bobbies on horse and on foot directed traffic. Inside, a tremendous scoreboard blazed, "Jesus said, I am the Way, the Truth and the Life."

More than one hundred twenty thousand people packed the stadium. Ruth was seated behind the platform in the royal box with eleven members of the House of Commons, the mayor of the City of London and his wife, and the wife of Archbishop of Canterbury Geoffrey Fisher. Cold, damp air seeped through Ruth's wicker chair and under the edge of the wool rug draped over her knees, chilling her to the marrow. Clouds were ponderous, the air shimmering as though the sky would split any moment and release a downpour. She surveyed the multicolored flecks stretching out before her. That this many people would file into a stadium and stand shoulder to shoulder to hear a man preach overwhelmed her and filled her eyes with tears.

There was a sudden flurry of movement below as her husband and the Archbishop of Canterbury passed through an entrance, a pack of photographers surrounding them.

"There ought to be a law stating how close a photographer can get to one's face," the mayor said in Ruth's ear.

Billy's sermon was simple, the message of salvation clear. Realizing that the crowd and immensity of the stadium would prevent thousands of people from coming forward, if they wished, he asked those who wanted to make a decision for Christ to wave their handkerchiefs. Billy Graham bowed his head before a fluttering white sea.

1. John Pollack, *Billy Graham* (New York: McGraw-Hill, 1966), 116.
2. Records of the Billy Graham Evangelistic Association, Limited, Folder 1, Box 4, Collection 9, Archives of the Billy Graham Center, Wheaton, Illinois.
3. One night after the service, Ruth ran into famous American photographer Carl Maddens. He was rushing out of the Inquiry Room as she was going in. Moved by what he had seen inside, he blurted, "Let me out of here! This is no place for a photographer."

Courtesy of Ruth Bell Graham Personal Collection

FAMILY ON THE MOUNTAIN

11
CHAPTER

Little Piney Cove

I surrendered for the obscurity of the mission field. I thought the height and depth of surrender was to lose myself in heathen obscurity for God. I find my surrender was neither high enough nor deep enough.

All summer I have rebelled at this publicity. I've climbed into a shell. I've tacked Private, No Admittance over my life, and it won't work. I belong to God and He placed me here, and He will undertake for me and give me poise, grace, love, wisdom all I need to bring Him honour in the life He has appointed.

—Ruth Bell Graham, summer of 1954

After Harringay, Billy Graham's life belonged to the public, and tourists descended upon the rustic house like pigeons on a monument.

On Sunday afternoons in the summer of 1954, commercial buses lumbered through Black Mountain from local religious conference centers and approached the town gate, built of native stone with MONTREAT spelled in small white rocks. Visitors had to pass through its twin arches to come and go, and from time to time truck drivers lulled by thrumming diesel engines forgot themselves and crashed through the top of it. During the weeks before repairs, it always looked as if someone had knocked out the town's teeth.

Rumbling up Assembly Drive, the buses parked across the road from the Grahams' house. Bus doors flapped open, disgorging curiosity seekers in a flood of rumpled suits, sunglasses, grins, and cameras. They flocked into the yard, shutters clicking. The evangelist's fans picked splinters off the rustic gate, snatched stones, leaves, twigs, anything that might serve as a souvenir, and they summoned the Graham children to come outside and have their pictures taken.

Ruth and Billy shielded the family from the public, refusing to place them on display for tourists or Billy's audiences. Requests to parade the children to the platform to give their Christian testimonies were denied. Although Billy wasn't home enough to shield them from his admirers and critics, Ruth was fiercely protective. Journalists were forbidden to interview the children and take their photographs, but she could not keep an eye on four rambunctious youngsters every minute. The summer of 1954 she began noticing that three-year-old Bunny, by nature more gregarious than her two sisters, had more change than her small allowance could explain. Questions were asked, and GiGi tattled: "Well, Mother, just watch the next time a bus stops." The following Sunday, Ruth watched Bunny slip from the house to the front gate.

"Are you Billy Graham's little girl?" one of the tourists asked.

She nodded innocently, her red pocketbook yawning at her wrist as she waited for the expected nickel or quarter in exchange for each picture taken. Her mother put a quick halt to Bunny's entrepreneurial endeavors. Training nine-year-old GiGi was a different matter. "She was a timid, enchanting child with a proclivity for mischief. She tried harder to be good than anyone but couldn't," recalled Ruth, who very well may have been the genetic source of her oldest child's spirit. GiGi's sins included scampering through the backyard and tying a rope across Assembly Drive, then dispatching six-year-old Anne to try to collect a dollar toll from passing cars. Crouched behind a large rotten stump, GiGi hurled mud balls and crabapples at tourists. One afternoon when someone stopped her on the roadside and asked, "Could you please tell me where Billy Graham lives?" she sweetly replied, "Who's he?"

Ruth decided it was time to move when she discovered someone peeping over her bedroom windowsill while she was drying her hair one morning. She was jittery, exhausted, and unable to sleep. Her own responsibilities had dramatically increased from the growing demands on her husband's life. He was too busy to manage the family budget, and the job had become hers. He no longer saw his paychecks, and Ruth was all too frequently summoned to the bank to take care of their overdrawn account. William Hickey, the president of Northwestern Bank, would telephone her himself:

"Ruth, this is William Hickey . . ."

"I'll be right down," she would interrupt.

Handling the finances was further complicated by the reality that she not only had to make ends meet, but needed to remember that the world was watching every penny she spent. She could never indulge herself in jewelry or expensive clothing, even if the items were gifts, and refusing extravagant presents was sometimes quite troublesome. For example, when she requested that a group she had addressed send her thousand-dollar honorarium to an orphanage in Mexico, they complied and sent her a Neiman Marcus gift certificate for the amount. Ruth bought a gold bracelet and gave it to a relief organization with the stipulation that they sell it for twice its value and use the money for mission work in Third World countries.

One Christmas, good friend and country music star June Carter Cash sent Ruth a hooded, full-length autumn haze mink coat (she had noticed Ruth shivering on crusade platforms). Ruth explained that she couldn't exactly appear in public, much less on Billy's platforms, wearing the fur.

"Look," June said, "wear it to the barn. Wear it to the car. Wear it out walking with Billy in the snow on the mountain. But stay warm!"

Ruth wore the coat on the mountain or in the car, once appearing at a friend's house on a bitterly cold day wearing the coat and a pair of asbestos gloves. Finally, with June's permission, Ruth auctioned the coat as she had the bracelet, only to have a friend buy it for twice its value and give it back to her for her birthday. Somewhere in a closet, this mink no doubt remains, most recently sighted in the winter of 1995 when friends arriving by helicopter spotted Ruth, the air traffic controller, bundled in fur in the field below. She was waving her arms to make sure her visitors didn't hit any wires.

Though no one offered Billy a fur coat, he had plenty of other rewards to resist and always would. In the late fifties he rejected NBC's offer of a million dollars a year to host a two-hour Sunday morning talk show. He said no to Paramount Pictures Corporation executives who wanted to make him a movie star. He declined ABC's offer of a starting salary of $150,000 if he would serve as a consultant, and he donated personal gifts, such as prime real estate in Florida and California, to the BGEA and Wheaton College. A year's lease of a private jet and pilot were refused, and he donated about half of his estimated five-hundred-thousand-dollar family inheritance to various Christian organizations.

Ruth wondered how she would overcome the tensions imposed by fame. She anguished over the importance of providing the children with a normal environment. Typically, she kept her anxieties to herself, talking about them in her prayers and journals. She fought the resentment that boiled to the surface when tourists invaded their property and their privacy, and she also knew that any unkindness on her part would not be forgiven.

"It's an odd kind of cross to bear," she wrote at the time. "Yet those who have not been through it would consider it some kind of glory."

In early 1954, the Grahams had been offered a good deal on a hundred-and-fifty-acre cove, located two miles from their house between two ridges, or hogbacks, on one of the Seven Sisters. The land was occupied by two mountain families who grew corn on one slope and culled timber on the other. They decided to sell out, and the cove was offered to the Grahams for a mere forty-three hundred dollars.

Shortly after the turn of the century, a six foot six mountain man named Solomon Morris built the narrow dirt road that wound from the hogbacks' base to a level area several hundred yards below the summit, where the mountain families later built their pole cabins. Morris hacked a clearing in the brush halfway to the top.

He followed with a mule-pulled plow and drag pan, and cut and smoothed a road wide enough for a wagon. Morris planted more than a hundred apple, pear, cherry, and black walnut trees and carried dozens of white pine seedlings from nearby Mt. Mitchell. These and a thousand white pines the Grahams received for a Forestry Incentive Program reseeded many times over until their full, pungent branches eventually cloaked the mountain.

Before the Grahams agreed to buy the property they drove there to inspect it and were greeted by suspicious eyes peeking through cabin windows on a slope thick with rhododendrons, mountain laurel, and wildflowers. The red-clay-chinked stone foundation of Solomon Morris's original house reclined in the moist, fragrant shade of the white pines he had planted almost half a century earlier.

Billy surveyed the property with skepticism, while Ruth felt her blood race at the potential.

"I leave it up to you to decide," he said just before he left for the West Coast.

She borrowed money from the bank and bought the cove while he was gone. When he returned he was incredulous.

"You *what?*" he asked.

After he recovered from his initial shock, they began making plans, deciding they would build behind the tall bank of white pines Morris had planted. Billy wanted to cut the evergreens to afford them a view of the valley. Ruth believed that no tree should be cut unless it was absolutely necessary. They compromised by deciding to build farther up the ridge. The mountain people evacuated the property, leaving a tarpaper shack, two pole cabins, three lean-tos, a hog pen, a potato cellar, and foundations of other cabins that had burned to the ground over the years. Bulldozers began gouging a shelf in the hogback.

Ruth's first project was a surprise for Billy. She would remodel one of the pole cabins so the family could escape the tourists on weekends while the house was being built. Workmen tore out partitions, opening the cabin into one spacious,

L-shaped room. They built a fireplace from fieldstone found on the property, replaced the asbestos roof, and scoured the rooms from beams to floorboards. Ruth furnished the cabin with a double bed and covered the loft with mattresses for the children. The kitchen was a fireplace and an outdoor grill. Spring water was piped into a wooden tub at the back door, and the bathroom was an outhouse some hundred paces beyond the secondhand wraparound porch Ruth had bought from a carpenter.

Shortly after she finished her secret project, Billy returned home. She drove him up the mountain at dusk, not telling him where she was taking him or why. Hugging the rutted, unpaved road around sharp bends, the jeep finally crunched to a halt in front of the remodeled cabin. Oil lamps glowed in windows and a wisp of gray wood smoke drifted up from the chimney. They sat at the hearth drinking cocoa she had heated over the open flames, their romantic mood dissolving into laughter when he drained his cup and discovered the chewing gum she thought she had tossed into the fire moments earlier. As construction continued, the cabin was a welcome refuge where Ruth's family, parents, and friends convened for picnics of fried chicken, biscuits, potato salad, and apple pie before the open fire.

In the weeks that followed, Ruth designed her new home. It would be U-shaped and two stories, facing a small semicircle of lawn and a vista of Black Mountain, the Swannanoa Valley, and row after row of hazy ranges. This would be Billy's retreat from the frenetic world, it was her hope. But as years passed, her accomplishment would prove, most significantly, to be a striking manifestation of her own sensibilities and spirit. She built and furnished the Graham home with materials from her past and cemented them with her imagination. It would be her artistic masterpiece, and she would spend a lifetime loving it as he continued to travel.

She studied books on architecture and discovered that she felt most strongly drawn to the chapters about log cabins. Like the red jeep she drove up and down the mountain and the face of the man she loved, ruggedness attracted her. She preferred the natural beauty of old wood and stone. Cracks, nail scars, and weather-beaten materials "had character," she explained, "as if they'd existed for a long time and seen a lot of living."

Billy, it would turn out, was not at home in rusticity. His idea of comfort was a hotel. "When Bill gets to Heaven and finds it's not like a Holiday Inn or a Marriott," Ruth would joke over the years, "he'll be back." His only request regarding the new house was that it have comfortable chairs and adequate lighting.

Ruth hired the same mountain men who had remodeled her parents' home. Her fondness for the neighboring clans had begun when she hired "Old Dad" Roberts to come work for her at her first house. He was a short, wiry man with black hair and a busy mustache, and dark eyes like volcanic glass. He raised his voice almost to a chant when he talked about religion, and he had a talent for tracking rattlesnakes, which smelled like cucumbers, he claimed. When he detected a snake, Roberts would freeze and sniff as he slowly laid down his hoe or rake. "I smell me a rattlesnake," he would announce. Workmen gathered around as he began stalking. When the enemy was spotted, Roberts would snatch it up behind its head and snap its neck like a raw green bean. Slitting the carcass with a penknife, he would tie a string to the tail and hang the rattlesnake over a tin can to drain it for "snake oil."

"It's good for the rheumatiz," he would explain.

Roberts was as honest as a tuning fork, and when Ruth began building her home, he went to the mountain with her. Ambling through the property, he took apart old still furnaces, for moonshiners were no strangers to this part of the world. He rolled boulders along a streambed to the construction site, where they became part of the native rock walls around the house.

The contractor was Gregg Sawyer, a mellow, good-natured man. Unlike several of the temperamental artisans who worked for him, he submitted to Ruth's preferences. A taut leather belt encircled his ample middle, holding up a pair of perpetually wrinkled khaki trousers. Usually he wore a plaid flannel shirt, sleeves rolled up to the elbows, and he had a habit of cleaning his wire-framed spectacles between his thumb and forefinger, smudging the lenses until it was a wonder that he could see a blueprint or drive a wooden peg into a floorboard. His chin was sandy with stubble and he wore a battered felt porkpie hat. Zeb Sawyer, his brother and partner, was the best fireplace builder in the valley. Both were craftsmen of the first order and in later years would be commissioned to restore former Governor Zebulon B. Vance's birthplace in nearby Weaverville.

Zeb Sawyer's skill in building fireplaces and clean-drawing chimneys reached its zenith with the construction of Ruth's house. Billy basically wanted none, and conceded that Ruth could build two. The instant he went out of town, she ordered Sawyer to build five as fast as he could. While a bootlegger mixed the mortar, Sawyer fashioned fireplaces in the guest room and Ruth's bedroom. Those in the living room and the family room were as cavernous as they would have been in the seventeenth and eighteenth centuries, when the family baking and cooking were done over the fire. The fireplace in Billy's bedroom unfortunately smoked the first time he came home and saw what his wife had done.

All but the frame of the new house was built of old wood, most from log cabins Ruth discovered in the mountains. Dressed in blue jeans and an army jacket, she drove her jeep through western North Carolina, stopping at gas stations to leave her telephone number with attendants in the event they heard of cabins for sale. Six months after her first inquiry, she began getting calls. She bought a two-story cabin for four hundred dollars. A dog-trot, or two cabins connected by a breezeway, she picked up for a hundred and twenty. Most cabins sold for about fifty dollars, and when she didn't buy the entire building, she would pay several dollars per wormy chestnut, oak, or yellow poplar log. Often the owners of the cabins would throw in a few bonuses with the sales, such as an old lazy Susan table with a broken leg, a smokehouse, or a broadax that had been used to hew logs in a century past.

She discovered a large, century-old Victorian house being torn down near Asheville and for forty-five dollars per thousand feet bought all of its usable heart-of-pine lumber. "Couldn't buy it new for a hundred and twenty dollars a thousand," Gregg Sawyer chuckled as he eyed her find. She became an expert at hand-staining new lumber, rubbing such curiosities as leftover lipsticks and shoe polishes into the wood until it was highlighted with subtle shades of red, gray, and brown, like the old wood she preferred. From a school razed in Asheville, she salvaged tons of old brick and floored the living room, a porch, and the glassed-in hallway that connected two wings of the house. She bought miscellaneous items from a salvage yard.

Her building philosophy baffled and annoyed many of her workmen. "Use the new lumber for framing and the old lumber for finishing," she reminded them daily.

It didn't make a bit of sense. They had all been born in log cabins, spending every night of their childhoods sleeping on feather beds with stars shining through the gaps in the shingles. They had worked hard to leave all that behind. Prosperity meant linoleum floors and department store furniture. They couldn't understand why Ruth wanted the hundred-year-old lumber on the outside where everyone could see it. They could not figure out why she wanted the massive exposed beams in the living room roughed up with a broadax. Two rock masons quit on the spot when she asked them to build walls without the mortar showing, "to look like dry rock walls," she explained.

"If I can't lay rock the way it's sposed to be laid," one mason told his boss, "then I'm not a-going to lay it."

A carpenter quit when she gave him weather-beaten log cabin doors and asked him to install them in the front hall closets. He picked up his satchel and stalked outside to the Sawyers. "I weren't mad at none of you men," he explained after announcing he was leaving. "But everything I done up there, I had to do wrong. A man can't take no pride in this kind of work."

Troy Fortner, a tall, broad-shouldered plasterer, came close to quitting. He was respected as a master craftsman, his ceilings smooth as beaverboard. Ruth told him she wanted her ceilings imperfect, the wide sweeps of the trowel visible as they would have been two hundred years ago.

"Go on back to the boiler room and practice," she told him cheerfully.

"OK, Mrs. Graham," he said, "I'll do it for you on one condition. You won't tell anybody who did it."

The other men stayed on the job after Ruth volunteered to replace all broken drill bits and pay for the extra time it took to sharpen saw teeth dulled by nails embedded in the old wood. They continued muttering behind her back, saying they hoped nobody ever found out who had built her house, for they feared it just might ruin their reputations.

As Ruth's creation began to rise from the earth, Billy once more became suspicious that he had been relieved of all home responsibility. It was obvious, especially when the workmen would walk right past him to discuss business with his wife. His frustration began to surface.

"Why is it," he demanded one afternoon, "that my authority seems to end at home?"

"Listen," she said, "do you want me to call you every time a door needs painting, the furnace needs repairing, the septic tank needs emptying, the drains need cleaning . . . ?"

"No," he had to admit.

"I'm assuming the home responsibilities," she explained, "to free you for your more important ones."

By late 1955, old logs were in place and chinked with rust-colored brixment, resembling the less durable red-clay chinking of the mountain cabins. The men built a split-rail fence around the yard and from the leftover lumber constructed Ruth's and the guest rooms' beds. Damming the stream below the house, they built a small swimming hole so cold it took your breath away when you first jumped in. Like the small pool Dr. Bell had built in Qingjiang, the one on the Graham property became the center of entertainment in the warm months. It was enjoyed by family, friends, tadpoles, water bugs, frogs, and an occasional water snake.

Ruth furnished her home with castoffs, hunting in such unlikely places as the town dump, where the workmen found a heavy slab of wood that had once been Lake Susan's diving board. It soon had been fashioned into the fireplace mantel in the living room and carved with "Eine Feste Burg Ist Unser Gott" (A Mighty Fortress Is Our God). She rummaged through furniture stores, antique shops, and junk shops. One day, she and a local antique dealer named Tom Rezutto followed a seldom-traveled dirt road to look at an old bench on a cabin porch. Hewn from solid board and complete with legs with Chippendale turnings, the bench was covered with dirt and chicken droppings, its only squatters obviously of the feathered variety. The owner, an old mountain man with a face like a dried apple, was sitting on the porch when Ruth parked her jeep beside his yard.

"Would you like to sell your bench?" Rezutto asked him.

"Nope, don't think I care to sell it," he said, staring past them with faded eyes. "I like to sit on it of an evenin' and watch the cars go by."

"How about thirty dollars?" Ruth suggested.

"Give me the money and take the bench," he said.

She made a deal with the workmen that for every old possum lantern they brought her she would buy them a new one. The old tin lanterns were wired and hung beside the outer doors, in hallways, and on the front porch. Visitors now will find the kitchen and its adjoining keeping room haven't changed. Hand-forged tools and copper pots hang from the fireplace, and an old black-iron Betty lamp tapers above the musket over the mantel. Colorful braided rugs cover the floors. Indian corn and a wrought-iron smokehouse hook hang from the exposed beams, and the furniture is overstuffed and inviting.

The living room is full of light, the ceiling high, and floors made of old brick are oiled to a soft shine. Two walls are built of cabin logs and the others from leftover chestnut paneling. An expansive, deep-set window overlooks the lawn, and two smaller ones overlook the ridge. Treasures from Ruth's rummages in English junk shops are scattered about. On the hand-carved mantel is a medieval helmet with bittersweet flowing from the mask like a misplaced plume. A pair of coach horns is propped in a corner, and a heavy jousting helmet turned upside down on a wooden base serves as a wastepaper basket. Framed on walls are two original letters by John Wesley, the Graham coat of arms, an etching of the Madonna and Child, an oil painting of a Chinese peasant, and a brass plaque that reads, "Pray for China." Old leather-bound volumes, acquired through years of visiting English and Scottish antiquarian shops, fill bookcases on either side of the fireplace. It is a warm, comfortable room that encourages folks to sit and stay awhile.

Over the years Ruth's creation would come as a surprise to people who had heard tales of Billy Graham's mythical mansion, which the IRS once listed as including a hundred acres of arable land and an Olympic-sized swimming pool. The first time singer Stuart Hamblen visited the Graham homestead he unfolded himself from the car and surveyed the place for a moment. "I thought you lived in a fine mansion," he drawled. "Thank God for all them logs." When the retired three-time world champion heavyweight boxer Muhammad Ali visited in the fall of 1979, his reaction wasn't quite as approving. "I thought he lived on a thousand-acre farm," he marveled to the press. "And we drove up to this house made of logs; [it was] the kind of house a man of God would live in." He politely refused Billy's invitation to spend the night there.[1]

In early 1956, the Grahams moved to the mountain. They named their homestead Little Piney Cove. By this time the workmen had reconsidered their early negative attitudes about their lady boss's notions. They were so proud of what they had wrought that some of them asked if their wives could see it, and soon women arrived with housewarming presents of a Dutch oven and a handmade quilt. "This place sort of grows on you," said workman James Sawyer, "and before you know it you catch yourself a-liking it."

Ruth and the mountain people had developed a mutual affection and respect. She admired their honesty and craftsmanship. Their skills were virtually lost arts, and so was their native gentleness. Likewise, the mountain folk found Ruth to be trustworthy, appreciative, and deferential. Her loyalty, they sensed, was nondiscriminating. She wasn't scared of a thing and spoke her mind.

One workman, Joe Tolliver, was a tall, husky man who had been an alcoholic before he got saved, as the natives put it. No sooner had Ruth moved up the mountain than Tolliver slid back to the bottom, drinking like a wild man and staggering home covered with blood after barroom brawls he didn't recall. Darlene, his slender, pretty wife, would wait for him and then clean his wounds, hoping with every breath that he would change. Finally, she began visiting Ruth and pouring out her despair. One day, as a last resort, she asked Ruth if she would talk to him.

Ruth found him stretched out on his bed, pale and weak.

"Why?" she asked him.

A veil of shame dropped over his eyes. "I'm guilty of ever' sin in the book, Miz Graham," he admitted. "I'm too weak to resist."

"I'm scared for you," she told him softly.

Soon after, Ruth received a plain white dime-store envelope containing a short note written by Darlene: "In case anything happens to me, will you keep my baby?"

Ruth told her she would.

Then there was Bud Lominac, whom Tolliver had introduced to Ruth in early 1956. Lominac, Tolliver told her, was a drunk, but if she would just take him on as a caretaker he would surely mend his ways. Ruth needed a man to cut the firewood, mow the lawn, and do other odd jobs around the house. She let Lominac move into one of the cabins.

Early one morning, as he and Ruth headed to a distant valley where they were dismantling an old cabin, she offered him a cup of coffee.

"Don't mind if I do."

"Do you like it strong or weak?" she asked.

"Strong!" exclaimed Lominac. "You know, Miz Graham, it don't take near as much water to make coffee as some folks think."

Over the months his cabin became so filthy that the other workmen mentioned it to Ruth.

"Mr. Lominac," Ruth told him one day, "you have two choices. Either clean that cabin or get you a wife."

"Iffen you don't mind," he replied with a grin, "I'll clean up the cabin."

He did and spent many hours there, propped up in bed with his bottle of whiskey. Days would pass without his showing up at work, and when he did put in a token effort, he cheated on his time. One week he didn't appear for five days and Ruth sent a workman to check on him. When the man returned from

the cabin, he reported sheepishly that he had found Lominac in bed, "a-readin' the Bible."

"You should have looked under the Bible," Ruth retorted.

Lominac would never admit that he drank. He might reek of whiskey yet he would look Ruth squarely in the eye and say thickly, "Before Gawd, Miz Graham, I don't drink." With reluctance, she fired him, replacing him with Floyd Roberts, Old Dad Robert's son, who with his wife and five children lived in a small cabin just outside the Montreat gate on Rainbow Mountain. Their brick-colored, unpaved road snaked up from Assembly Drive and disappeared into the woods.

Ruth had become acquainted with him when she lived in the house across the street from her parents. She often joked that she kept him around just to hear him talk and engage him in lively bantering sessions. Pontificating about politics, he would launch into a diatribe about the evil deeds of "Adof Hilter" and "Joe Stallion." Ruth chided him because he refused to take his family to church.

"Church's full of hypocrites," he usually replied.

"Well, Floyd," she would say, "there's always room for one more."

Roberts became so fond of the Grahams that he named his sixth and seventh children after them. So it was that the real Billy and Ruth Graham lived up a steep road to the left after one entered the Montreat gate, and their namesakes lived up a steep road to the left after one exited. Unsurprisingly, some of Montreat's younger and more devilish neighbors occasionally directed unsuspecting Graham fans to the wrong Billy and Ruth.

Needless to say, the mountain folk didn't always appreciate the thousands of cheery Presbyterians and Baptists who stampeded below their mountain into Montreat each summer for conferences and perhaps a peek at where the "Baptist pope of the Presbyterian Heaven lived," as one minister referred to Billy. If a misguided tourist strayed from the herd and lumbered up Rainbow Mountain instead of Little Piney Cove, he couldn't count on any sympathy. He most likely would pass by a certain unpainted cabin where there lived a woman who didn't exactly qualify as the hostess of a welcome station. Worn out from too much work and too little comfort, she had little regard for tourists. On a typical summer day, she could be found sitting on her front porch, unperturbed, a shotgun propped on a nearby chair.

Legend has it that one sweltering summer day, two men in a Cadillac made that wrong turn. When they reached the cabin and the unfriendly old woman who lived in it, the fancy car rocked to a quick halt, stirring up pinging gravel and billowing red dust. A window was rapidly rolled down and a smiling face greeted the woman's inscrutable one.

"'Scuse me, ma'am, but could you please tell me where Billy Graham's . . ." the man's voice trailed off as the oddity of the situation

struck him. "We must have made a wrong turn, 'cause this doesn't look like . . ." he added lamely.

Seconds later, the Cadillac was careening down the mountain, a double-barreled shotgun load of rock salt whizzing past the rear bumper. With so many tourists violating the local residents' territory in search of Billy Graham, it was a wonder that the mountain folk and their neighbors didn't resent the Graham family. But they were fiercely loyal to them. Ruth was known to carry casseroles or pots of soup to them when there was illness in a family, and she was always there to offer comfort in bereavement.

She did the same for her Montreat neighbors. On one occasion a widow returned home from church to find that Ruth not only had left her a pot roast for dinner but had cleaned the oven. If a journalist made the mistake of telephoning one of the mountain folk to ask about the Grahams, he was answered by a resounding click. If a neighbor was asked, he likely answered with a smile and a platitude.

Floyd Roberts eventually quit his job with the Grahams when Ruth repeatedly told him that she needed him to work inside the house as well as in the yard. "But indoor chores," he often reminded her, "are woman's work." It was an amiable parting.

He was succeeded by John Rickman, a gentle, kindly man who also lived on Rainbow Mountain. A recovering alcoholic, Rickman had been converted to Christ after Nelson Bell found him unconscious in the woods. Dr. Bell carried him into his own home, sobered him up, and hired him to do odd jobs around the house. Later he sent Rickman up the mountain to work for the Grahams. They took him on, provided he wouldn't drink. After a few slips, which they pretended not to notice, he kept his promise. An uncle of sorts to Franklin and Ned, he taught them how to handle guns. He taught all of the children how to drive.

In the late seventies, Ruth began noticing that Rickman was pale and listless. She caught him leaning on his rake, panting and wiping his brow when he thought no one was looking. Finally, she persuaded him to see a doctor, and it was discovered that his years of chain smoking had finally exacted their toll. He had cancer of the throat. She visited him in the hospital the day before his death.

"Let not your heart be troubled," she read to him. "Ye believe in God, believe also in me. In my Father's house are many mansions . . ."

A rough hand covered hers and she looked up to see Rickman, whose larynx had been removed, carefully mouthing, "many, *many* mansions." They prayed, his face crinkled into a smile, a finger pointing heavenward.

The next day, his daughter Shirley watched him struggle in his hospital bed as he tried to hold on.

"Papa," she said gently, "don't fight it. Go on to heaven."

His face smoothed as he passed on.

In the early sixties Ruth noticed that Gregg Sawyer's skin was yellowish and it was discovered that he had a fatal pancreatic disorder. One afternoon as they worked on a gate, he began thinking out loud.

"I figure I'm not good enough for Heaven," he told his boss.

Ruth smiled and her hands never stopped as she worked on the rocks. She told him a true story.

"Well, you know, Mr. Sawyer, when Mr. [Dwight L.] Moody was in Scotland holding meetings, a little boy wanted to get into the building. He was a little urchin. Now when I say a little urchin, I mean his face was dirty, his clothes were ragged. And every door he went to was closed because the place was jammed. He was turned away. Maybe if he'd come in top hat and tails they would have been a little more respectful to him.

"But anyway, the little guy got turned away and turned away until finally he wound up at the back door with tears running down his little face. And just about that time a carriage pulled up. People went to help the gentleman out of the carriage and a big, tall man stepped down. And he noticed this little guy with the dirty face and tears running down and he put his hand on his shoulder and said, 'Sonny, what's wrong?'

"The boy said, 'I want to hear Mr. Moody and it's full up and nobody will let me in.'

"And the big man took his hand and said, 'Come with me.'

"When they got to the door it was thrown wide and people bowed him in. The big man found the little boy a seat in the front row. Then he mounted the platform. It was Mr. Moody.

"When we get to Heaven, Mr. Sawyer," she concluded, "that's the only way any of us are going to get in, if Jesus takes us by the hand. None of us are good enough. We're too dirty."

Cocking his head to one side, he studied her over his glasses for a moment. "Well, now," he said, "that makes sense. A man can understand that."

1. "The Greatest Meet: Graham, Ali Discuss Problems," *Asheville Citizen Times*, September 17, 1979.

12

CHAPTER

Her Jungle

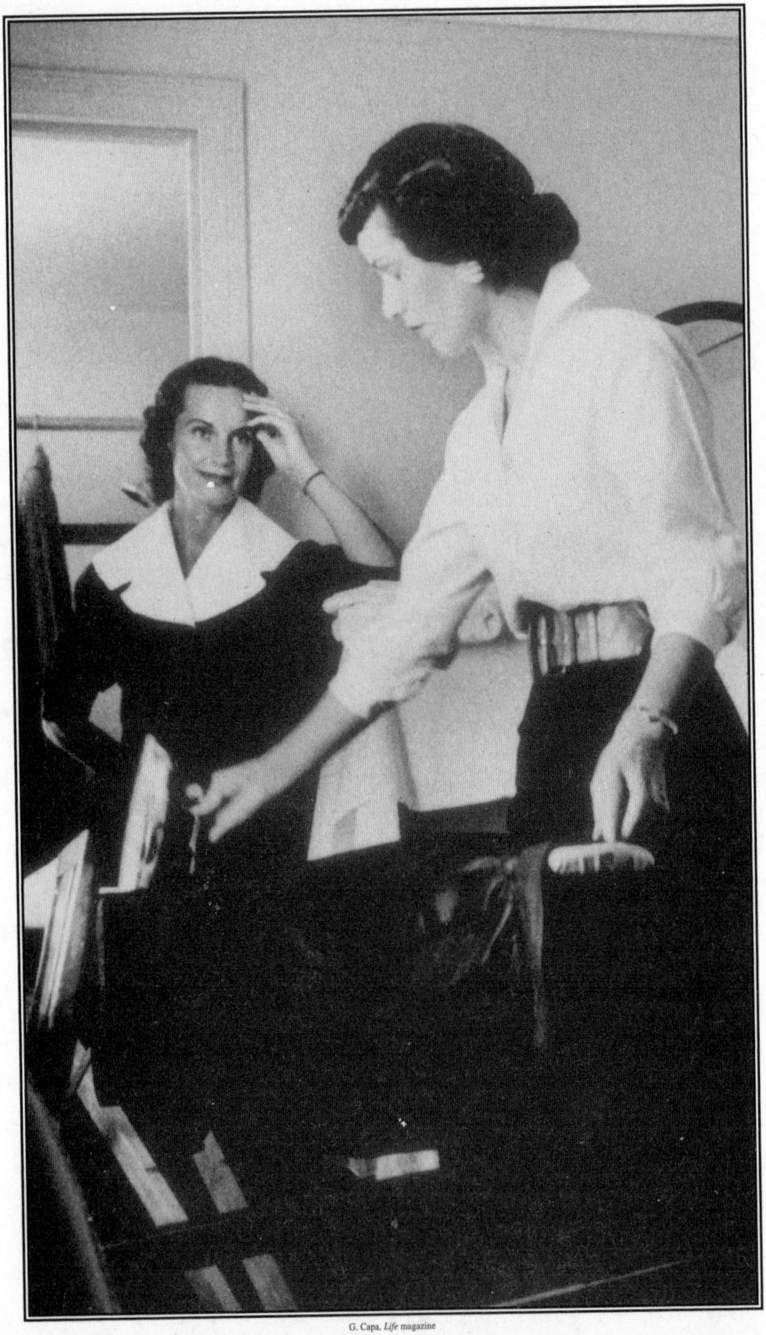

G. Capa, *Life* magazine

THE NEW YORK CRUSADE, 1957

Having always longed to do pioneer missionary work, I must keep reminding myself as I look out over the New York skyline this is our jungle.

—Ruth Bell Graham, 1957

On Saturday, May 11, 1957, Ruth leaned against pillows in her Pullman car as soft lamplight shone on the blanket tousled over her legs and her open, battered King James Bible. Two and a half hours had passed in hypnotic beats since she had awakened at 2:00 A.M.

The train lurched to a halt in Washington, where the day before Billy had met with President Eisenhower and Vice President Nixon. Billy boarded the train and greeted Ruth with a hug in their two-bunk stateroom. As the train lumbered to New York, they talked and then slept until the porter brought them coffee and toast at 9:00 A.M.

Two years earlier, John Sutherland Bonnell, pastor of New York's Fifth Avenue Presbyterian Church, had approached Billy with an interesting question.

"Billy," Bonnell asked, "when will you begin a crusade in New York?"

"I am not ready for that," Billy replied. "I want more time for study and prayer before tackling that project."[1]

That same year, the Protestant Council of the City of New York, representing seventeen hundred churches and thirty-one denominations, invited him to hold a crusade in Madison Square Garden. He accepted and his organization began setting it up. As the train sped that way, the city was plastered with six hundred fifty billboards, forty thousand telephone dials reading "Pray for Billy Graham," thirty-five thousand window posters, and forty thousand bumper stickers. The BGEA's marketing arsenal included one million letterheads, two and a half million envelope stuffers, two hundred fifty thousand crusade songbooks, and one hundred thousand Gospels of John.[2]

Vice President Nixon would attend the crusade on behalf of the president and speak to one hundred thousand people in Yankee Stadium for ten minutes on July 21. Many of the country's top entertainers and jet setters would come. It would be the longest, most expensive, and exhausting crusade Billy had yet held, as the scheduled six weeks of services stretched into sixteen. By the time it was over, more than two and a quarter million people would have attended, with one hundred sixty thousand jamming Times Square for the first meeting September 1. But the phenomenon that would change the course of history for Billy, and for the Graham family, was that on June 1 Billy's ministry would be televised, launching him as one of the nation's pioneer "televangelists."

As the Grahams sat in their Pullman car, journalists from virtually every major magazine and newspaper in the United States and Europe were trickling into Manhattan. Billy was restless, unnerved by the task ahead. To him, his mission was not necessarily one of choice, but of obedience. He knew it was God propelling him along a ribbon of steel to the central nervous system of the nation, the hub of sophistication, art, and fashion.

Politically, it was a volatile time in the United States. On May 17, 1954, the U.S. Supreme Court had declared that racial segregation in public schools was unconstitutional. Violence and controversy erupted in the already stormy South. In September of 1957 President Eisenhower would send a thousand federal troops to Little Rock, Arkansas, to quell Governor Orval E. Faubus's attempt to block the integration of a local school. Reporters wanted to know why Billy Graham didn't stay home and help his people solve the racial problem instead of traveling north to "save" New York City.

Over the past four years he had gained increasing respect in the country for his stance on racial segregation. During the 1953 Chattanooga, Tennessee, crusade he had instructed his ushers that blacks were to sit wherever they pleased. There was no segregation at the foot of the Cross, he maintained repeatedly. Many people fancied that he was moving in rhythm with a twenty-eight-year-old black Baptist named Martin Luther King Jr., who had mounted his own platform in 1955 when Rosa Parks, a black woman, had been arrested in Montgomery, Alabama, for refusing to surrender her bus seat to a white man. While Billy Graham rebelled against the ungodliness of racial discrimination, King set in motion the first mass civil rights movement in American history.

At the 1957 New York crusade King would sit on Billy's platform. Three years later the two men would fly together to Brazil to attend a banquet for

Baptist leaders. There King said, "If it had not been for the ministry of Billy Graham, my civil rights work in the United States would have been much harder."

Shortly before Billy left Montreat for Washington, and then New York, he and Ruth had hiked to the small mountainside field near their house, a quiet spot where he often wandered alone to pray. They stretched out on the grass, sleepily watching their four sheep graze. As they talked and prayed about New York, he confessed to her that though he was challenged, he was frightened. She shared his feelings, she told him. "But at the same time," she simply added, "self-confidence would be worse."

Now, as they ate breakfast on the train, they were talking and praying again. She gently peeled back the fragile pages of her Bible, smoothing them when she found each verse. "If Thy Presence go not with me carry us not up hence. . . . My Presence shall go with Thee. . . . Lo, I am with you always," she read. This opportunity came from God, she told him. And He would be with them.

In a steady, dreary rain, the train stopped briefly in Newark, New Jersey, an hour late. The press, much to Ruth's relief, had tired of waiting and had left. But in Manhattan they were greeted by a mob of reporters, friends, and, for the first time, police. A burly sergeant and a detective stood sentry on the station platform while the Grahams left the train. Ruth was surprised, for it had not occurred to her that there was any possibility of violence. The presence of guards was the beginning of what was soon to become commonplace.

Moments after they arrived at the New Yorker Hotel, one of Billy's associates began ushering Ruth to her quarters, away from the hundreds of journalists who had been waiting more than an hour for her husband.

"Oh, no," Billy said, grinning as he scotched Ruth's getaway. "She goes to the press conference with me."

She sat beside him, feeling "like a fool," as she recalled, while he answered the reporters' ten pages of questions:

"How sinful do you think New York is?"

"Is it a criticism of the church today that people respond to you as an evangelist and not to the churches themselves?"

"Why is a revival needed when the membership in churches is zooming?"

Drained, he remarked to a reporter as he walked toward the elevator, "My wife and I have lost our privacy. And I don't think anyone who has lost their privacy doesn't long to have it back. You don't realize what a priceless possession it is to be a private individual. To be looked at, to be stared at everywhere one goes, never to go into a restaurant without being looked at . . ."[3]

During this crusade many of the wealthy and famous showed interest in Billy as never before. Jackie Gleason invited him to lunch. Tallulah Bankhead invited the Grahams to tea. Billy was a frequent guest on talk shows. On Sunday, May 12, Ruth sat on a balcony and watched him on the set of the *Steve Allen*

Show, along with Dean Jones, Milton Berle, Tallulah Bankhead, and Pearl Bailey. Amid the dancing, fanfares, and one-liners, he emerged in a simple gabardine suit.

"And the presence of God was there," Ruth observed. "Right in the midst of all that fun & foolishness. . . . Bill sat and God was with him. . . . Oh, the consuming . . . ambition of the stage and even when you reach the top, what do you have? Full lives and empty hearts."

She couldn't wait to escape the crowds, the flashbulbs. Whenever possible she would sequester herself in her hotel suite and read and meditate. Along with her Bible, she read Frank W. Boreham's essays and the recently published *Through Gates of Splendor*, written by Elisabeth Elliot, whose husband Jim was one of five missionaries murdered by the Auca Indians in Ecuador. "I have never been more deeply moved or challenged," she wrote at the time.

Her life had radically changed over the past fourteen years, evolving in a way she could never have imagined in those early days in Illinois. Her priorities, nonetheless, had not wavered. They burned like a quiet inner flame, making her who she was. She had redefined her notion of her mission field. It was not Tibet; it was everywhere.

The moment the Grahams would emerge from their room, they were hounded by journalists and television crews. Everywhere they turned, it seemed, someone was snapping their picture.

"After so much publicity you begin to feel exposed," Ruth wrote on May 13. "Every paper you pick up has a picture or a story or both. And you feel a bit like a beetle under a stone when the stones have just been removed. Well, I was feeling very uncovered when I picked up my Bible and read, 'He shall cover thee with His feathers, and under His wings shalt thou trust.' I can't say what a comfortable thought that was. All I needed."

Journalists crowded into the BGEA team prayer meetings. They wandered through the crowds at night, hunting for celebrities to photograph. Ruth's annoyance with the press mounted when the "czar of the Los Angeles underworld," as Mickey Cohen was called, appeared in Manhattan. She had recently seen the tough-talking ex-convict on television, where he referred to gangsters and racketeers as "fine men," and law enforcement officers as "degenerates." She feared that he was attempting to reestablish himself in the underworld. She also suspected that his interest in the crusade was only a publicity stunt. She hoped he would come to know Christ during the services, but she didn't see how that was possible when the press was between him and the pulpit.

She watched the assault the night of May 21 and her indignation peaked. Julie Nixon Eisenhower, at the service with her father, later recalled it was the "angriest" she ever saw Ruth. Sitting in the lower tier, just in front of Cohen, Ruth noticed an Associated Press photographer stalking the front row like a cat. Oblivious of the woman inches away from him, he squatted and focused his camera on Cohen. Smiling, Ruth blocked the lens with her songbook just as the shutter clicked. She shook her head at him like a mother reprimanding a naughty child.

"It's my job," the photographer explained when Ruth bumped into him after the service. "And I will do all I can to get the pictures."

"And it's our job to do all we can to stop you from getting them," she replied, again with a smile.

"So at least we understand one another," he said as he walked away.

Moments later she met Cohen in Billy's stadium office. She had been praying for him since the 1949 Los Angeles crusade when his wiretapper Jim Vaus had accepted Christ and Billy had unsuccessfully urged Cohen to do likewise.

"We're praying for you," she said.

He smiled nervously, kissed her on the cheek, and left.

"He has not given in to God, he would not that night," she recorded. "As he said good-bye, I felt like that verse in the Scriptures, 'He went out. And it was night.'"

While Billy Graham, "the fair-haired evangelist with that clean collared look," was "fighting the roughest battle in his phenomenal career,"[4] as columnist Dorothy Kilgallen wrote, he was chosen Father of the Year in Religion. On May 23, he took time off from his usual fourteen-hour workday to escort Ruth to the awards dinner at the Waldorf-Astoria. Guests included Ronald Reagan, who with his wife Nancy would one day invite the Grahams to the White House, and the parents of Grace Kelly, as well as Ed Sullivan, Charles and Mark Van Doren, and Mickey Mantle, who was wearily signing autographs. When Billy rose to accept his award, he told the guests that it was his wife who deserved it, not he, because she had been both mother and father to their children.

After the dinner, Ruth returned to the hotel and discovered that the AP photographer she had confronted days earlier had left her a message. He wanted her to sit in the front row that night so he could take her picture. She sent him a message back.

"Yes, I will, if you promise not to photograph any celebrities."

He never showed up.

Saturday, June 1, marked the beginning of Billy's television career. The month before, American Broadcasting Company executives had approached him with their idea of televising the services. Soon, seventeen broadcasts had been scheduled for the crusade, a modern miracle made possible by a one-hundred-thousand-dollar donation. The Grahams rode the train back home and gathered with the Bells before the television set, switching the channels past Jackie

Gleason and Perry Como until Billy floated onto the grayish screen before them. He preached on John 3:16, his face pale, his gestures too energetic for the small box.

Yet his words carried power, and as Ruth watched hundreds of people come forward, she was overwhelmed. "Thank God for the incomparable opportunities of preaching Christ these days," she wrote. "For men's willingness to listen. It may not be but for a time. But thank God for it! And may we all take advantage of every opportunity while the time lasts."

Six million people tuned in for the first broadcast, three times as many as had attended the sum of all Graham crusades the year before. Ruth knew then that if television was to become his new pulpit, their lives would be laid bare before the world as never before. It was, however, but a small exchange for transformed lives, she believed. A Presbyterian minister, a Roman Catholic priest, a bartender, a calypso dancer, a prostitute, and one of her customers all had made that walk through the Garden as a gesture of their desire to make peace with God. "One watches, lost in wonder, love and praise," Ruth wrote.

Joy and pain, blessings and bitterness, are usually yoked together. The New York crusade was not exempt. By 1957 Billy had reached a point in his career where he was rapidly polarizing his fellow Americans. He was evolving into the most powerful religious figure of the century. That alone made him controversial, and a target for criticism.

In a *Life* magazine article published during the crusade, Reinhold Niebuhr, prominent theologian and vice president of Union Theological Seminary in New York, took the evangelist to task.

The success of mass evangelism, Niebuhr said, "depends upon oversimplifying every issue of life." Billy Graham's preaching, he added, "promised new life, not through painful religious experience but merely by signing a decision card. Thus, a miracle of regeneration is promised at a painless price by an obviously sincere evangelist. It is a bargain."

Niebuhr's first point was perhaps relevant; his next one was questionable. Though Billy Graham said his "present crusade is aimed at New York City," Niebuhr wrote, "relatively few New Yorkers attend the Graham meetings. The bulk of his nightly audience comes from out of town."[5] Had his assertion been correct—and it was not—one wonders if it really mattered whether the people flowing into Madison Square Garden were from New York City, Yonkers, or New Jersey. During the services following the July 1 article, members of the audience were asked to raise their hands if they lived in New York City. At least eighty percent of the people did.

Attacks also came from extreme liberals of various denominations who claimed that Billy's crusade was a sort of religious circus where the evangelist instead of the Holy Spirit was the ringmaster. Criticism came from the extreme Fundamentalists who condemned Billy for cooperating with "Christ deniers, radicals, and liberals," referring to the high-powered businessmen and clergy who made up the crusade's Executive Committee. The attacks upset Ruth. She ventilated her anger in a journal, then tore out the pages and burned them because "God would give me no peace of heart. We must leave them to Him. These men are, after all, God's anointed. May we like David refuse to lift our hand (or tongue) against them."

One of the most noted developments in Billy himself, one that was largely responsible for his losing some supporters and winning others, was his growing ecumenism. His father-in-law was partly responsible for this change. Billy later claimed that he "never took a major step without asking [Nelson Bell's] counsel and advice." Bell's influence, along with Billy's own experience as a minister, had given him a respect and understanding for different denominations. "Even though I was a Southern Baptist," Billy recalled, "I still had an independent streak in me that came from my days at the Florida Bible Institute. Dr. Bell showed me that the strength of my future ministry would be in the church. He actually taught me to be a churchman."

Ironically, Billy's toleration for other denominations stopped just outside his front door. If someone else chose to be a Presbyterian or a Methodist, that was fine with him, as long as that someone wasn't his wife. For fourteen years he had listened to the badgering of his Baptist friends who thought it was mighty sorry if a man's wife wouldn't join his church. He tended to agree and had tried to tug Ruth away from the Presbyterian Church more than once. But pulling her away from that tradition was like uprooting kudzu. No matter how much or how hard he yanked, it was always there, hearty and happy come rain or sun.

The attacks were tenacious and clever, and not all of them were made by Billy. Once a Baptist friend appeared for breakfast and spent the morning proselytizing. After each battle, Ruth remained steadfast and smiling like Mona Lisa. Finally realizing what he was up against, Billy jokingly announced that he would give a hundred dollars to whoever could make a Baptist out of her. Though the reward would forever go uncollected, more than a few Baptists offered to split the money with her if she would allow them to immerse her.

Not everyone appreciated the role Nelson Bell and his daughter Ruth were playing in Billy's life. In 1954, Dr. Bell and Billy had worked together to found the evangelical magazine *Christianity Today*. The magazine had a rather unusual beginning. One morning in 1954, after a sleepless night spent at his desk, Billy came downstairs and made an abrupt announcement to Ruth.

"God has given me a vision," he said, "the plans for a new magazine which I am to call *Christianity Today*.

"The magazine is necessary, for there is not an intellectually respected magazine for evangelicals" in existence at the time. He immediately shared his idea with Dr. Bell and found to his amazement that his father-in-law had been thinking about the same thing. Working side by side, the two men turned their dream into a reality. As Ruth recalled, "I watched and listened as my husband and my father talked and planned, marveling at the vision and wisdom God had given them, each one respecting the other, each one so beautifully balancing the other." With Dr. Bell as its executive editor, the magazine's first issues had begun circulating less than a year before the New York crusade.

To some observers, the organization was a dynasty, not a business. It was built of old, trusted friends who had banded together over the years. "The BGEA wasn't formed," Ruth often asserted, "it simply evolved much as a family evolves." Over the years, she would develop warm friendships with the wives of Billy's associates. "Though scattered around the world," Ruth noted, "we share a sense of family love and fellowship. There is mutual support, and any of us facing some difficulty is backed by the others' prayers. If one of our children strays, the prayers of not one but dozens of mothers will follow that child."

Jerry Beavan, who helped plan the early crusades and who would resign from the BGEA in 1963, recalled that he resented Billy's treating Ruth and her father as his chief advisers. To him, it was rather like Jimmy Carter's asking Amy for advice. "It's no secret," Beavan said, "that I, in all my years, didn't agree always with their advice and didn't always feel they were the best people to advise him on anything." Ruth, he said, had grown up in China, then retreated to the sheltered world of Wheaton College, and had finally "retired" to the mountaintop in Montreat. Dr. Bell, meanwhile, had spent most of his life in China, "which is not exactly in the mainstream of the world's affairs. So I felt that those two were not the best ones to advise Billy on how to conduct his life, his ministry, his gradually growing world influence. I felt [theirs] was a very narrow view. There were times my advice didn't concur with theirs and Billy almost always took theirs. And if you're very pragmatic and look at success, it must have worked. He's done pretty well."

On Saturday, June 15, Ruth returned to Montreat for several days and was greeted with the chilling news that her four children and a friend had plunged over the mountain in the jeep. There were no serious injuries, just cuts, scratches, bruises, and one fractured arm. The jeep was virtually demolished. The same day, however, there was a photograph in the local newspaper of a Thunderbird and a twenty-ton tractor-trailer that had collided in nearby O'teen. The car's three occupants had been killed. She couldn't help feeling as though her own family had been spared. "I had cold chills to think what might have happened," she wrote. "My heart was speechless with gratitude."

That same day, she found a note on her pillow telling her to telephone Darlene Tolliver: Joe Tolliver was dead. He had died alone, a hand groping toward the telephone as though he were trying to cry for help.

On Sunday, Ruth drove to the Tolliver home to pay her respects to his family. The living room was small but well kept. The casket was heavy and lustrous, and she stood looking at it, thinking about a day many years ago when Billy had knelt on the floor beside Tolliver's bed, praying for him, leading him to Christ. Tolliver had won the war then, and lost every skirmish leading up to what he knew was to be his reward. It was a glory without honor.

At the small hillside cemetery, Bud Lominac lurched up the hill toward the church, his body twitching uncomfortably in his Sunday suit. Ruth headed toward him up the grassy slope and took his big, rough hand. As in the case of the Thunderbird and her jeep, she was again confronted with a fatality and a close call. Lominac had not changed his hard-drinking ways, and yet he had been spared Tolliver's fate. His turn might be next.

"God loves you wherever you are, Mr. Lominac," she told him with feeling. "Whatever happens to you, remember God loves you."

"Yes, ma'am, Miz Graham," he muttered, staring blankly past her. "How's Franklin?"

1. "Dedicated Deciders in Billy Graham Crusade," *Life*, July 1, 1957, 92.
2. Curtis Mitchell, *God in the Garden* (New York: Doubleday, 1957), 32.
3. Ibid., 36–37.
4. Dorothy Kilgallen, "D. Kilgallen Goes behind the Scenes to Tell Life Story," *Los Angeles Herald Examiner*, May 20, 1957.
5. "Dedicated Deciders in Billy Graham Crusade," *Life*, July 1, 1957, 52.

13

CHAPTER

Home on the Mountain

Tom Blau, Camera Press Ltd.

RING AROUND THE ROSIE

When God asks someone to do something for Him entailing sacrifice, He makes up for it in surprising ways. God has not let me down. Though He had led Bill all over the world to preach the gospel, He had not forgotten the little family in the mountains of North Carolina. I have watched with gratitude as God has guided each child.

—Ruth Bell Graham

Beside the bedroom fireplace bordered in old blue and white Dutch tiles, the empty antique cradle waited. The wedding veil had disappeared long ago. On January 12, 1958, Ruth's fifth and last child was born. She named him Nelson Edman, or Ned, after her father and Dr. V. Raymond Edman, former president of Wheaton College. In an eerie fulfillment of her dream of being a "pioneer missionary alone," she found she was virtually on her own in the large responsibility of raising a family. She would have to be both mother and father.

Ruth was no longer the young bride whose feelings were easily hurt. She had learned to laugh at most things, including Billy's chronic preoccupation. One day the Grahams were expecting guests for dinner and she asked him, "What would you like to have on the menu?"

"Uh-huh," came the reply.

"I thought we'd start off with tadpole soup," she said.

"Uh-huh."

"And there's some lovely poison ivy growing in the next cove which would make a delightful salad."

"Uh-huh."

"For the main dish, I could try roasting some of those wharf rats we've been seeing around the smokehouse lately, and serve them with boiled crabgrass and baked birdseed."

"Uh-huh."

"And for dessert we could have mud soufflé and . . ."

His eyes finally focused. "What were you saying about wharf rats?" he asked.[1]

She still had her opinions, and Billy remained unaccustomed to a woman countering him. One day, the two of them were arguing over something his aide T. W. Wilson had suggested. Finally, in frustration, Billy blurted, "I spend more time with him than I do with you!"

"And you haven't had five children with him" was her rejoinder.

Ruth began modeling her home after the familiar, the nest she had known in her childhood in China. She attempted to revisit her own childhood, playing many of the same games with her children and emphasizing the same values. There were interesting parallels. The Bells were less than two miles away, and Ruth saw them daily when she wasn't traveling. To the children Nelson Bell was an attentive, caring grandfather who advised and sometimes disciplined them while Billy was away.

Montreat, like Ruth's childhood compound, was a Presbyterian oasis populated largely of retired and furloughed missionaries, clergymen, and people who simply wished to live in a secure, peaceful environment. With the exception of some of the students at Montreat-Anderson, the small junior college clustered around Lake Susan, most Montreaters were genteel Southern Presbyterians. The town had a zero crime rate, according to North Carolina annual crime statistics. There was only one town drunk, as best anybody knew.

In the beginning Ruth would rely on the childrearing principles of her missionary parents, and she assumed the results would be the same. But soon enough she discovered that the differences between the environments were considerable. In China, much that wasn't Christian was blatantly evil and unattractive. In the world of Ruth's children, sin wasn't always easily recognizable. Often, it was attractive. Ruth could not completely shield her family from the world beyond the Montreat gate, and there were times when she felt the bite of frustration.

With the exception of the usual childish spats, her childhood home in Qingjiang had been a happy, peaceful one, as she recalled. Her new home sometimes seemed unmanageable and unsettled. The children bickered and pecked at each other. "We can lick this evil," she confided in her journal in 1959. "With His help we *will.* A happy, well-disciplined, well-ordered, loving home is our spiritual right." In fact, there were no rats or scorpions to battle, no bandits shooting guns or Japanese bombers droning over the roof day and night. As it was, the flying squirrels and hoot owls offered little diversion for restless young minds.

During Ruth's early childhood, she rarely went a day without seeing both parents. The dangers and hardships common to the China mission field served to bring people closer. But now, Father's long and frequent absences and his fame threatened to fragment the family. His often neglected and overloaded wife might easily have become resentful and demanding, evolving into a selfish, brittle woman whose love was conditional. Ruth's own childrearing philosophy began to evolve, and it was rather simple. She did her best to make each child feel special. She respected their individual rights and considered herself their guardian, not their owner. "Each child had to be dealt with differently," she recalled telling herself.

In her journals she often reminded herself of George MacDonald's warning that the quickest way to make someone bad is to try to make him good. She could, she later discovered, change only herself. She wanted to be an example, not a judge, and the focus of her personal life became the old rolltop desk in her bedroom. Cluttering it were numerous translations of the Bible and concordances, devotional books, notepads, and her poetry and sentiments written in her distinctive hand. It was here that Ruth came from time to time throughout each day, with a cup of coffee. She would sit and study and remind herself of her "reference point," as she would say.

Prior to the mid-fifties Ruth had been able to help Billy by traveling with him whenever possible, leaving the children with the Bells. After the 1954 Harringay crusade, she realized she could not afford to stay away from the children for long stretches. When she returned from London in the late spring of 1954 she found a resentful Franklin and an even more insecure and unmanageable GiGi.

Monday, June 14, of that year was typical. Ruth loaded GiGi, Anne, and Bunny into the jeep and drove them up to the cabin below the then-unfinished house. They sat in the sun and read, picked cherries, and hunted turtles. Hanging a blue and white bedspread from the loft for a curtain, GiGi and Anne performed skits based on nursery rhymes. Ruth and Bunny were the audience. When Anne performed "Little Miss Muffet," GiGi climbed a ladder to act out the "spider beside her" and hurled a lump of manure.

"It's the only thing I could find that was brown and we could pretend was a spider," GiGi explained as her mother scrubbed a teary Anne.

One naughty scene led to another, and Mother ended GiGi's escapades with a spanking. After a supper of hot dogs roasted over the fire, she read the children a Bible story and GiGi began asking questions.

"Mommy," she asked, "if I die, will I go to heaven?"

"You tell me," Ruth replied.

"I don't know."

"Want me to tell you how you can know?"

"I don't think you can know for sure."

"I do," Ruth said.

"OK, how?"

"First, you know you are a sinner, don't you?"

"Oh, I know that." GiGi was quite sure of this.

"Then you confess your sins to Him."

"I do that. You know when I got so mad at you this afternoon I told Him I was sorry three times just to make sure, in case He didn't hear me the first time."

"He heard you the first time," Ruth said. "If we confess our sins, He is faithful and just to forgive us our sins and cleanse us from all unrighteousness."

"Are you sure He heard me?"

"I know He did," Ruth said.

"But it doesn't say GiGi."

"It says whosoever."

GiGi said nothing and her mother continued. "Now you have done the first two. You have become a child of God. You are born into God's family, just as eight years ago you were born into our family. Your body was born then, your soul is born again now."

"But I still am not sure," GiGi said.

"GiGi, would you call God a liar?"

"Of course not!"

"But you are. He said if you confess He will forgive. If you believe, you have eternal life. You have done both, but you don't think He will keep his promise. That is the same as calling Him a liar." Ruth held up a piece of paper and said, "Whoever wants it can have it."

GiGi snatched it from her fingers.

"What makes you think I said you?" Ruth demanded.

"You said whoever," GiGi let her know.

"Exactly."

At bedtime they knelt and prayed, and GiGi exclaimed, "I feel like a new person."

The next day, GiGi the *new person* skipped down Assembly Drive to the Montreat gate and uprooted a dozen water lilies that had been planted in time for the arrival of the season's first tourists and conferees. Ruth escorted her to the town manager's office, the evidence wilting in a tight little fist. GiGi's face was pale as she worried aloud that she was going to be thrown into jail. Her mother said nothing to dispel the fear. GiGi confessed and apologized, and as she was tucked into bed that night, she plaintively asked, "Mommy, have I been good enough today to go to heaven?"

"Now how much," Ruth wrote at the time, "should I impress on her

Salvation by Grace when really for a child of her disposition one could be tempted to think salvation by works would be more effective on her behavior?"

The training of the Graham children began early in more ways than one. Days started with a Bible lesson and devotions at the breakfast table. Education was a priority, and when GiGi turned twelve she was sent to a boarding school in Florida. The results were mixed. Going away at such a young age added to GiGi's insecurity, ironically repeating her mother's own homesickness when she had been sent to Japan. GiGi was frightened. She missed her family terribly. It all served to prepare her for marrying and moving to Switzerland at the age of seventeen, just as Ruth's separations in her own early life steeled her for what lay ahead.

The foundation for Ruth's method of childrearing, unsurprisingly, was the Bible. Her upbringing had taught her a love for the Scriptures. She studied for insight, to be corrected, informed, and inspired. From the Bible she drew ideas like this one: "Because sentence against an evil work is not executed speedily, therefore the heart of the sons of men is fully set in them to do evil" (Ecclesiastes 8:11). From that verse Ruth determined that punishment, when needed, should be prompt.

Had she made a habit of threatening "Wait until your father gets home," the children most likely would have dreaded his return. Billy probably wouldn't have looked forward to returning home either. Ruth had a catalog of punishments for different offenses:

First Fight—ten minutes in room
Second Fight—fifteen minutes in room
Sassing and Rudeness—switching with a shoe tree or flyswatter
Procrastinating Going to Bed—earlier to bed the following night

Often her chastisements were more humorous than severe. Occasionally, when two of the children had a spat, Ruth would sit them together nose to nose until they kissed and made up. Once when Franklin was insufferable while his mother drove the children to a fast-food restaurant in Asheville, she finally stopped the car and locked him in the well-ventilated trunk.

"Don't worry," she assured the startled carhop who appeared just as the trunk yawned open. "He enjoyed it."

"I'll have a cheeseburger without the meat," Franklin ordered as he dusted off his jeans.

"The children misbehave," Ruth wrote. "I reprimand them sharply, more probably peevishly. The very tone of voice irritates them (I know because if it were used on me it would irritate me). They answer back probably in the same tone. I turn on them savagely (I hate to think how often! And how savage a loving mother can be at times). And I snap Don't you speak to your mother like that. It isn't respectful. Nothing about my actions, tone of voice, etc. commanded respect. It doesn't mean I am to tolerate sass or back-talk. But then I must be very careful not to inspire it either."

Not long after GiGi left for boarding school she wrote her mother and said she had fallen in love. Ruth kept her concern to herself. It was not her way to lecture or meddle. Later, when Anne was a teenager and bleached her hair and began wearing makeup, Ruth let her alone. Anne began modeling for several of Asheville's finer clothing stores, and her mother granted her freedom.

"These weren't moral issues," Anne recalled. "Mother totally trusted me and encouraged me and loved me. Therefore I was always the person she thought I was. She used to say, 'If you trust a person, they'll live up to that trust.'" Even so, the fighting, the disobedience, and the rebelliousness raged on. GiGi, Anne, Bunny, Franklin, and Ned certainly were not the saints the public "Billy Graham's kids" ought to be. Then, in the middle of the day-to-day turbulence, Billy would come home and peace would be restored.

The scene in the early years was always the same. Ruth and the children stood on the wooden depot platform, watching the glassy ribbon of train windows flow by while they waited, hearts racing, in the damp mountain air. Billy, his rumpled suit hanging more loosely than it had when he was last home, would emerge, his face beaming but weary. In his suitcases there were certain to be stuffed animals or dolls and toy cars.

Life on the mountaintop would change. The children would temporarily lose interest in their neighborhood playmates. They were better behaved. Billy did not tolerate impertinence or disobedience, but he would never be much of a disciplinarian. Spankings from him were rare. GiGi can recall but two, the last one the more memorable. She sassed him, stomped her foot, slammed her bedroom door, and locked it. When she finally let him in, he began spanking her.

"Some father you are!" GiGi cried. "You go away and leave us alone all the time."

Suddenly he stopped, his eyes filling with tears.

"It just broke my heart," GiGi recalled. "I'll never forget that because I realized that this was a sacrifice he was making."

In the main, strictness was rather much forgotten when Billy was on the scene. "Daddy would come home from a trip and break all the rules," GiGi said.

"Oh, let them stay up a little later," he'd say to Ruth when it was time to turn the television off and tuck the children in bed. "I hardly get to see them." He'd give them candy, gum, and soda pop during the week when he knew the rule was that they were to get such treats only on Sundays. The five young faces would look up to their mother after Father had just granted them permission to break her rules, and she would concede, "Whatever your daddy says is fine with me."

When he was home he conducted family devotions and told the children stories and played games with them, especially at bedtime. Billy would play spider and creep through the house as the children scattered and screamed in delight. He was affectionate, stopping them in the hallway to hug or kiss them, or perhaps sneak them away for a hike on the mountain. It delighted them when he and Ruth would "smooch," as the children called it. He was boyishly demonstrative, sometimes whisking Ruth away from the stove to waltz her around the kitchen. Throughout the day he held her hand or sat her in his lap, the two of them laughing and teasing like high school sweethearts.

"His love and tenderness toward her were something we daughters looked for in our husbands," Bunny remarked.

Billy's presence, however, did not ensure his undivided attention. Usually, he slept through his first two days at home. "It's like being in a hurricane," he once explained, "and all of a sudden it stops and there is nothing but quiet." He would confide in Ruth, telling her details of a life that she had not been on hand to witness. He would voice his joys, plans, and discouragements. Though she had worries of her own, she kept them to herself. She listened, encouraged, and soothed his anxieties and doubts. One evening as she and Billy sat on the porch watching the setting sun ignite thunderclouds piiing over Rainbow Mountain, he began fretting aloud.

"God has never failed you yet, has He?" Ruth asked.

"No," Billy said. "But He's come pretty close to it sometimes."

Business did not stop when he was home. There were always telephone calls and letters to answer. Television crews and journalists would arrive for their "thirty-minute" sessions, which characteristically stretched into half-day marathons with Ruth hovering nearby, smiling, appearing calm, as she listened. Behind her cool, gracious façade, she was stressed and uneasy. Her hands trembled as she served coffee. She was poised to attack, ever ready to protect those she loved from what she viewed as the irresponsibility of the press.

In the late fifties and early sixties, anyone could and often did show up on the Graham mountain. One Sunday morning Ruth took the children to church while Billy stayed home and rested. He decided to surprise the family with a picnic lunch and met them on the driveway with seven peanut butter and jelly sandwiches and an unopened can of pork and beans. They were eating as an old car full of admirers chugged up the mountain, past the PRIVATE PROPERTY signs. It overheated in front of the swimming pool.

Billy was quick to offer help. Magnanimously, to his uninvited guests he said, "Come on up and share our picnic lunch. There's plenty of food for everyone."

"Sharing always makes a picnic more fun," Ruth uneasily assured the children.

There were unwelcome visitors who bore special messages from God, or, worse, who thought they were God. When Ruth was pregnant with Ned, her housekeeper Beatrice Long entered the living room one day, characteristically calm and never in a hurry.

"Mrs. Graham, there's a man at the door who says he's Jesus Christ and Mr. Graham is expecting him."

Ruth went to the door and found a heavy, perspiring man who immediately repeated his claim.

"You are not Jesus Christ," she told him firmly, "and my husband is not expecting you."

An argument ensued and the man announced he was coming in.

"You are not. And besides," she unwisely added, "you must remember, after the Resurrection, Jesus didn't knock on doors, he walked through them."

The man paused to lift eyes heavenward for instruction. Ruth grabbed the opportunity and quickly shut the door and latched it. He drove his green Chrysler New Yorker to Assembly Inn on Lake Susan and told the desk clerk his story. "My only mistake," he concluded, "was I knocked on the door instead of walking through it."

"Don't you realize," the clerk responded, "Jesus made no mistakes?"

The man announced that the end of the world was upon them. He tossed his wallet and wristwatch into the lake and rolled his car in after them. There were other encounters, and Ruth handled them firmly whether Billy was out of town or in his study.

"Before they put that gate up," recalled Beatrice Long, "cars would come up there every day and pretend they were lost. Some of them would wander around the yard hoping someone would come out and speak. Sometimes she'd go out. Sometimes she wouldn't. She was never rude. She was nice and kind to them but they never did see him. He wouldn't know what was going on."

In the sixties, a man toting a large Bible appeared at the Billy Graham office in Montreat. The man bore a message from God, he claimed. He wasn't leaving until he delivered it. After he had camped in front of the office for three days, a secretary telephoned Billy, informed him of the situation, and asked him what should be done. In no time, Billy was down the mountain, shirtless, sitting on a tree stump in the sun. For hours he patiently listened to the man's rather deranged prophecies. Billy shook his hand and thanked him. It was a scene that would have been common had Ruth not intervened.

Then Billy would go away again, hastily piling packed baggage into the car trunk and heading to the train station or the airport. Often one of his aides would pick him up. As his fame grew, it became futile for the family to say good-bye to him in public, where he was inundated with those who wanted his autograph or a handshake. Once Anne accompanied him to the airport and was immediately swept to the background by well-wishers flooding her father. Rapidly shaking one hand after another, he finally turned to his daughter, shyly standing behind him. Pumping her hand, he blurted, "Nice to meet you!" before bolting toward his gate.

When it was time to say good-bye neither Ruth nor Billy displayed emotion. There was the tight hug and kiss. But in private, their individual reactions were quite different.

Many a time, Billy said, "I've driven down that driveway with tears coming down my cheeks, not wanting to leave."

No matter what part of the world he was in, whenever possible he would telephone Ruth every night. His feelings were best expressed in a letter he wrote her from Los Angeles on August 11, 1963, two days before their twentieth wedding anniversary:

> How can I find words to express my appreciation for all you have meant to me. Your love and patience with me in my ups and downs . . . have meant more to me than you will ever know. Your counsel, advice, encouragement and prayer have been my mainstay and at times I have almost clung to you in my weakness, in hours of obsession, problems and difficulties. Whoso findeth a wife findeth a good thing, and obtaineth favor of the Lord. One reason that in spite of my own lack of spirituality, discipline and consecration I have found favor of the Lord is because of you. I found a good wife and as a result have found favor with God. . . . It seems that in the recent months my capacity to love you has been increased. I did not think that age would bring greater and deeper love but it has and is. I love the wife of my youth more every day! When we are apart, I miss you so much more than I used to. A week seems like a month. Yes, I am thankful to God for you. What a wonderful helpmeet He provided; certainly our marriage was planned in heaven. I am thankful for the five precious children you bore me each one a bundle of joy. And what a wonderful mother you have been to them! No child ever had a greater mother than our children. You may compare yourself to Susanna Wesley and think you are a failure but she did not rear her

family in a modern secular society. For our generation you are near perfection.

Ruth's emotions were revealed in her poetry:

We live a time
secure;
sure
It cannot last
for long
then
the goodbyes come
again again
like a small death,
the closing of a door.
One learns to live
with pain.
One looks ahead,
not back,
. . . never back,
only before.
And joy will come again
warm and secure,
if only for the now,
laughing,
we endure.[2]

On rare occasions her feelings escaped in front of close friends, such as actress Joan Winmill Brown, who was visiting her while Billy was out of the country on a long campaign. One morning, Ruth received a letter from a missionary acquaintance whom she had not seen in years. Joan later recalled what it said: "Oh, I guess you don't remember me, Ruth, now that you are married to such a famous evangelist. It must be a very glamorous life. Here I am stuck in the mission field with my husband."

"Well, at least she's with him," Ruth said, her eyes bright with tears as she quickly left the room.

"Maybe she cried in her room," GiGi speculated, "but we did not know it at all. When Daddy would leave she would get busy doing something. We'd have projects like hunting for antiques and we'd right then begin looking forward to his coming home."

After he was gone and his physical presence was a memory, Billy was the figure they saw on television, in magazines and the paper. He was the authority figure who was no longer there to enforce rules or break them. Once while Billy was gone, his secretary entered the kitchen and discovered Franklin playing with matches.

"Franklin," she said sternly, "you know your daddy told you not to play with matches!"

"No he didn't," Franklin countered. "He told me not to let him catch me playing with matches. And I'm not going to let him catch me."[3]

Billy was the husband who was gone an average of six months of each year. Ruth never really got used to it. Even at the end of the century, after they had been married more than fifty years, she would find somewhere to go or something to do right after a car drove him away. Anne, who stayed home during high school and saw her mother the most, remembered that no matter how late it was at night, she could see her mother's bedroom light shining in the trees at the rim of the yard.

"She'd be studying her Bible. And if I entered her room at these times and found her on her knees, there was no use saying anything to her then because she wouldn't hear me," said Anne. "That's how Mother coped with Daddy's being gone so much."

1. Ruth Bell Graham, *It's My Turn* (Old Tappan, N.J.: Fleming Revell, 1982), 67.
2. Ruth Bell Graham, *Sitting by My Laughing Fire* (Waco, Tex.: Word Books, 1977), 153.
3. Chris Jarrett Kyle, letter to Ruth Bell Graham, 1982, Ruth Bell Graham Papers, Montreat, North Carolina.

14

CHAPTER

The Beginning of a Mission

Russ Busby, BGEA

RUTH'S DESK

I am grateful not even one little sparrow falls to the ground but what He knows and understands. This is our opportunity to explain to the world.

—Ruth Bell Graham, 1966

On a ridge between the Red and Sulphur Rivers, a hundred miles northeast of Dallas and just south of Oklahoma, stood a two-room log cabin on a small patch of weather-beaten dirt. It was Lamar County, near Paris, Texas, August 15, 1930, and the heat slammed down like a hammer as Mae Thielman gave birth to her second set of twins. She named the youngest of her seven children Calvin Coolidge and Malvin Joe.

For the next thirty-two years Calvin Thielman and Ruth Graham would move in their separate orbits and finally connect in an obscure thumbprint in the Blue Ridge called Montreat. They would become partners in their personal war against the poverty, pain, and loneliness they had witnessed in their childhoods and seemed from then on to discover in every pocket of the world.

The cabin rested on a small cotton farm run by Calvin's father, Charlie, an alcoholic who became abusive during his binges. He died when Calvin was fourteen months old, leaving his mother to chop cotton and later work in a factory, eking out a bare survival for herself and her children. She was a devout Presbyterian and wanted more than all else to instill a love of God and learning in her children. By the time Calvin graduated from West Texas University, he was a respected student and athlete. He was headed for a career in law until he felt the unmistakable call to the ministry.

In 1952, he and his wife, a petite blonde named Dorothy Barnette, moved to Columbia Seminary in Decatur, Georgia. There Calvin became friends with Billy Graham's brother-in-law Leighton Ford and Ruth's brother Clayton. Through them he became well acquainted with the Grahams and the Bells. In 1961, he was hired to fill the double post of Montreat-Anderson College chaplain and minister of the Presbyterian church, which sat on the top of a hill at the center of the school's raw fieldstone buildings. The grounds, which in the summer bustled with conferees and vacationers escaping the heat, had changed little since that waning afternoon almost twenty years earlier when Ruth Bell and Billy Graham had been married there. Ruth had attended the church regularly since. Shortly after he was hired, Calvin gave her charge of the college Sunday school class, consisting almost exclusively of Montreat-Anderson students.

From the beginning her class was popular. A gifted teacher, she was adept at sensing the mood of the group and responding impulsively with her blend of homespun logic, candor, and piercing humor. She stirred the students until they rallied to her causes, which included holding street meetings, helping the poor, and distributing hundreds of large, bright yellow DON'T MISS CALVIN buttons throughout the campus when church attendance had dropped.

Hers was no mean task. The small college was not immune to the rebellion and hostility that had infected the people of the so-called generation gap. In fact, since Montreat-Anderson College was known as the place where you go if you can't go anywhere else, a sizable band of society's rebels, along with those afflicted by academic indolence, landed there. "Ruth," Calvin said, "never paid any attention to the generation gap. For her, it didn't exist. She was not shocked by anyone's hair to his knees or clothes. I can remember some people that were very physically unattractive or terrible misfits that other people would not like, would not want to be around and would not work with. And yet, she would take time with these people and show them kindness."

One day Calvin said to her, "Don't you think you could more profitably put your time on some other people where you could get more mileage?"

"Well, God loves these people too," she replied. "Just because they're unattractive or warped in their thinking doesn't mean the Lord doesn't love them. And if we don't take them, who is going to take them?"

It was as though the Qingjiang mission station had been relocated in Montreat. The new minister rooted out the needs and then telephoned Ruth.

"I sometimes feel guilty for calling her so much," he later admitted as he sat in his small, paneled church office, where autographed portraits of astronauts, baseball players, and LBJ were propped on crowded bookshelves around his cluttered desk. He was typically dressed in a shapeless sweater, baggy Levis, and Wallabees, an unruly shock of gray hair falling over his brow. "But I've always got kids who have medical payments to be made, who are about to flunk out

or don't get their grades because they can't make their final payment. And she has always assisted. She's very generous with other people, but not with herself." He would later speculate that she had helped hundreds of people through college.

When Calvin wasn't telephoning Ruth, he was calling on her father. Dr. Bell had retired from a successful surgical practice in 1955 and was respected for his professionalism and his humanity. He was known to charge the poor only what they could pay, or nothing at all, just as he had done in Qingjiang. Observers speculated that he gave away at least a third of his gross income. His load had not lightened upon leaving the mission field. A doctor, he was on call at night. A prominent Presbyterian layman, he was often out of town. Sometimes he worked around the clock while his wife sat up anxiously, crocheting or reading, until fatigue or one of her headaches drove her to bed.

Though Virginia Bell began her daily entries with "head," "no head," or "terrible head," she rarely mentioned her pain to others. Likewise, Ruth was stoical. She rarely admitted even in her journals that she was ill.

"You never really see her down or depressed," Calvin said, "or if she is, she covers it in such a way that you don't know it. I've seen her when she's had migraine headaches that were so severe that she was almost unable to see how to walk and yet she wouldn't complain. I'd say, 'Do you have a headache?' because she was glassy-eyed and it was evident the light hurt her eyes and she was really in pain. She would brush it aside with the comment that it didn't amount to anything. The only time I've known her to hide out is when she gets one of those severe headaches. She's been plagued with them and she never made a to-do over them at all. And she always works very hard at beating the schedule of getting well."

In fact, Ruth was a terrible medical frustration. Cheerful, cooperative, and stoical in the hospital or clinic, she was quite another sort of patient at home, denying ailments and treating them herself. A few of her unsavory remedies were buttermilk with a twist of lemon and blackstrap molasses over toast, which had all the appeal of bread dipped into a bucket of tar. She derived infinite delight from offering these awful creations to houseguests. She experimented with different types of analgesics and swallowed a variety of obscure vitamins, lecithin, and alfalfa, conveniently storing the tablets in empty lipstick tubes which she carried in her pocket or purse.

If a doctor ordered her to stay in bed for two weeks and do "absolutely nothing," her notion of compliance was to putter about the house in a flowing robe and do all the chores she normally did. "What the doctors don't know won't hurt them," she would say. That attitude prevailed in most of her dealings with people. She avoided confrontations, gently if not humorously contradicting only once in her mellow Virginia accent. If her antagonist of the moment remained obstinate, Ruth would simply smile and say no more. What she would do next, no one

could predict. She was as quietly stubborn as the Sphinx and just about as inscrutable.

If all else failed, that wit of hers could sting, just a little. In 1996, when she almost died from spinal meningitis, GiGi was at the hospital helping her frail mother from the bathroom back to the bed, and daughter could not get mother to slow down. Finally, GiGi impatiently blurted, "Mother, why do you have to walk so fast?"

"To get it over with," Ruth shot back, as she walked on without pause.

When a visitor appeared and chided Ruth that she wasn't taking good care of herself and was too eager to get home, this was met with smiling silence. The guest went on to fix Ruth a high-vitamin, healthy drink, not known for being savory. Ruth took one sip.

"I guess it tastes better if you drink it fast," she said, setting it down on the tray and not touching it again.

"I'll be back to see you soon," promised the visitor. "Unless you tell them not to let me in."

"Now that's an idea," said Ruth.

Her children used her extended hospital stay as an opportunity to clean out and organize their mother's house. Since Ruth rarely threw anything away, the job was daunting, and not the least bit appreciated.

"Anybody who goes into someone's drawers and cabinets should be thanked with a switch," Ruth announced from her sickbed.

She would always have a mind of her own, but her rather profound stubbornness was not completely born of self-interest. Rather, it was part of her determination to keep on course, to carry on with her duties no matter how she felt or who or what was interfering. She had observed the missionaries' self-sacrifice and tenacity in China and expected no less from herself. Like her childhood heroes, she enjoyed an extraterritoriality of sorts, for she was not always guided by the standards of the society she lived in. Her sense of justice was bigger than the law, which in her mind wasn't always moral, and she didn't necessarily do the practical or the expected. She followed her own impulses, signals transmitted by her faith, her tenderheartedness, her eccentricities, and her spiritedness.

The result was an unpredictable, disorganized, baffling human being, far more loving than legalistic, but never to be underestimated. She had an unusual live-and-let-live attitude toward nature, allowing bats, cobwebs, flying squirrels, goats, nonpoisonous snakes, or perhaps a runaway turkey to inhabit her homestead with impunity. Creatures, like children, seemed strangely drawn to her, and a guest marveled one morning when a tiger swallowtail alighted on Ruth's shoulder and rested there a good minute before floating away.

Hummingbirds sometimes watched her eye to eye as she planted geraniums. Flying squirrels carried Christmas yarns from the attic and built nests in old jeep

tires. Field mice hid birdseed in her shoes. Once a train of ducklings followed her from a lake shore, across a lawn, and through the front door of a nearby house. Harmful creatures were not tolerated. Nor were they feared, at least not by her. Copperheads and rattlesnakes she killed with a marshmallow fork kept by the family room fireplace.

She was spontaneous, impulsive, and delightfully uninhibited, walking into a shop in the Atlanta airport on one occasion and requesting a psychedelic package of rolling papers behind the counter.

"These are great to write notes on and stick in your Bible," she cheerfully explained to the clerk.

"Oh yeah," the young woman sarcastically drawled.

A practical joker, she was not above squirting Grady Wilson's new pastel suit with disappearing ink or sneaking a slice of rubber Swiss cheese into his sandwich. She cooked beef bouillon with tiny meatballs for lunch and placed a bowl of tinted water and live tadpoles in front of associate Lee Fisher. He didn't notice anything odd until he dipped for a meatball and it swam away from his spoon. She served a guest a slice of pie covered with shaving cream and left a dead black snake inside a bag outside a friend's kitchen door and hid behind a tree to watch her open it.

Her life, like her dresser drawers and closets, was dominated by clutter. It was common for her to have twenty or thirty books scattered around the house, each in some stage of being read. She might devour a volume from beginning to end or abandon it after the first twenty pages if it lost her interest. Finishing a book just because she had started it, she once said, "was like going into the pantry and thinking you had to eat all the peas before you could open anything else."

Though she eventually had a bona fide office upstairs, complete with a desk, library, and disarray of knickknacks, her "office" was wherever she was. Often, particularly when she was weary, she worked on her bed, propped up amid her jumbled projects. When she traveled, the clutter traveled with her like iron filings after a magnet and relocated where she next slept. The dining room table also made a fine desk, and on it one might find a heap of maps, scrapbooks, and photographs. Wherever she had been there was a trail of notes, written in her unique calligraphy on snippets of white or yellow paper or Post-its. These included grocery lists, reminders, telephone numbers, spiritual insights, sermon ideas and illustrations, quotations that she found particularly amusing or profound, and ideas for improving the house. Reminders might be stuck on a cupboard door, next to a telephone, inside a book, under bed covers, in her Bible, on a table, taped to a car visor or wall, or perched on a log in a cold fireplace.

Ruth's proclivity for disorganization wasn't helped by her reluctance to throw anything away. Most of her memorabilia, including ticket stubs, dried wedding bouquets, her wedding dress, cartoons, poems, and letters, eventually migrated to the attic. Billy was nothing like her in this department, as in most others. After he left home for his next frontier, Ruth would rummage through the garbage to retrieve items, such as his college diploma and a hundred-dollar check, that had been lost amid other "trash" he had pitched into his wastepaper basket.

Ruth's unfinished projects included people. She opened her door to all, and was known to invite into her living room the sort her neighbors would have feared to let into their yards. Had she ever kept a guest book, it would have held the names of drug addicts, thieves, the delusional and deranged, and juvenile delinquents from the local detention center who had committed crimes of vandalism or murder. She would buy pizzas, barrels of fried chicken, or bags of hamburgers for her scarred, skeptical acquaintances, and challenge them with the Christian faith.

Through her own ministry, she kept her husband in touch with students, on occasion coaxing him to speak at the local college and small community gatherings, or teach her Sunday school class. Important people, ranging from celebrities to politicians, visited the Graham house. But it was the lonely, the misfits, Ruth welcomed with special warmth. They were the people she virtually adopted.

Her first "orphan" was an elderly man named Arthur Radcliffe, a midwesterner who had taught horticulture in North Carolina and later managed a flower shop. An eccentric bachelor, "Old Man Art," as he was called, was as sinewy as a licorice stick. Ruth had become acquainted with him through the Montreat Presbyterian Church, where he was an usher.

When Radcliffe reached his seventies, about the time Ruth started teaching her Sunday school class, he was placed in a Greensboro, North Carolina, nursing home. Miserable when separated from the soil and plants he loved, he ran away and hitchhiked back to western North Carolina. One day he appeared on Ruth's doorstep.

"I'm not going to let the highway patrol take me back!" he declared in a desperate voice. "I'll die before I'll go back to that nursing home. Why don't you just let me die right here in this old cabin you got at the end of the road?"

She renovated it and he moved in. He papered the walls with magazine photographs of flowers and plugged the cove with plants and shrubbery. Whenever a friend would drive up to visit, Radcliffe could be found stretched out in the loamy soil, digging and planting, because he was too feeble to stand or squat. He died two years after moving into the cabin, and Ruth carried out the wishes of his handwritten will. His body was given to science and a white pine was planted on the ridge in remembrance of him.

At Christmastime, not long after Radcliffe had become part of the earth that once was so much a part of him, a rumor circulated about a family virtually starving in an abandoned toolshed on a brambly patch of dirt in Black Mountain. On a raw December day, Calvin Thielman and two deacons investigated. They found the unheated shanty and a mother and five small children living inside. There was no plumbing. The only convenience was an electric lightbulb glaring over a crazed mosaic of broken concrete flooring. The father, a carpenter named Luther Dover, was dying of cancer in Asheville's Memorial Mission Hospital. When Calvin visited the ward several days later, he found Dover on his back, the skin covering his gaunt face as thin as cigarette paper.

"I went up to your house and went out to your family," Calvin finally drawled after moments of small talk. "It looks like it's going to be a pretty rough Christmas for the children. And some people at our church have more than they know what to do with. They would be glad to help give the children some things for Christmas and to help you have a place to live if that would be all right with you. We don't want to do anything without your permission and I guarantee you it won't take anything away from anybody else, it won't take anything away from them."

Dover's eyes filled with tears. "I reckon they would appreciate that," he whispered.

When Billy Graham heard the story of the Dovers, he sent for Calvin. "I'm always hearing that the government is giving away money right and left," he said. "Find out if they're receiving the aid they should be." He handed Calvin a generous check, adding, "There's more where that came from."

Ruth discovered the ages of the Dover children and bought clothing and toys for them. By mid-December, the Dover family had been moved into an abandoned house. Plumbers had replaced its rusty water pipes. Rooms were furnished and Dover's doctor allowed him to come home for the holiday. Shortly after the family moved in, Ruth's Sunday school class arrived with sacks of groceries. Christmas Eve she sent her husband and the children down the mountain to deliver the gifts she had chosen and wrapped.

Several days later, Dover, gasping for breath, was carried back to the hospital in the bed of a pickup truck. Calvin went to see him and found him wracked with pain and receiving little attention.

"Can't you give him oxygen or something to make him more comfortable?" Calvin asked an orderly.

"Well," the man stalled, "I have to get clearance from the head doctor and I don't know where to get him . . ."

Outraged, the preacher stormed through the hall, telephoned Ruth, and told her the situation.

"You let me handle it," she told him.

She knew when to throw her weight around and didn't hesitate when the need arose. She was calmly settling the matter over the telephone before Calvin had walked twenty paces. "And boy!" he recalled, "when I went back down the hall the nurses were moving and everybody else was moving. A private nurse was by Dover's side and a doctor had arrived."

The last moments of Dover's life he held his wife's hand. "I'm gonna die," he whispered. "I want you to see that all my debts are paid. And I want my children raised as Christians."

Cloaked in wool, her breath turning to smoke against the wintry air, Ruth stood at the edge of the small crowd when he was buried in the mountainside cemetery. Not known to all who clustered around the new gash in the frozen earth, she had paid for the funeral.

Ed Clark, *Life* magazine

WALKING THE MOUNTAIN PATH WITH FRANKLIN

15

CHAPTER

The Terror by Night

Whether it was a loud car or motorcycles I loved these things when I was growing up. I never pretended to be the stereotype of a fellow with a Bible under my arm. But my parents pretty much let me be me.

—William Franklin Graham III

The six of them, children and mother, perched around the kitchen table, beginning the day with readings from a box of multicolored Bible verses. Momentarily they heard the heavy, booted feet of Gregg Sawyer in the foyer, arriving to begin his chores.

"Morning," he said.

Ruth invited him to read the Scripture lesson, something she always did if one of the workmen appeared during breakfast. He shyly withdrew one of the cards from the box she handed him, seated himself, and commenced cleaning his glasses between his thumb and forefinger.

He read Hebrews 12:6: "Whom the Lord loveth, he *chaseth* . . ."

His misreading was a harbinger of life with Franklin when he reached his teens. It would indeed seem that the Lord would chase him as he veered from the straight and narrow, his problems and temptations nipping at his heels.

Franklin would require his mother's full attention, something she could not always give. He needed the strong hand of a father, but the pressure of Billy's ministry was staggering. By the time Franklin was old enough to drive, more than thirty million people had attended his father's crusades, while millions more had heard him over the radio or on television. Billy was so recognizable that he could no longer eat in restaurants without people lining up ten and twelve deep to ask for his autograph. He could not appear in an American hotel lobby or airport without being mobbed.

Frequently, he resorted to disguises, rarely leaving the house without a pair of large sunglasses and a cap pulled low. Perpetually preoccupied, sometimes he didn't pay as much attention to his camouflages as he ought to have, and some of them were rather curious. He wore a wide-brimmed hat in Mexico and an autograph hound thought he was James Arness. In a European airport he discovered with alarm that he had lost his sunglasses, and quickly bought a pair off a rack. Ruth later noticed, to her horror, the Playboy bunny insignia on the frames. He walked along a crowded beach in Europe, clad in fire-engine-red shorts, a blue windbreaker, yellow socks, Hush Puppies, a denim cap, and sunglasses. "That's the dumbest looking human being I've ever seen," Ruth thought to herself as she watched him amble in her direction. "Oh, no!" it dawned on her. "He's mine!"

Without disguises, he was painfully vulnerable. In the mid-seventies the Grahams were on a boat in Acapulco Bay, Mexico, with future President George Bush and his wife, Barbara. After a picnic of raw oysters on a deserted beach, it was time to swim back to the boat. It would take an hour to follow the shoreline to their hotel.

"Since the trip back will take so long," said Billy, in the midst of writing a sermon, "I think I'll just walk back along the beach."

Without wallet or sunglasses, and clad in nothing but a pair of white swim trunks he had borrowed from Bush, he set out, not realizing that the beach he was walking along was the property of a Mexican naval station and off limits to civilians. He rounded a corner and was greeted by two submachine guns backed by unsmiling Mexican soldiers. Billy spoke no Spanish and did his best to explain, and the guards, who spoke no English, tried to understand.

He was directed to sit on a nearby bench and wait for one of their English-speaking superiors. The officer arrived, heard Billy's explanation, and released him, with the order that he could not walk along the restricted beach. When Billy stood, he realized he had been sitting on wet green paint. He could trot barefoot along the scorching sidewalk to the first hotel and get back to the nonrestricted beaches by darting through the lobby, where he would be recognized. Or he could stay on the sidewalk the entire distance and burn his feet but remain anonymous, which was what he did.

As early as 1961, there were signs of what Franklin's life held. On November 27 the *Indianapolis Times* printed this: "Columnist Charlie McHarry writes that the handsome lad nightclubbing in New York with Gayle Horne, Lena's daughter, was Billy Graham, Jr., son of the evangelist." Franklin was nine years old at the time.

"But the sobering fact," Ruth observed, "is that it shows none of our children can ever live privately, conquer privately, or sin privately." She and Billy prayed, she recorded, "that God would mercifully spare [the children] any sowing of wild oats. . . . Unless committed to Thee, they will react violently against this enforced publicity and turn against Bill in bitterness as tho he were to blame. . . . As Christians they will take all this as an opportunity for witnessing. As pagans they would seek to camouflage themselves with worldliness to escape notice."

A rakish-looking boy with strong features and a mop of black hair, Franklin had inherited his grandfather Bell's sturdy build and love of adventure. He was happiest when scaling Suicide Trail on Montreat's Lookout Mountain or hunting with Calvin Thielman, who taught him much about guns and preached that he mustn't kill songbirds. One day, after hearing complaints that Franklin was indeed committing this crime, Calvin firmly reprimanded him.

"Aw, Calvin," Franklin assured him, "don't worry! I draw a bead on a bird and I say, Sing. If he sings, I let him go. And if he doesn't I let him have it."

The shooting lessons came to an end one day when Calvin was demonstrating how to handle a high-caliber pistol and accidentally shot himself in the leg.

Out of sorts in a Sunday suit, Franklin preferred faded jeans and flannel shirts, his hands usually covered with black grease from tinkering with automobile or motorcycle engines. He was energetic and witty, more attracted to vice than virtue. He began his flirtation with cigarettes at age three, supplying himself with the butts dropped by the workmen while they were building the house. One day, after he had gathered a tidy little pile, he heard his father coming.

"Pretend they're yours," Franklin whispered loudly to Wallace Walker, the electrician.

"Franklin," the man laughed, "your daddy knows I don't smoke."

Several years later, Ruth asked caretaker Floyd Roberts to let Franklin try one of his cigarettes, thinking it would make the boy so sick that he would never again want to smoke. Franklin inhaled the first one down to the filter and proceeded to help Roberts finish the pack. The next day Ruth asked John Rickman to give him a cigar. That plan backfired as well.

"Why are you doing this?" Franklin asked his mother at bedtime.

"The things are bad for you," Ruth said. "I don't want you to get the habit."

Perhaps it was a little late.

When Franklin was ten, Ruth recorded that he had asked Christ to come into his heart while hiking with Chuck Gieser, the son of a former missionary Ruth's family had known in China. Instead of ensuring peace, it seemed to give him something else to fight. His mother's anxieties became acute.

"I cannot sleep," she wrote at the time. "For a while I sat here in bed with the lights off, and thought and prayed. I have a headache. It would be so easy to take a sleeping pill but He knows I need sleep and how much. And sometimes there are things more important like seeing the world outside flooded with moonlight and watching the last log in my fireplace flicker and die; watching the shadows of the ceiling beams leaping in the firelight. And knowing He is here. I've taken time out to remember all this because of one special thing He said. He had told it to me before, many times in one way or another. It's about Franklin. Every time I pray especially for him God says: Love him. . . . Which seems odd because I love every bone of him. But God means show it. Let him in on the fact. Enjoy him. You think he's the greatest let him know you think so."

Ruth agonized over her older son. She felt frustrated as her other responsibilities wrestled for her attention. Insomnia became common, and by 1965, the year John Pollock was finishing his first authorized biography of Billy, life was becoming as complex and fast as a circuit board. Frequently, Ruth lay awake at night, her mind streaking down her list of chores.

November 10, 1965, was a typical frenetic day. Ruth drove Anne twenty miles to the dentist, then to the oral surgeon. Ruth carried clothing to the dry cleaner, shopped, and returned home in time to serve tea to radio commentator Paul Harvey and five other guests. At spare moments, Ruth packed her bags for London, read snatches of Pollock's galley proofs, answered mail, paid bills, and bought traveler's checks. Still ahead were two talks and a Sunday school lesson to prepare and Sunday dinner to plan. "And running thru my mind," she wrote, "are there not twenty-four hours in the day?"

It seemed that the only time she had to herself was the sleepless early morning hours when everyone else on the mountain was unconscious. She studied her Bible and meditated, her thoughts turning to God, Whose presence was silently and invisibly there. "It may be," she wrote, "that the night seasons are the only times He can get in a word edgewise."

From time to time, her experiences were almost mystical. On February 17, 1965, she awoke at 2:30 in the morning, disturbed and dejected. Feeling the impulse to pray, she knelt beside her bed. Inexplicably, tears flowed as she found herself petitioning God for two men, Kenneth Strachan, a Latin American missionary whose wife, Elizabeth, had gone to college with Ruth, and Tom Allen, a pastor in Glasgow, Scotland, whom the Grahams had come to know during crusades in the British Isles. She prayed, unaware of the men's circumstances, for "a reprieve for both. An extension of their lives and services on earth." After a few minutes the impulse was gone. She returned to bed. One week later, forty-nine-year-old Strachan was dead from cancer. Allen, also forty-nine, died soon after from a heart attack.

There were periods when the rhythm continued, day and night, night and day, light giving way to darkness, darkness giving way to dawn. "INSOMNIA," scrawled in black ink and underlined, scarred pages of her journals. In the cool dark her senses became refined, a radar detecting something more. Through parted curtains she watched the moon hanging over Rainbow Mountain, pallid, a ghostly face. The stream whispered to the west of her window, and anxieties, failures, and unfinished tasks would not be silenced.

She began climbing out of bed at two, three, and four o'clock in the morning to write letters, pay bills, or finish work that worried her. She prayed and read her Bible, and began to dread the turning off of her light at the hour for bed. One night, she felt a tugging as she read Psalm 91:5. The words were lifted from the page: "Thou shalt not be afraid for the terror by night." She emerged from her worries, strengthened.

In 1969, Franklin hit the white water of his rebellion. "In looking back," Ruth wrote, "I think I would say this is the summer Franklin began to walk his own road." He turned seventeen that July. He seemed unwilling, his parents saw, to take a stand for Christ. Despite their concern, their talks with him were amiable.

"I remember when long hair became a big issue I wanted my hair to touch my ears," Franklin recalled. "When I smoked I knew they disagreed for health reasons. But they never preached at me. They wished I'd do it at home and not behind their backs. They didn't want me to make alcohol, tobacco, or long hair an issue."

Franklin would not smoke in front of his family, but he couldn't fool his mother. He sneaked by smoking out his upstairs window, not realizing that an updraft from the valley simply carried the evidence around to her bedroom. Academically, he continued his nosedive, and his parents sent him to the Stony Brook School, an all-male private school in New York. There he kept a brotherly eye on Bunny, nearby in the Stony Brook Girls School. Both of them were miserably homesick, and in an effort to cheer themselves up, he visited her on a regular basis, bringing her candy he bought with money he earned from selling popcorn on campus. When his parents realized how much he loved his home and the mountains, they did not insist that he return to Stony Brook his senior year.

Instead, he enrolled in Charles D. Owen, the local public high school, where he struggled with his studies and the gang of students who thought it great sport to goad the shaggy, denim-clad fellow widely known as Billy Graham's son. One classmate, determined to harass him into violence, sat behind him in class and jiggled the desk every time Franklin attempted to write. After repeated warnings, Franklin finally jumped to his feet and took a big swing, knocking the young man over the teacher's desk. Moments later Franklin was in the principal's office. He was expeditiously sent home. "He walked in, grinning like a possum totally unrepentant," Ruth recalled.

He wasn't exactly a calming influence in the house. Franklin tormented Ned unmercifully, and fired his shotgun out his bedroom window, and set stereo speakers in front of the intercom to rock the house with Janis Joplin. In summer, he stayed out late. Again his mother did not confront him. "I'd come in at one or two o'clock," Franklin recalled. "And her light would still be on. But she never would get on me for being up late." It was often at these times, when she was calmly waiting for him, that they would have their most meaningful talks. But sometimes her presence annoyed him.

"You only wait up so you can smell my breath," he accused her one night.

"If that's how you feel," she replied, "I'll hit the sack. I'm tired."

At least in Franklin's mind, it was sometimes his mother, not God, who was doing the "chasing." One Sunday afternoon at lunch the family was discussing spirits and wondering if it were possible that some Christians returned to earth after death, no longer restrained by bodily limitations. "Too many people who have lost loved ones," Ruth remarked, "have said that at times they have had such a sense of their loved one's presence as if they were breathing down their necks."

"I sure hope *you* don't die," Franklin pointedly remarked to her.

In the main, Ruth allowed him to do as he pleased, making it clear that she expected much from him regardless of how little he expected from himself. Her attitude about sin in general was that people who break the law or one of God's commandments should confess and accept the punishment. Then they should accept forgiveness. If her son chose to be irresponsible, he had to live with consequences, such as feeling cranky and exhausted when his mother awakened him at 7:30 each morning by banging a broom against the copper stove hood below his second-story bedroom. When that failed, she dumped his ashtray on his head.

He began locking his door. Ruth did not believe she had met her match. She climbed onto the roof one morning and crept across shingles. A tin cup of water was clamped in her teeth and she planned to dash it in his face when she reached the open window. Franklin heard her coming and feigned sleep until she was just outside his room. He slammed down the sash and grinned at her through the glass.

16

CHAPTER

Other Children

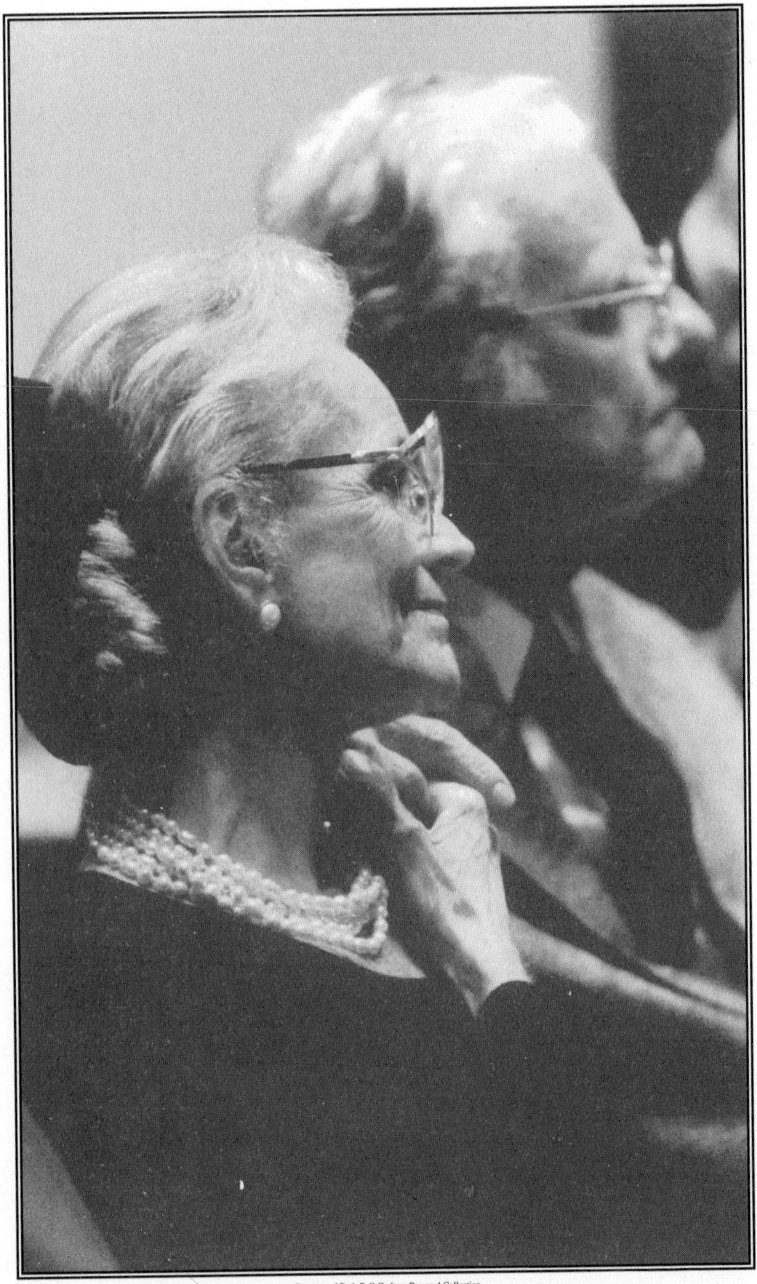

Courtesy of Ruth Bell Graham Personal Collection

THE MOTHER

Ruth picks some peculiar ones.

—Pete Post, Chief of Police, Montreat

There were her "other children," waifs who drifted, lost in life, like dandelion seeds. She had an eye for them, snatching them in midflight for a moment, more a mother than a missionary, and a tender friend, not a judge. The years, really, had not changed the heartbroken little girl who buried Tar Baby beside the compound wall and dug him up three weeks later to see how he was doing.

Her empathy was her weakness, for often she involved herself with people who were beyond help. No matter how often they fell, her optimism was unflagging. No matter how often they took advantage of her kindness, she did not see it.

On Wednesday, May 18, 1966, the Grahams boarded the *Queen Mary* in New York and set sail for the month-long crusade at Earls Court, London. The afternoon was cool, the clouds ponderous over the Verrazano-Narrows Bridge as the ship passed under it toward the open sea. The night before the ship docked Ruth tossed anxiously in their cabin, sleep eluding her until 4:30 A.M. when she dreamed they were in the Earls Court stadium and only thirty people had appeared for the first service.

As they prepared to dock in Southampton on Tuesday, May 24, seventy-five reporters boarded. Unlike the mob twelve years before, this crew was courteous and friendly. From Southampton the Grahams traveled by train to

Waterloo Station in London, where they were greeted by a large, cheering crowd. Many had first heard Billy at Harringay. The people sang spirited hymns as a convertible whisked the famous couple away.

"It's hard just to smile and wave when there's a lump in your throat," Ruth wrote at the time. "It would be all right if only they wouldn't sing. Then memories of Harringay come crowding back and that overwhelming sense of the presence of God. And you know you should be down there among them, lost in the crowd, singing with them . . . not riding in a convertible."

On May 28, a warm, cloudless Saturday, the Grahams arrived in Oxford at midafternoon, commotion rippling from them as they were besieged by newsmen, well-wishers, and the curious. Oxonians glanced up quizzically as the party moved along narrow, winding streets, where flower vendors peddled paper-wrapped roses, and pale, bespectacled dons pedaled bicycles. They passed dark, towering churches with headstones leaning and stained from centuries of rain and wind. Europeans, Africans with crisp English accents, ragged beggars, and tourists teemed beneath spires.

The next day Billy was to speak at Saint Aldate's, an evangelical Anglican church. A long line of Oxford students wrapped around the imposing stone building, some still in their evening clothes from revels the night before. Others were passing out humanist tracts. As he went through the crowd to the church door he was escorted by hecklers. "I'm glad to have you here," Billy affably let them know as he passed into the cool silence of the sanctuary. Afterward he and Ruth drove to Cambridge, stopping midway for a picnic lunch, for once alone. "The press," Ruth wrote, "missed two good shots of Bill. One of him going into the Ladies restroom by mistake and the other, his hat brim turned down all around, raincoat on . . . [as he leaned] on the fence like an old farmer."

He spoke at Great Saint Mary's that night, and again, hundreds of students were queued outside, many there to make sport of this American evangelist who dared to violate their refined minds with his simple message.

"I bless you in the name of Billy Graham," a young man wearing his shirt backward chanted as he sprinkled water on his friends. In the hall next to the church residents played their radios full volume until the police intervened. A row of students sitting behind Ruth whispered insults about her husband throughout the service. The vicar forgot to turn on the pulpit light and Billy could not see to read one word of his notes.

Abroad, Ruth was no different from the Sunday school teacher at home. It was the young cynics, the confused, often troublesome people who drew her.

On Sunday, June 12, her husband was to speak at a church in Brixton. She sat in the family pew of the elegant woman beside her, a patrician and an acknowledged force in the congregation. Two young men, bearded, wearing blue jeans, their arms tattooed, moved down the aisle and stood with uncertainty just yards from Ruth. She glanced at them empathetically and later wrote in her journal, "I wished so that someone would welcome them warmly and offer them seats." The woman next to her stared at the men with obvious suspicion and disapproval.

"That kind sometimes disturbs meetings," she whispered to Ruth.

Heads turned as Billy appeared at an entrance. He walked down the aisle, stopping long enough to shake hands with the two young men and welcome them. The moment he moved on, the woman instructed an usher to show the men out.

Later, when Billy preached to ten thousand at Victoria Park in London's East End, Ruth wandered through the crowd and noticed a group of irreverent teenagers. When Cliff Barrows suggested a song, they yelled "No!" They wadded their song sheets and pelted people, a stockpile of eggs nearby and ready to hurl. Billy preached on John 3:16 while his wife, dressed in a trench coat and dark glasses, slipped toward the offenders, her strategy planned.

When she reached them she would say, "I'm much more interested in what you have to say than in what he has to say. Let's get off where he won't disturb us and explain what you've got on your mind." Before she could open her mouth she felt a hand on her arm. Three BGEA team members flanked her, thwarting her plan, and the teenagers scattered. This was not unusual, and the preacher's wife would forever be rather much a security nightmare to whoever's chore it was to watch her.

She was irrepressible, spontaneous, even reckless. Ruth, in later years, would confide to a friend that she was never free to be socially and politically uninhibited. She felt she had to constrain herself for the sake of her husband's ministry. In spiritual matters she was open and irrepressible, and carried her beliefs wherever she went. She shared her faith with whoever seemed receptive, whether it was teenagers, hotel maids, or taxicab drivers.

One morning in London she hired a taxi to carry her to Foyle's Bookstore and soon discovered the driver was Jewish. As he whizzed Ruth past cars, careening through side streets and around pedestrians, she invited him to Earls Court.

"You must be kidding or something," he turned around and said. "In my faith, we have our own beliefs. And I know what you people would do. You'd try to convert me. And me, I don't want to get involved."

"Are you Orthodox, Conservative, or Reformed?" she asked, clinging to the back of the seat as he darted down another street to avoid a traffic jam at Trafalgar Square.

"The synagogue I go to is Orthodox," he replied. "It's the only one around. I wish it was Reformed. Me, I don't go to synagogue any more than I have to. I say, why should I go to church and confess my sins to God when I know I'll go right back the next week and sin all over again?"

"I wonder why you bother to eat a meal since you will have to turn around and eat another," she replied.

"Hey!" he said, laughing, cutting into another lane. "That's a good answer!"

He began attacking religious formalism, legalism, and hypocrisy, punctuating each remark with dramatic gestures, looking at her over his shoulder for what seemed alarmingly long moments. He buzzed past her address, braked to a screeching halt, and backed up.

"Your comments on religion sound very much like Christ's," she smiled as she paid him.

"How's that?" he asked, startled.

"Christ said many similar things in the New Testament."

"Never read the New Testament," he said thoughtfully. "But I'll get one."

On Wednesday, June 29, the radio brought the news that the United States had bombed Hanoi, and war protesters retaliated by announcing they would set off firecrackers in the counseling room at Earls Court after that night's service. As Ruth sat in the stadium and police stood sentry outside the counseling room, an usher slipped her a note. It was from Meg Spalding, a young woman Ruth had recently become acquainted with, and it read: "Dear Mrs. Graham. Please could you come and see me as I need your help. I will wait for you outside the exit where you sit. Thank you very much. Meg. P.S. It is about dope."

She was a wan young woman with frizzy red hair, and had noticed Ruth walk in with Billy before the service a week earlier. She had oddly and desperately rushed to introduce herself to the evangelist's wife. Since then, Meg had forlornly sought out the lovely woman in the stands, her nervous small talk masking her misery and interminable loneliness. One of five children, Meg had been born to a prostitute. Eventually, her home became the streets, her trade the same as her mother's, and she was a lesbian.

Ruth immediately left the service and found Meg huddled at the bottom of the steps. Wearing jeans, sandals, and the same brown jacket she had worn every day, she looked blankly at Ruth. Her eyes were dark and dull, her face blanched. Meg dug inside her brown satchel and she pulled out a square of cloth. She spread it open next to her for Ruth to sit on.

"I'm doped," Meg said.

"What happened?" Ruth asked, sitting near her.

"It's me girlfriend Pat. She died in hospital today. Drugs."

"You can't go on escaping from problems and hurts by taking dope," Ruth told her gently. "You'll have to choose between escaping to Christ or escaping to dope. Jesus loves you, Meg."

She hung her head, staring at her hands. "I wish I had a mother like you."

"Listen," Ruth told her, "you have Jesus. He's always with you. He loves you. He understands. He's more powerful than dope. I'll be gone next week. Earls Court will be over. You'll have disappointments but He's there with you."

"I have more dope," she confessed.

"Give it to me," Ruth said.

"You want it?"

"No, I don't, but I don't want you to have it."

She again rummaged inside her satchel and handed Ruth a small knot of something wrapped inside a handkerchief. In the distance Billy's words echoed off the stadium walls as though there were two voices preaching instead of one. The service seemed unreal and far away as his wife sat in the damp air watching a young prostitute drift deeper into a stupor.

It was the beginning of a sad, seemingly futile friendship. Ruth attended to Meg, and would exchange letters with her for many years, though her troubled friend was the sort of person very few in Ruth's position would have cultivated. She wished for her an end of aloneness and abandonment. It was what Ruth wanted for all her other children. Two years later, she met Tony Mendez. He was a Puerto Rican from the Bronx, where he was known as "the Kid." Compactly built and bearded, he was usually armed with a pool cue and a switchblade. Mendez liked platform shoes and multicolored Indian cottons, and was uninhibited and mercurial.

His parents had divorced shortly after immigrating to the United States, and his mother had raised him and two sisters in a shabby tenement on Prospect Avenue, a drug-infested strip between the Harlem and East Rivers. Early on, Mendez mastered the art of survival, picking up a dollar any way he could, and rarely buying anything if he could steal it. He hustled in smoky, boozy pool halls, earning sometimes a hundred dollars a day, and feeding his hunger for cocaine and heroin.

On a whim, he enrolled in a few courses at nearby Fordham University shortly after graduating from high school. There he fell under the watchful eye of his guidance counselor, a man who had grown up in the ghetto and escaped. In early 1968 he urged Mendez to leave New York and told him about a tiny two-year school in western North Carolina called Montreat-Anderson College. Maybe Mendez should give it a try.

"Those people are out in the sticks," Mendez retorted, laughing ruefully as southern stereotypes came to mind. "Man, they're backward!"

To please his counselor, Mendez filled out the application, though he had no intention of ever going south. But when he received word that he had been accepted, the thought of heading there for some reason warmed his heart, he recalled. That fall he stuffed his few garish belongings into a suitcase and flew to Asheville.

It was a shock from the moment the prop plane began circling for landing. The runway seemed no bigger than a racetrack, a solitary wind sock swaying languidly from a pole. Inside a terminal so small that baggage was simply set on the floor, he looked about in sinking disbelief. The lobby was a small square of shag carpet scattered with plastic chairs, and a mounted television set blinked in a corner. The gift shop sold no duty-free cameras, liquors, and perfumes, but saltwater taffy, jars of dark sourwood honey, and Cherokee Indian souvenirs.

But it was the mountains that left him speechless. Fall had peaked, and hills were dashed with gold, orange, yellow, and red. The few pitiful trees Mendez had seen along Prospect Avenue had already lost their leaves. He had never before seen the magic of autumn.

"Did someone paint the leaves?" he asked the college employee who picked him up at the airport.

"No, Tony," the man replied. "They change that way."

As a student, Mendez was a loner, working as a janitor in the post office and in the student center, where he hustled at pool and spent his profits on drugs. Gambling in Asheville as well as in Montreat, he earned a reputation, and soon outsiders were driving through the rustic stone gate to challenge him. The college's Presbyterian administration began to wonder at the wisdom of importing this inner-city student.

On a Sunday morning during the fall of his first semester, Mendez crawled out of bed, headachy and dizzy after drinking the night away. He pulled on a white Nehru jacket and slacks, tied a red sash around his waist and a scarf around his head. He ambled along the cracked cement walkway, passing beneath gnarled apple and pine trees on the rim of Lake Susan, Montreat's stream-fed swimming hole. Docks were warped and painted the same dark green that seemed to coat every resort porch and rocking chair in western North Carolina. On a diving platform in the center of the lake was the graffiti "PLEASE DON'T WALK ON THE WATER."

On the lake's western bank, over the dam, the student center was a modest building filled with brightly colored plastic chairs and round, Formica-covered tables. The oily smell of a million hamburgers clung to the stale air. Mendez considered this his turf, and found it was being violated by a gang of students who were seated around the pool tables—*his* pool tables. A handsome woman with a large black Bible was the ringleader. It seemed her name was Ruth.

She glanced with friendly curiosity at the glassy-eyed, wildly dressed Hispanic stumbling through the line of chairs in front of her, and she thought, "That's got to be the most pitiful individual I ever saw." Bleary and confused, he dropped into an empty chair and watched her through bloodshot eyes.

"I'll never forget," he recalled, "she must have had Billy Graham's Bible because it was so big." She abandoned her Sunday school lesson and directed her comments toward him. Afterward, she introduced herself and invited him to come again.

"Well, I've got to go continue my game," he said, hurrying away.

As the days unrolled, Mendez's reputation worsened, an unsurprising phenomenon in a town the size of Montreat, where news spreads like an echo in a telephone booth. Calvin Thielman was determined to reach the college's hippies and invited Mendez and several others to his house on December 9. Billy Graham's Indian associate Akbar Abdul-Haqq talked with them and answered questions. Afterward, Mendez stayed for more than an hour and said he wanted to change his life. The next day, Ruth, or "Roof" as Mendez called her, sent him a copy of the J. B. Phillips translation of the New Testament. Reading the simple prose in the student cafeteria, he understood the words for the first time and became so excited that several students reported him drunk.

Two days later, he and his best friend broke into a heated argument in the dormitory.

"I could cut your face! I could cut your face!" the friend menaced, waving a scalpel, a recent gift from Mendez, who had stolen it from the biology lab.

Mendez, the street fighter, slipped a bone-handled knife from his belt and plunged it into the man's stomach. When the police arrived moments later, they found the two men clinging to each other.

"Buddy, I didn't mean to do it," Mendez cried.

"It's okay, buddy. It's okay," said his bleeding friend.

Though the friend dropped all charges, the college wouldn't be so generous. Montreat-Anderson's Disciplinary Committee advocated kicking Mendez out of school. They summoned him and interrogated him about the fight, about his past, their opinion of him darkening by degrees. Ruth was a member of the college's board of trustees at the time and was instrumental in saving Mendez from being shipped back to the ghetto.

"Do anything," she told the committee, "but don't send him back to the Bronx. He'll slide down the drain."

Reluctantly, the committee agreed to place him on probation and let him stay.

After hearing his wife talk about Mendez, Billy invited him to the house and they spent an afternoon talking in the living room. As he left, Billy wrapped an arm around him and said, "Tony, I want you to know that your friends are my friends, and my home is always open to you."

Mendez took him at his word, and the next day he loaded a bus and a van with drug addicts and the worst on the street, as he called them, and led the way to Little Piney Cove. The caravan halted at the lower locked gate, an obstacle Mendez had not anticipated. He reassured his disappointed companions, climbed on top of the bus, and began yelling as loudly as he could until they were granted entrance. The Grahams watched from the porch as the crew arrived, not knowing how they would fit all of them inside the house.

In the late spring of 1969 Billy held a crusade in Madison Square Garden, and Mendez, home for the summer, decided to attend. The night of the first service he and a group of rough-looking men showed up in gang colors, shaggy hair, tattoos, obscene patches, and frayed blue jeans. The stadium was full, said the security guard as he looked them up and down, and Mendez assumed he was being discriminated against.

"Listen," Mendez said, his voice rising, "Billy Graham and Ruth, they're just like my parents. I've eaten at their home, I've slept there . . ."

"Yeah, yeah, yeah," the guard said sarcastically. "Listen, he's my brother." Then he got hard and ordered, "Listen buddy, keep walking."

"Come on!" Mendez motioned to his friends. They pushed past the guard and bolted through the entrance. What Mendez didn't know was that the Black Panthers had threatened Billy's life that day and security was unusually tight. By the time he and his buddies had made it to the fourth tier they were surrounded by plainclothesmen, and in moments they found themselves back on the street.

"Yeah, yeah, you know him, sure," his friends taunted him.

Two nights later Mendez brought his sisters to the service, and when the invitation was given, Ruth saw the three of them go forward. She headed toward the counseling room to welcome them.

"Hey Ruth," Mendez said nervously, "I've got to see you, I've got to talk to you."

They met the next night outside the loge entrance.

"What's the trouble, Tony?" she asked, studying his troubled face.

"Well, Ruth," he said, "I've done something bad. Really bad."

"Not again," Ruth said. "What this time?"

"Well, Ruth," he said, "I have a buddy. He needed some money and, Ruth, he had never robbed a filling station before and needed some help. So I thought it was my Christian responsibility to teach him how to rob a gas station."

"How much did you get?"

"A hundred and twenty-five dollars."

"Okay," she said. "You have to pay back your share."

He blanched.

"Was your buddy a Christian?" she asked.

"No," he said.

"Okay," she said, "then you have to pay back his share as well."

He stared at her in pained disbelief.

"Tony, do you have anything else in your possession that you've stolen?"

"Everything I got," he said.

"It's a good thing it's summer," she told him, "because you're going to have to give everything back."

When he returned to Montreat that fall Ruth asked him, "Did you pay back the service station owner?"

"I couldn't," he replied, shrugging his shoulders innocently. "I went to the filling station and it was closed down."

"Well, I guess so if he had many customers like you," she said.

17

CHAPTER

Power and Influence

Courtesy of Ruth Bell Graham Personal Collection

WITH THE PRESIDENT

I don't think Ruth cares a hoot about whether or not she meets a celebrity.

—Julie Nixon Eisenhower

On a clear, balmy March evening in 1950, Strom Thurmond and his wife, Jean, invited the Grahams to the governor's mansion at Columbia, South Carolina. It was one of the first occasions when a prominent politician showed interest in this evangelist who had become so well known during the pivotal Los Angeles crusade the year before. Ironically, after an evening of mingling with a number of the state's prominent citizens, the names Ruth recorded in her diary were those of the domestic staff.

This was typical. The Grahams' association with the famous and influential has been a source of curiosity and controversy. In 1950, President Harry Truman invited Billy to the White House for the first time. Five years later, the Grahams were invited to Clarence House to be presented to the Queen Mother. Later that spring they were invited to Windsor Castle to have lunch with the Queen and the Duke of Edinburgh. This would go on for the rest of their lives, for never has an evangelist been of such interest to contemporary world leaders.

Ruth occasionally accompanied her husband on his visits to places of importance. In general, she was observant and unassertive. She rarely discussed the details of such events with friends or even family. In the mid-nineties, when there was increasing pressure for Billy and Ruth to reveal details about their famous associations, they would not. Confidential conversations, whether with presidents or neighbors, were privileged.

In later years, Ruth would often bemoan the growing loss of loyalty and grace in a world where every confession, indiscretion, and peccadillo was a disgrace for all to see. She would never have a taste for *Court TV* or psychobabble talk shows, and she would never get used to worrying about reporters and the curious who began rummaging in the old galvanized garbage cans at the bottom of the Graham road.

She would learn to soak labels off jars or prescription bottles that were nobody's business. She would buy a trash compactor and burn personal bills, notes, itineraries, and other paperwork in a barrel behind the house. It was simply wise, she would say with a smile that did not belie her indignation. Such precautions, in her mind, were one more irritating and unwanted invoice from fame, and a violation of what should have been an individual's reasonable right to privacy.

As far as celebrities, royalty, and world leaders were concerned, Ruth simply treated them as she wished to be treated, and exploitation was rude, if not immoral. Her retelling of celebrity encounters, for the most part, would always be restricted to harmless and often humorous anecdotes. On the Grahams' first visit to Clarence House in 1955, for example, a butler reached for Billy's hat and Billy shook his hand with a "Pleased to meet you." When the Queen Mother appeared, Ruth didn't know which to do first, curtsy or bow. "Her indecision," Billy remarked afterward, "made it seem she had tripped over the rug."

Though the Grahams were quiet about these visits, the British press was not. Reporters usually found out about what had gone on and printed detailed, often fictitious reports in the newspapers. After the 1955 lunch in Windsor Castle, reporters demanded a statement from Billy. When he refused, they printed that as the Grahams left the castle, the evangelist patted Prince Charles on the head and remarked, "God bless you, sonny. I have a little boy just like you at home." Neither Billy nor Ruth had even seen Prince Charles.

Billy's associations with world leaders began generating criticism from other ministers and theologians, many of whom had never agreed with the evangelist or his message. One critic was theologian Karl Barth, whom the Grahams became acquainted with in the summer of 1960 while Billy was preaching in Switzerland and Germany and his family was staying near Montreux on Lake Geneva. One afternoon the Grahams met Barth and his son Markus for a chat at a provincial inn. On August 26, Ruth wrote her parents:

> Dr. Karl Barth came down from the little inn porch big, kindly, rumpled man. Like most great men, he doesn't look the part. . . . We had a very interesting two-hour visit. . . . Really, his graciousness, his geniality, his kindliness, make one feel he is a near and dear relative like

> an uncle or a grandfather. There is nothing of the austere or unapproachable scholar one might expect.
>
> They are all deeply disturbed by and concerned over Bill's giving an invitation. As far as I could see Dr. Karl Barth felt the "convert" would confuse the act of coming forward with conversion itself. Dr. Markus Barth felt it was "separating" the believer from the unbeliever and he feels there is a great danger in Christians "separating." I felt the language barrier accounted for some misunderstandings and the fact that none of them had ever attended a meeting.

They talked around the table, and Billy asked Karl Barth what he would say to a sinner if one came to him for help.

"I would say to him," Barth replied, raising his shoulders and upturned palms in an eloquent shrug, "friend, you are in great danger . . . but then, so am I."

Ruth observed, "One could not help but feel that was a rather dreary outlook with nothing of hope and certainty in it. I could hardly believe he meant it as he said it, and perhaps he didn't. His English is very broken. But none of the others offered to contradict or supplement what he said. Trying to follow their profound reasoning I felt myself getting thoroughly confused."

Toward the end of the conversation Karl Barth suggested to Billy, "You should come to Basel and teach theology for six months. And I will go out and hold your meetings for six months." A smile tugged at the corner of Barth's lips as he concluded, "And anyway, I should love to have lunch with the Queen and meet President Eisenhower and people like that."

Ruth was not awed by glamour and fame. In truth, she was most comfortable sitting before the fire in her rustic house, chatting with a friend from her past or, perhaps, a neighbor. To her, greatness was measured by service, not office.

Shortly after a tea with the royal family in 1961, she was in Belfast for a crusade at Saint Andrew's Hall. There, on June 27, she visited a former missionary to China whom she remembered from her childhood. The woman lived in a nearby rest home. Her small apartment was washed with sunlight, and warm with symbols from her past. The quilt covering her bed was made of Chinese silk scraps. Favorite books filled the bookshelves, and yellowed photographs of family were neatly pasted on the walls. The packing crates used to carry her belongings home from China had been turned into furniture, and her desk was a card table. She was packing boxes with empty plastic bottles, notepads made from greeting cards and paper, a crib sheet made from bits of damask, and cans and trinkets she would soon ship to missionaries in Africa to distribute to needy children.

"You certainly manage to keep busy and get a lot done!" Ruth marveled.

The missionary straightened proudly, meeting her eyes. "I don't belong to myself," she said.

"I couldn't help remembering another room just five days before," Ruth wrote in her diary that night, referring to her earlier visit to Buckingham Palace. "It also had family pictures all around the wall, books, and a desk. And boxes piled on boxes. Red dispatch boxes. They were a world apart. But for all the royal elegance of one and simple poverty of the other, there was a similarity. And I couldn't help but feel I had tea with royalty twice in one week."

By the late fifties Billy was receiving invitations to White House prayer breakfasts, beginning a tradition that would continue through the Clinton presidency. It was at such a breakfast that he and Ruth became acquainted with Senator Lyndon B. Johnson and his wife, Lady Bird. When John F. Kennedy was assassinated in 1963, Johnson became president, and soon Billy Graham became known as the White House chaplain and counselor to presidents.

Forthcoming were telephone calls from President Johnson and invitations to the White House and to the ranch on the north bank of the Pedernales River, fifty miles west of Austin. Ruth was adamantly opposed to her husband's becoming involved in politics. She reminded him of this whenever she could. In 1964, they dined with the Johnsons the weekend of the Democratic convention.

"Who should I take as my running mate?" Johnson asked Billy.

Before Billy could reply he got a swift kick under the table. "Why did you kick me?" he blurted to Ruth.

Johnson looked at her quizzically, his eyes amused as he waited for her response.

"Because," she said firmly to her husband, "you are supposed to limit your advice to moral and spiritual issues and stay out of politics."

"I agree with you," Johnson said to her.

As they left the dining room, preceded by the women, Johnson whispered to Billy, "Now, what do you really think?"

Johnson had no hesitation in letting the world know that he and Billy were friends. On May 20, 1965, the Associated Press reported that when the president was tired or worried he often called Billy to get a new injection. When he "was being called a crook and a thug and all," he said, he spent a weekend with Billy and "we bragged on each other. I told him he was the greatest religious leader in the world and he said I was the greatest political leader."

Ideally, it was not the Grahams' place to judge the president, they believed. Nor were they to endorse him. Of course, being frequently seen with a president might have been perceived by some as endorsement enough. But the friendships between Johnson and clergymen were more than political, claimed those who had reason to know. Calvin Thielman was of such an opinion. By a strange twist of fate, he had been Johnson's campaign manager in his race against Coke Stevenson for a seat in the Senate in 1948.

Calvin was seventeen, a respected orator in his high school, when the Lamar County attorney, Royce Whitten, summoned him to his spacious courthouse office and asked him to be Johnson's campaign manager. Calvin accepted and with this gangly, jug-eared Texan, forever known as LBJ, buzzed the Lone Star State in a newfangled contraption called a helicopter. It was just the two of them and a pilot, their bubble with flying blades agitating skies above rural towns, a Texas drawl booming such messages from the P.A. system: "THIS IS LYNDON JOHNSON, YOUR NEXT U.S. SENATOR. MEET ME AT THE MARKET SQUARE AT THREE O'CLOCK."

One afternoon they landed in Calvin's hometown of Paris. Knowing that Calvin dreamed of one day being a politician, Johnson, amid a square thick with people, wrapped an arm around him and announced, "If Wright Patman ever dies, this boy will be the next congressman from this district." Ironically, thirty-five years later, Calvin and Patman would stand side by side at Johnson's funeral. Johnson campaigned for five months in thirty-six precincts, and won the runoff by eighty-seven votes out of nine hundred thousand cast. "Landslide Lyndon" was accused of stuffing the ballot boxes.

Many years later, when Johnson was in the White House, he called upon Calvin as many as half a dozen times to sit by his bed and pray or read the Bible to him. The president had a vulnerability that caused him to crave approval and have "a soft spot for preachers," Calvin observed. Billy's affection seemed especially important to Johnson. In 1971, Johnson told Walter Cronkite, "Not many people in this country love me, but that preacher there loves me."

CBS anchorman Dan Rather, a native Texan who covered the Johnson presidency, believed that Johnson's interest in Billy was not entirely opportunistic. "Johnson had a strong strain of religion in him," he mused, staring over black reading glasses in his New York CBS studio. "I think Johnson, in a way, was a believer in what Graham was doing and what Graham was trying to do. . . . In street language, he put a move on Graham. But it would be a mistake to see it as entirely cynical."

To Lady Bird Johnson, it was all very simple. "I know, at least my feeling is, that Lyndon sought counsel of an awful lot of folks from our cook on up to Dean Rusk, and the wealthy or most academic to the lowest. Lyndon had a very strong sense of need, certainly he did in the presidency—a need for being sure he was on the right path, a need for comfort, a need for an anchor. Billy was a comfort. And Lyndon believed in him and respected him. . . . And if there ever is a position in the world where you feel you need all the help you can get it's the presidency."

It was during the Johnson friendship that Ruth became familiar with the White House. Of those who observed her, Lady Bird Johnson, the press, and later Barbara Bush commented that it was not her modus operandi to elbow her way to the forefront and introduce herself to the important people. Rather, she would drift to the edge of the crowd, blending into the background like one of the dark oil portraits, unobtrusive amid heavy draperies and chandeliers. The Ruth who lost herself in the masses at crusades, the Ruth who disliked sitting on the platform, remained in character in places of power. Indeed, she would remain an enigmatic paradox of withdrawn whimsy and fire that seemed the wrong combination for such an overwhelming role in life.

She was "quiet, gentle, observant," recalled Rather, who occasionally saw her at the White House and later at events involving Nixon. "As a professional observer myself, maybe I recognize that. She was watching people, watching events. Listening very carefully. She was not one of these people whose minds are elsewhere."

Ruth Bell Graham was not a politician and never would come close. Her discomfort in front of the camera, if one watched carefully, sometimes broached anger, which manifested itself as mischief, acceptably harmless, but with a steely edge. Why this might have been the case for one so physically lovely and charming can only be guessed, but Billy himself would say many years later that Ruth had always been uncomfortable with her beauty.

"She always has been as long as I've known her," he said on a Saturday in the spring of 1996, while browsing through old family photographs and holding up one of her that took him back to Wheaton.

It could simply be that, like other women who have so much more to offer than their looks, Ruth wanted to be taken seriously and demanded it in her own quirky way. For sure, she always dismissed compliments with a laugh and immediately changed the subject. She had a flair for style and could look stunning upon easy command. Or when it came time to cast her likeness on the Congressional Gold Medal, she might pin back her hair severely and look like the old maid missionary she never became. Newt Gingrich and Senator Strom Thurmond presented the medal, which truly did not bear a likeness to Billy either, and Ruth slipped to one side of her husband, where no one could see her. Then she sat down, slipping farther out of view as the accolades and honors went on.

What she did not do was slip out on individuals, and one might argue that this was what mattered, for Ruth believed that if she touched a single life, she had accomplished something too important to measure with a medal. She was most present when alone with another human being who needed her help or attention.

In the spring of 1994 when televangelist Jim Bakker was about to be released from prison, Ruth invited him to sit with her in church his first Sunday after he was freed. She called the Asheville paper and admonished the publisher about harassing Bakker any further and warned that she had better not see any reporters in church. She didn't. Two years later, a celebrity friend whose alleged sexual behavior was worldwide news hid out at Ruth's house one weekend and spent hours talking.

It really did not matter whether Ruth agreed with a person's behavior or convictions. What was vital was that she listened and offered kindness and understanding. Unlike many people brought up in strict environments, Ruth would spend her later years trying to be open-minded about matters that in earlier times may have been beyond her ken.

"If she's talking to you, she's talking to you, she's not looking past you," recalled Dan Rather. "You may only have her for a few seconds, but you've got her attention and she's listening to what you're saying."

In 1968 Johnson announced he would not run for reelection. He asked the Grahams to stay with him on his last night in the White House in January of 1969. The friendship did not end with his term of office. On Sunday, October 18, 1970, the Grahams flew to Austin, and Secret Service agents drove them within two miles of the LBJ ranch. Johnson escorted them the rest of the way. He was thinner since leaving the White House, his silver hair untrimmed and curling down the back of his neck.

Ruth found the former president more relaxed and playful. He yowled cheek to cheek singing duets with his white mongrel, Yuki, reducing guests to teary laughter. He told long stories, ambling through the colorful turns of his imagination, savoring every detail like the raconteur he was, and he read aloud long sections from his new book, *The Vantage Point*. When he tired of talking, he would ride around the ranch, checking on the guinea hens, hawks, deer, tractor blades, and his airport runway.

During the October 18 visit Ruth met Madame Shoumatoff, the Russian artist who was painting President Franklin D. Roosevelt's portrait when he died at Warm Springs on April 12, 1945. She was now in the midst of painting Mrs. Johnson's portrait, and on this Sunday she rode with the Secret Service man who picked up the Grahams in Austin. En route to the ranch, Ruth and Madame Shoumatoff discussed her leaving Russia just before the Bolshevik Revolution in 1917, and Grigori Efimovich Rasputin.

"It is quite an experience to find oneself in a new country with nothing," she told Ruth. "Suddenly one realizes one has absolutely nothing. It is a strange sensation, a sort of lightness. It's a great privilege to be deprived of all one's possessions when one is twenty and in good health."

Madame Shoumatoff's father, the artist went on, had once ridden a train with Rasputin and conversed with him for two hours. He was a compelling personality, repulsively dirty but with strange, piercing eyes. Very light with small, dark pupils, she said. During this train ride, Rasputin claimed that as a young man he had committed every sin and was consummately evil. One day in a field, he had seen the glory of God and he repented. When Madame Shoumatoff's father asked him bluntly about the stories of his immorality, his debauchery, Rasputin replied as the train lumbered on, "I repented once. I can sin and repent again."

As their car carried them farther away from Austin, Ruth wondered aloud if Rasputin could have been possessed by demons.

"But of course," Madame Shoumatoff replied. "One knows, but one cannot speak of certain things in polite society."

In contrast with some of the more prominent people Ruth had met, she found Madame Shoumatoff interested in others, and therefore interesting. Perhaps for this same reason Ruth held Mrs. Johnson in high esteem. In the former first lady, Ruth found a kindred spirit, and the two would remain close for the rest of their lives. Mrs. Johnson was a kind, gracious woman, lacking the veneer of self-importance one might expect of a president's wife. She was humble, almost self-effacing, aggressive in her interest in others and quick to steer the interest away from herself. Beneath a soft exterior was a fortitude and intelligence, a keen perception, that was all the more powerful because it usually went unnoticed.

"Sometimes beautiful women develop from adjusting to difficult men," Ruth noted in her journal.

The two women became friends. Both knew the pressure of having the world view them with expectation and curiosity. "I don't want to be anybody's role model, don't think I'm that good," explained Mrs. Johnson. "And Ruth wouldn't want to be a role model, but you are forced into it willy-nilly."

It was a winter morning in Richmond, Virginia, and the former first lady was seated on an indigo couch on the second floor of the governor's mansion, where she was visiting her son-in-law Governor Chuck Robb, her daughter Lynda, and the grandchildren. Mrs. Johnson's hair was a bit grayer; she was erect, yet unassuming, dressed in a navy skirt and creamy satin blouse, and weary from greeting various groups touring the mansion.

She was a troublesome interview, especially for someone twenty-four years old and writing a first book. More interested in asking questions about Ruth than in answering them, she was masterful at shifting the focus from herself to others, including this interviewer. Mrs. Johnson said she had unsuccessfully tried for years to learn more about her friend Ruth. The problem was that because of their husbands, the two women could rarely get a word in edgewise. It may also be that they were so much alike, neither would focus on herself.

"It's not easy to get [Ruth] to talk about herself," Mrs. Johnson observed. "The conversation around Billy is always very substantive and exciting. And I like to hear him talk too about the places he has been and all these crusades he has conducted and his feelings about a country, its culture, its economy, its stability. And pretty soon I've lost the thread about her childhood and I've found we're listening to these other things."

Ruth was accustomed to being her husband's second priority. His ministry came first and she wanted it that way, even if she didn't always like it. Sometimes she came in third, for if a world leader needed her husband, Billy felt it was his patriotic duty to be there. Johnson certainly saw the logic of this reasoning and demonstrated as much on August 13, 1972, the Grahams' twenty-ninth wedding anniversary, when Billy and Grady Wilson were on the ranch with him. That night Billy telephoned Ruth to wish her a happy anniversary and Johnson picked up another extension.

"I sure do want to thank you for letting us have Billy today," he told her. "But I needed him more than you did. We've been having a time riding around. Grady's here doing a good job keeping the dogs in the backseat, but he's a damn poor substitute for you."

On Monday, January 22, 1973, two days after Nixon's second inauguration and the day before a cease-fire was announced in Vietnam, Johnson, alone in his bedroom, suffered a fatal heart attack. For years he had expressed his wish that Billy would preach at the funeral. The last time the evangelist was with him on the Johnson ranch, the former president had taken him to the family cemetery, about a mile from the house. He showed Billy the spot where he wanted to be buried, and gave specific instructions about the service.

"Don't use any notes," Johnson told him. "The wind will blow them away. And I don't want a lot of fancy eulogizing, but be sure to mention my name."

On January 24, a raw, overcast Wednesday, Johnson's body was flown to Washington in *Air Force One*. The next day the flag-draped casket moved slowly up the steps of the Capitol, where Billy led the prayer. The Grahams flew to San Antonio and waited in a private lounge for the presidential jet to arrive with the body, and for a while Ruth talked with one of Johnson's sisters.

Air Force One arrived and the Grahams and others waiting moved from the lounge to take their positions outside. Anonymous onlookers lined the fence around the runway, hunched in the cold. The jet taxied into place near a waiting hearse. Friends, officials, military officers lined up behind Billy as he stood bareheaded in the icy rain, a black robe over his winter coat. An elevator platform was rolled into place at the plane's rear exit and the casket was lifted. Billy stepped forward to meet the Johnson family as they deplaned from the front and stood together, somberly facing the crowd while a band played hymns and white-gloved hands smoothly slid the casket inside the hearse.

People dispersed to private cars or limousines to make the hour's drive to the ranch. Protocol directed that Billy was to ride alone behind the hearse, but Mrs. Johnson requested that he stay with her family. Ruth rode with John Connally's family. People lined the road on both sides for miles, and traffic stopped, cars pulling off the road to let the procession pass. Each small town and farm along the way had its own cluster of spectators, some of them holding signs that read, "We love you, Mr. President" and "Forgive us, Mr. President."

The small cemetery was surrounded by a low stone wall and shaded by massive oaks, and it was filled this hour with generations of family, living and dead. Thousands had gathered outside it, standing in the rain and mud. Ruth was to follow the Connallys through a barrier of Secret Service agents and stand inside. Instead, she lingered just beyond the gate while her husband read John 14:1–3 and briefly eulogized Johnson. He pronounced the benediction and the honor guard folded the American flag, then presented it to Mrs. Johnson. She kissed it.

Hundreds of friends had been invited to the ranch afterward for coffee. Mrs. Johnson had asked the Grahams to spend the night, "but we felt the kindest thing we could do was to leave as quickly as possible," Ruth wrote at the time. Inside, the carpeting had been covered with heavy plastic and the furniture had been pushed back. Yuki was curled up on the couch.

"I wanted so much to say something to let Mrs. Johnson know how we loved and admired her, how our hearts went out to her," Ruth recorded. "Instead she hugged me and said something about reading everything I wrote or that had been written about me. And we hugged again and I slipped away. I, who had come to love, had been loved. I, who had come to give, had been given to. Such is the stuff of which she is made. Nor was I the exception. There was a word, a hug, a cordial greeting, or a warm smile for each." Ruth wrote of the occasion:

Of this historic moment
two things I kept:
that earth was gray
and cold,
and heaven wept.[1]

The Grahams, T. W. Wilson, Grady Wilson, and Calvin Thielman left the ranch late that afternoon by car, heading for San Antonio as the setting sun broke through the black clouds, splashing red and gold over wet pavement. The next morning, when no cameras or microphones were there to record events, the small group sat in the San Antonio airport eating breakfast. A woman across the room eyed Billy for several minutes, her face bleak as though the wretchedness of all the world were held in her heart. Finally, she mustered enough courage to approach him.

"May I talk to you for just a minute?" she asked shakily.

Billy nodded for Calvin to move aside. Billy listened to her, then prayed with her. When she left, tears in her eyes, Calvin apologized to Billy for not shielding him so he could finish his breakfast before his eggs got cold.

"No," Billy said. "You did the right thing. Her mother is dying from cancer and her heart is very heavy. She wanted me to pray for her."

President Richard Nixon moved into the White House in January of 1969, and right away established church services in the East Room.

"In those years President Nixon, whether rightly or wrongly, thought that church was so important that you should emphasize it by having it in the White House," recalled Barbara Bush as she sipped coffee in a sitting room of the vice-presidential mansion on a raw morning in February of 1982. "And of course it also, in all honesty, kept an awful lot of people from going to an awful lot of trouble. If you had church at the White House you didn't have to have the church sniffed and security all checked, and eighty people have to do all of that when the president moves. So he had church at the White House for security reasons. And then he asked leaders in the church to come and preach Jewish, Catholic, whatever."

Billy Graham was one of the leaders Nixon occasionally invited to preach, and Ruth often went along. The couple had a deep affection and admiration for Nixon. In the same way that Nixon admired Billy's Christian integrity and fortitude, Billy, who had always been interested in world affairs, admired Nixon's genius. Though Ruth never became close to Nixon, she was later grateful for his breakthrough in China, believing his skill at foreign policy to be unmatched.

She did strike up a warm friendship with Julie Nixon and, in fact, had a significant influence on her. One early Sunday morning before Billy was to speak at the White House, Julie asked Ruth about her faith, about prayer, and if God really listened. Together they talked until church time, with Julie asking questions in her high-strung, perceptive manner and Ruth calmly replying, her leather-bound King James Bible open in her lap.

"She's been an inspiration to me," Julie said later. "She's so real. She's one of the few persons I've known who really live their faith."

Ruth inspired Julie enough to become the subject of a chapter in Julie's book *Special People*.[2] She shares page space with Prince Charles, Golda Meir, and Anne Morrow Lindbergh, among other notables.

Nixon had first heard about Billy in the forties when his mother, Hannah Nixon, had attended a Billy Graham crusade in Southern California and had written her son about how impressed she was. Senator Clyde Hoey introduced the two men in 1950 and, through Billy's friendship with President Eisenhower, they became well acquainted.

By the late sixties, the days of Ruth's kicking her husband under the table for discussing politics were long gone. "Bill was supposed to limit his advice to spiritual and moral matters," she said.

> Knowing Bill, knowing myself and how prone we are to give free advice even when unasked for, I wouldn't be at all surprised if when he was with the president, if the president asked his opinions, he would tell him what he thought, and give him advice that wasn't limited to spiritual, moral things.
>
> He wouldn't say, "I'm sorry, Mr. President, that's out of my field." And frankly, I don't see what's wrong in asking the advice of a clergyman if he's got a good clear head on him. The media's taking exception to what they are afraid Bill might be saying doesn't make sense to me. I would think they would be happy to have as many good, decent men as Bill as possible at the White House. . . . Christianity is above ideology. It's for Democrats and Republicans alike. It's for sinners and I think the press would be the first to admit there are sinners in politics.

William F. Buckley Jr. summarized it rather well: "It seems to me plain that presidents should have access to religious figures. Plain also that there will be attempted abuses, in both directions, in many cases."

"Whatever Nixon's intentions towards Billy Graham," Ruth said in retrospect, "the president impressed the Grahams as being a religious man who did not wear his religion on his sleeve."

"Nixon," said Billy during an interview in Montreat on a raw, blustery November afternoon in 1982, "is a very serious person and a very deep person and a very intellectual person." He added that Nixon was surprisingly sensitive and thoughtful. For example, he would never forget a birthday.

"I was playing golf in France," Billy recalled, "and I had an old set of clubs that I had rented. And I played one of the best games I've ever played and I wanted to buy those clubs. The golf pro would not sell them to me. So when I got home and was playing golf with Mr. Nixon in California one day, I told him about this and I didn't think anything more of it. And did you know I got those golf clubs for Christmas? He had sent over there and gotten them. He was just always kind, courteous, and thoughtful. I never felt he was using me—*ever*."

It is hard to imagine Billy ever feeling used, really. For those who knew him well, he was not as naive as innocent, and, remarkably, his willingness to assign decent motives to all never really changed. Even when he was in his late seventies and halting with Parkinson's, he did not turn away strangers who approached him in hotel lobbies or during his dinner. Were Ruth not present and in a position to shield him, he would give his time to anyone, often kissing and patting hands, while his own trembled with exhaustion or, later, from disease.

He would never seem to know the meaning of suspicion or guardedness or his right to privacy, any more than his wife knew fear. She did not share his distilled view of motivation or the entitlement of another when it came to his availability. Ruth knew exploitation, agendas, and wickedness when she saw it, and she knew when her husband was dangerously wearing himself thin. But she could not always shield him, and neither Billy nor those around him always listened.

In May of 1970, Nixon appeared on the platform at Neyland Stadium at the University of Tennessee during the Knoxville crusade. It was the first time in history that a president had spoken on an evangelist's platform, and the first time Nixon had appeared on a university campus since he'd ordered troops into Cambodia the month before.[3]

Seventy-five thousand people crowded the stadium and another twenty-five thousand spilled into the parking lot and the grassy area around it. Three hundred antiwar demonstrators pooled toward the rear, unfurling banners and flags. Members of the University of Tennessee football team wanted to force the protesters back outside, but Secret Service agents shook their heads. It was wise, they said in agreement with Billy, "to avoid a confrontation."

The president and his wife, Pat, waited with the Grahams until all the platform guests had been seated. Then Nixon and Billy, followed by Mrs. Nixon and Ruth, filed up the platform steps to deafening applause and a standing ovation. The obscenities and boos of the dissenters, for a moment, were barely discernible.

"The rudeness, immaturity, and stupidity of the demonstrators was unbelievable," Ruth wrote at the time. "Whatever they think of Mr. Nixon they should respect the office of the presidency. During Nixon's speech the protesters stood time and time again, shouting and waving their banners. It was a strange mixture of feelings I had, mounting anger that the President of the United States cannot speak at a religious rally without being shouted down, pride in Mr. Nixon's dignity and graciousness . . . and profound gratification that the vast majority were solidly behind him and let him know it."

After Nixon's brief speech, Ethel Waters, the black singer and former actress who had been a frequent guest at Billy Graham crusades, was helped to the pulpit to sing.

"I've known my precious boy Dickie President Nixon and his precious Pat for many years," she said. "I expect the next time we meet, Mr. President," she added, turning toward him, "will be in heaven."

She turned her attention to the protesters and said, "If you knew them you'd really like them. They're just nice, fine people. And now, you precious children, I love you but if I could get close enough, I'd smack you!"

After the service Nixon asked the Grahams to ride out to *Air Force One* with him and Pat in the long, black, bulletproof limousine. For miles the road was lined with people. Dozens of reporters waited near the presidential jet, and Nixon, obviously in a good mood, quipped that he'd had to borrow money from Billy for the offering and that he would repay him later with golf balls. The reporters attempted to interview the evangelist, but their questions were swallowed up in the roar of the jet's engines as a silver door shut behind the president.

The Grahams discovered that Nixon had left orders for the limousine to drive them back through Knoxville to their hotel. Flanked by motorcycles with flashing blue lights, they cruised slowly through town, "feeling ridiculous," as Ruth remembered it.

The event was disturbing to Dan Rather, who was there with a press pool. Rather, an admirer of Billy's, could understand an evangelist's desire "for the opportunity to talk to and perhaps influence the country's leadership and world leadership." But, he recalled, "the Knoxville scene was personally troubling to me. I remember walking into the stadium and saying to myself, 'You know, this is just really not right. I mean, Billy Graham shouldn't be doing this,' or someone in Reverend Graham's position shouldn't be doing this, President Nixon shouldn't be doing this. I would think both of them would have a little embarrassment about that scene today. It had the appearance at least of being a little too calculated on both sides and a little too blatant on both sides using one another to each's advantage.

"There was a tremendous crowd and it was a little piece of Americana, great football crowd, all that big U.T. stuff hanging around the stadium and Reverend Graham running a crusade and Richard Nixon running his own crusade. Two crusaders meet—it was a bit much."

Ruth had her own private ambivalence about Nixon's appearance on her husband's platform. She was disappointed that Nixon had not given a spiritual message to the people. "I think to have [presidents] come and sit in the audience is one thing," she remarked in later years. "To have them speak from the platform is another."

In the spring of 1971 Nixon, with the argument of "national security," demanded that his campaign aides step up their political intelligence. In June a year later, five men were arrested in the Democratic National Committee headquarters at the Watergate complex. Three days later Nixon and his top aide, H. R. Haldeman, met to discuss the arrests. The scandals collectively known as Watergate were beginning to escalate, but in the public eye Nixon was untainted.

On October 15, a year before the presidential election, Nixon paid Billy an unusual tribute by appearing on the platform with him for Billy Graham Day in Charlotte. The prominent media executive and president of the Charlotte Chamber of Commerce Charles Crutchfield conceived the idea of having the city publicly honor its most celebrated son. When Crutchfield telephoned Billy about it, Billy refused, saying he'd been honored enough by the people of his birthplace.[4]

Crutchfield wouldn't take no for an answer. After Nixon had appeared with Billy in Knoxville, Crutchfield decided both that Billy Graham Day was a grand idea and that what would really make it spectacular, indeed historic, would be the appearance of Richard Nixon in Charlotte to honor his evangelist friend. Crutchfield contacted the White House. Next, Nixon telephoned Billy. He wanted Billy to accept the honor, he said, and Nixon wanted to be there with him to honor their years of friendship.

"If that is your wish, Mr. President," Billy replied, "then of course I'll accept."[5]

October 15 was designated a holiday in Charlotte. The children had a holiday from school. Tremendous crowds of cheering citizens lined East Independence Boulevard as such dignitaries as North Carolina Senators Sam Ervin[6] and B. Everett Jordan, South Carolina Senator Strom Thurmond and John Connally and his wife rumbled past in a motorcade. There was a public rally at the Coliseum, during which Billy spoke, followed by Nixon, who used no notes. He made comments such as "What I know about the law I owe to this state; and Greece, Rome, Ancient Persia, their civilizations died . . . because as they became wealthy, they became soft, as they became educated without principle they became weak. . . . It is the character of a nation that determines whether it survives.

"Let me just say this," he continued, "we all think of Billy Graham as a strong man. But as I look at the Graham family, if I am asked, who are the stronger, Billy Graham or the women in his family, I'll say the women every time. . . . God made man out of the soft earth but he made woman out of a hard rib—the woman is the stronger of the two.

"I think of his wife, Ruth, who has been by his side, born in China of missionary parents, lived there three hundred miles from Shanghai for seventeen years and now giving him the support, the strength, that any man who is in the arena needs, needs when he goes home."[7]

Ruth listened from her honored spot and silently worried more, as the political encroachment upon her husband's ministry continued.

On Monday, January 22, 1973, Nixon began his second term by having Billy speak at the White House church service. That morning people convened in the spacious East Room with its parquet floors, gold draperies, mirrors, and crystal chandeliers. Nixon stood at the podium, flanked by portraits of George and Martha Washington. He talked of his mother, her deep Christian faith, and how she loved to hear any new preacher in her area. When Nixon was a student at Duke Law School, he went on to say, he received a letter from his mother saying she'd heard a young preacher by the name of Billy Graham.

"'I think he is going to go places,'" Nixon quoted his mother. "I still have this letter."

A short time later, when Israeli Prime Minister Golda Meir was to appear at the White House for a dinner in her honor, she requested that Billy Graham be included on the guest list. On March 1, just before the 8:00 P.M. dinner, the Grahams mingled with the other guests in the East Room. When Billy greeted the prime minister in the receiving line, she reached up and kissed him. At dinner, Meir sat between Nixon and Billy at table 12. Ruth sat at table 9 next to Speaker of the House Carl Albert, where she watched the proceedings with a bit of bemusement. A Jewish woman sitting at Ruth's table stared suspiciously at Billy and Golda Meir, not realizing that the evangelist's wife was sitting inches away from her.

"What is Billy Graham doing sitting next to Madame Golda?" the woman asked of no one in particular as she picked at poached red snapper and wild rice. "Do you suppose he is proselytizing her?"

"I would put my money on Madame Golda Meir," Ruth replied dryly. "But never fear, when we get home tonight, I'll straighten him out."

On August 9, Nixon resigned the presidency. The man revealed on the Watergate tapes was a man the Grahams felt they had never met. They felt sick with disappointment and disbelief. The only Graham friend who seemed undaunted was Ethel Waters, who one day remarked to Grady Wilson, "If my baby Dick said damn, he damn well needed to say damn!"

The scandal, however, did not change the Grahams' affection for Nixon. After listening to his resignation speech Ruth wrote, "He spoke from his heart, quietly, movingly, eloquently. This was the man we [saw] on other private occasions. Warm, human. . . . I still wonder, what did he do to warrant this?"

Billy attempted repeatedly to reach Nixon but his telephone calls were never returned. It was as though an iron curtain had dropped between the Grahams and the Nixons. "I tried many times to get through to him, to just have prayer with him, to encourage him," Billy recalled. "He wouldn't have anything to do with me." Later, he learned that Nixon had told his aides, "Don't let Billy Graham near me. I don't want him tarred with Watergate."

That fall, while Nixon was hospitalized with thrombophlebitis, a rather bold idea occurred to Ruth one night. Why not fly an airplane carrying a message up and down the beach in front of Nixon's hospital? At her request, a friend arranged for an airplane to be rented in California. It pulled a banner that read: "NIXON, WE LOVE YOU—SO DOES GOD." Photographs of this spectacle appeared in newspapers and magazines throughout the country, but its perpetrator remained a mystery.

The Grahams' reaction to Watergate demonstrated a number of traits important to both of them. First, they were not likely to voice criticisms publicly, especially if their opinions risked breaking the pastoral promise of confidentiality.

Both seemed to have an inexhaustible supply of forgiveness, and neither turned a back on a friend.

As Barbara Bush observed, "They're close friends to the Nixons. I mean they really are, still. They're that kind of friend. They don't think we're perfect. And they don't think the Nixons are perfect. But that doesn't mean you drop a friend."

1. Ruth Bell Graham, *Sitting by My Laughing Fire* (Waco, Tex.: Word Books, 1977), 175.
2. Julie Nixon Eisenhower, *Special People* (New York: Simon and Schuster, 1977).
3. John Pollock, *Billy Graham: Evangelist to the World* (San Francisco: Harper and Row, 1979), 106.
4. Ibid., 174–75.
5. Ibid.
6. Ironically, Senator Sam Ervin would later head the Watergate investigation on Capitol Hill.
7. Records of the Blue Ridge Broadcasting Corp. (October 15, 1971), Tape 35, Collection 45, Archives of the Billy Graham Center, Wheaton, Illinois.

18

CHAPTER

A New Season

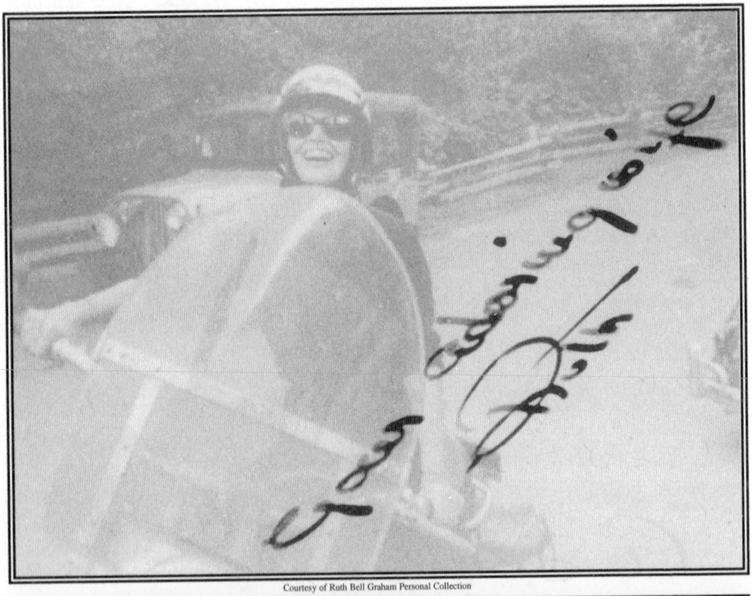

Courtesy of Ruth Bell Graham Personal Collection

Russ Busby, BGEA

Top: Ruth on Motorcycle

Bottom: Mother and Oldest Daughter

Oh, time! be slow!
it was a dawn ago
I was a child
dreaming of being grown;
a noon ago
I was
with children of my own;
and now
it's afternoon
and late,
and they are grown
and gone.
Time, wait!

—Ruth Bell Graham, 1974[1]

For her, it was autumn. It was the season when beauty rises with the sinking of the sap, igniting the hills in death. The moon, heavy and yellow, floats to the surface of night and sifts light over the cool features of the earth, illuminating what has been dark. It was the phase in a woman's life when she begins to look like herself, in the end transfigured by the life she has lived.

Ruth had become more lovely. Her face was older, and all she had ever been or done was etched there. It was the face of one who often smiles, her brow smooth with lines radiating from her eyes and fine creases lifting her cheeks in tucks. Her eyes were wide and expressive, flashing when she laughed and teased or felt fury she would not show. At pensive moments, when she was alone, weariness and wisdom wavered, a shadow. Her bones were more sharply defined and exquisite, her skin taut, and veins as prominent as a leaf's.

She was trim, if not a bit too thin, as she advanced into her seventies. More dapper and conservative in dress, she preferred tweedy suits with pocketed long skirts or trousers. She enjoyed simple leather boots and slippers, turtleneck sweaters, and long-sleeved blouses. Frequently, she wore a strand of pearls. The only jewelry she wore on her fingers was a wide gold band Ned had given to her, her wedding band and a guard ring. She wore simple pearl or gold earrings, and after her fiftieth wedding anniversary, a gold bracelet from Billy that was engraved with the names of their children and grandchildren. She disliked wristwatches, and few who had ever known her remembered seeing one. She pinned her silver-streaked hair in a French twist when her husband was away, occasionally tucking a fresh rose in the back. She wore it down, flipped up and brushing her shoulders, when he was home.

Her children were almost grown. Her parents and the missionaries from her childhood were dying or already dead. By 1970 her father had suffered four heart attacks. Her mother was losing her eyesight, her body wracked with pain. In 1963 GiGi married Stephan Tchividjian, a Swiss psychologist. In 1966 Anne married Danny Lotz, a dentist and former University of North Carolina basketball star. Three years later Bunny married Ted Dienert, an advertising executive, and later would marry again.

By 1983 Bunny and Anne would have three children each, and GiGi would have seven. The daughters implemented many of the childrearing techniques that had once been used with them. GiGi and Bunny had inherited a love of writing, publishing several books between them. Anne had inherited a zeal for teaching and would start a Bible class in Raleigh, North Carolina, with a weekly attendance of five hundred women. Later the numbers would grow, the outreach becoming international.

Franklin and Ned were growing up, too, and their friends became Ruth's friends, several of them visiting her when the boys weren't around. Ruth took an active interest in her sons' hobbies of rock climbing and automobiles, and attempted a few new ones of her own, such as motorcycles, hang gliding, and parasailing behind motorboats. This was not a great surprise to those around her. Family and friends had always known she was fearless, sometimes to the point of recklessness.

In the early seventies, Franklin enjoyed waking up the college students on early weekend mornings by roaring his motorcycle beneath dormitory windows until rounds of soda pop bottles sent him on his way. It was easy to figure where Franklin got his temerity. Three times his mother swung into the black leather seat, determined to master the sport. The first try she zoomed along Old U.S. 70 in Black Mountain, knowing how to do just about everything except brake. She plunged over a steep embankment. A big tattooed truck driver stopped and peered down at her from the road, more than a little surprised to discover that this trim woman dressed in black and riding a Harley-Davidson wasn't exactly a teenager.

"Lady," he asked, "can I help you?"

"Thanks," Ruth replied. "If you could just get it on the pavement headed in the other direction, I've a friend at the end of the road who'll help me stop."

The second try landed her in a lake. On her third attempt, she accelerated instead of braking and crashed through her split-rail fence, severing a vein in her leg. She wasn't exactly a benign influence in an automobile either. As coolies had scattered when Dr. Bell sped into sight in his Austin Healey, so Montreaters hugged the edge of the mountain roads for fear of meeting Ruth head-on around a curve. New drivers were warned to watch out for Mrs. Graham.

While her husband served on the National Safety Council, preaching on film, "Drive unto others as you would have them drive unto you," his wife was behind the wheel practicing situational ethics. She was known to careen around narrow, winding roads or fly along the highway, a shameless lawbreaker who got away with it, in her mind, by praying, "I'm sorry, but You understand." She was cited only twice for speeding. In her first brush with the law, the patrolman realized who she was and suggested she pay the ticket when the station opened early the next morning. So no one will see you, he hinted.

The second citation came after Ruth had driven fifty miles from Montreat to Waynesville to visit friends. At three o'clock that afternoon Billy telephoned her and said he was with a German businessman and wondered if she could serve them tea at four.

"Sure," she said.

She sped along Old U.S. 70, the red needle creeping past eighty, when suddenly the ominous blue light flashed in her rearview mirror.

"Could you please hurry with that?" she asked the trooper as he filled out the ticket. "And when you finish, please don't follow me, because I'm going to do it again."

When Franklin bought a used early-model green Triumph Spitfire, it was clear he had inherited his mother's race car talents and would outperform her. Not only did he drive fast, but he had a dangerous habit of zipping through the Montreat gate, entering through the exit arch, or exiting through the entrance. This seemed a good idea in the summer when he'd find himself locked into a long traffic jam of tourists who did not seem inclined to move along fast enough to suit him.

Police Chief Pete Post finally caught Franklin in the act one afternoon. With blue light flashing, he chased him up the road toward the Graham mountain.

At the lower remote-controlled gate, Franklin touched a button, accelerated through, and shut the gate in the policeman's face.

By virtue of his late arrival, Ned was more a second family than a fifth sibling. He was a sensitive, affectionate child with more than his share of charm and wild blood. A carbon copy of the young Billy Graham, he abounded in nervous energy and was as tall and thin as bamboo. He was persuasive and articulate, capable of talking his way in and out of anything. Perhaps the brightest child, he had a keenly analytical, inventive mind and was handsome, with sharp, refined features. His eyes were deep-set like his father's but mercurial like his mother's.

By age ten he was teasing the little girls in school. At twelve he was a dandy, admiring Italian boots, leather jackets, and designer-label clothes. Like his father during his formative years, Ned was known around town for his girlfriends, none of whom enjoyed much in the way of longevity, until he would later meet and marry Mayo Clinic nurse Carol.

Despite Ned's talents, he did poorly in school. His mind froze when he took examinations, a symptom that had begun in the primary grades when a teacher repeatedly punished him harshly for minor infractions. In the spring of 1972, when he was fourteen, his parents decided to send him to Felsted School in Essex, England, a stately but stern public school located on acres of playing fields not far from the North Sea.

That September, mother and son flew to London. Ruth checked into a dreary hotel near Hyde Park, where Donald Soper was again haranguing and a group of doomsayers were proclaiming that the end of the world was at hand. In some measure, it felt like the end of the world to Ruth, who did not want to leave her son and youngest child. On September 11, their last night together, they watched television in her hotel room and he briefly laid his hand over hers.

"And it came as a shock to feel the weight of it," she wrote in her journal that night, "and realize it was larger than mine. It was thirty-nine years ago this fall in Shanghai, China when a thirteen-year-old girl cried herself to sleep and prayed to die before morning. But morning came and she sailed for Japan and Korea. Today I'm glad. Only now it's tonight. And boys don't cry."

The next day they unpacked his belongings in the dormitory. It was a tiny room, scrubbed and Spartan with study desks, chairs, and space for little else. Honeysuckle grew on the wall outside his window, its sweet fragrance permeating the air. Nearby was a large room with rows of gray-blanketed iron cots where he would sleep with some twenty other boys. Later, Ruth stared through the taxicab window, watching him wave to her from the drive, clad in his navy blazer and gray slacks, lank and smiling. The ache in her heart was overwhelming, and as she flew home alone she could not really recognize that her life, her role, had forever changed.

Felsted was to be a rather cruel experience for Ned, more wretched than his mother had imagined. He soon discovered that academically he was three years behind the other boys his age, deepening the very discouragement his family had sent him there to overcome, and he was unaccustomed to the hazing traditional in English preparatory schools. Older classmates were tyrannical, prone to mete out harsh punishments for obscure infractions. Ruth was horrified when she later learned that more than a dozen times during the bitter winter months, Ned was forced to sit in a bathtub while it was slowly filled with icy water until it reached his chin and one of the upperclassmen would dunk his head.

More than ever before, Ruth was alone on the mountaintop. Even when her children were home for brief spells, she knew they were already gone. The world she had known was changing. Sometimes she wasn't sure if it was for the better. By now the BGEA had grown into a worldwide organization with more than five hundred full-time employees. It included a movie studio called World Wide Pictures and the weekly radio program "Hour of Decision."

The vastness of Billy's ministry made his family life more pressured and began taking him to remote, troubled areas of the world. In the fall of 1972 he ventured to Nagaland, the sparsely populated state between Assam and Burma, where headhunters and cannibals had once roamed the densely forested hills. Two nights before he was to leave, on October 29, he commented to Ruth as they were drifting off to sleep, "Well, a month from now you may be a widow."

"Life being what it is," she replied, "I might beat you to it."

His increased travels to totalitarian countries kept her alert and uneasy. Accompanying him on one trip, for example, she decided she would locate the bugs in their hotel room. She had read enough spy novels to conclude that there must be surveillance devices in everything from the ice cubes to the telephone. The latter, of course, was where she looked first. Unscrewing the mouthpiece, she held it up to the light, then close to one eye. She shook it a bit. No bug. Then the earpiece. Same procedure, no bug there either. Her husband, lounging on the bed with his hands behind his head, watched her with a somewhat dubious expression.

"They know exactly what you're doing," he said.

"There's no way they can tell," she retorted, holding up the telephone to show she had cleverly taped down the cradle so they couldn't detect that it was off the hook.

Satisfied that the telephone was bug-free, she peeled off the tape, pressed the receiver to her ear. To her dismay, there was no dial tone.

"I think it's dead," she let Billy know.

He sat up in a panic. Ordinarily he hated the telephone, but now that he was without one, he became obsessed with the thought of it. There were calls coming in, those to make, and itineraries to discuss. What if there was an emergency? He paced the length of the floor while she unscrewed, shook, banged, and rescrewed the mouth- and earpieces, unable to figure out what she had done wrong.

She would have to be his messenger, he announced. Ruth slung her black raincoat over her nightgown and dashed out the door to begin contacting people he had suddenly decided must be reached right this minute. After running around the large hotel for a considerable time, she returned to the room, where she found him attempting to fix the telephone. He was having no better luck, and if there were any spies listening to the dialogue and disgust generated, they were generously entertained, although certainly no national secrets were learned. At last, in the flash of brilliance, Ruth followed the cord behind a couch to the wall socket. It was unplugged.

It was unfortunate that as Billy's demands took him farther away, Ruth's private world continued to empty, threatening to leave her alone in a tiny mountain town that originally had drawn her to prevent just that. Her mountaintop house seemed to echo with voices gone and rooms no longer lived in. Her parents were also failing rapidly.

In 1972, Mrs. Bell was eighty and almost blind with inoperable cataracts. An unsuccessful hip replacement had virtually crippled her. A stroke had left her speech tortured, her mind substituting letters and words for ones she wished to use. It became almost impossible to understand what she said, and she measured her days by the pain and frustration she suffered. Though she rarely complained to others, the truth showed when she would scrawl comments in her diaries, such as "Oh woe. . . . It took me more than ten minutes to spell Ruth. Or I can't read, and I can't talk."[2]

Dr. Bell was seventy-nine and wracked with pain from an ulcer that had developed between two toes after he bought a three-dollar pair of imitation leather shoes. He was diabetic, and the ulcer would not heal, the pain so acute he could not sleep. In the summer of 1973, he visited the Mayo Clinic and begged the doctors to amputate the infected toe. They advised that his circulation was so poor that they would have to amputate his leg at the hip. He refused. Despite his suffering, he treated his wife like a queen, as she confided in a diary, and led an unusually active life. He never lacked in humor or smiles or tall tales when guests dropped by the shaded old house at the foot of the mountain where the Bells' famous daughter and son-in-law lived. Dr. Bell took neighborhood kids to baseball games in Asheville and to Sunday dinner at the Battery Park Hotel.

In 1972, Ruth's father was elected moderator of the Presbyterian Church in the United States, the highest office that could be held in the denomination and one that had eluded him twice since he had left the mission field.

"I don't know if your moderatorship will be able to stem the tide in our church today," Ruth told him at the time. "But at least for one year our church will get a glimpse of godliness."

After serving his one-year term he continued traveling throughout the South to address what he considered to be the growing ills of the Southern Presbyterian Church. A formidable proponent of the Presbyterian tradition of his youth, he was grieved by what he deemed the modern church's leaning toward humanism. He taught the adult Sunday school class in Montreat, which was broadcast over seven states, and several times each month he flew to Washington, D.C., for *Christianity Today* board meetings.

On Sunday, July 8, 1973, he preached at the Swannanoa Presbyterian Church, where he and his wife had first attended when they had moved to Montreat thirty years earlier. Ruth sat beside a window that stretched from eaves to floor. Beyond was the cemetery, lined with the granite markers and monuments of generations. Montreat had no place to bury its dead. Some residents, especially many of the retired missionaries, like her parents, had purchased plots here.

"I knew as I sat there listening," Ruth wrote at the time, "watching his loved figure, his white hair, his kindly face, that the next time he came to this church would be in his coffin."

Her prediction would soon come to pass. On Wednesday, August 1, she telephoned her parents, offering to bring them supper. They weren't hungry, they said. She did not see them that day.

The next morning Mrs. Bell awoke at 7:30. She lay very still, listening for the familiar murmur of the television playing in the living room, for Dr. Bell always got up before she did and turned on the news. The house was silent. She called out to him, lowering herself from her bed to her aluminum walker. Stumbling, almost falling, she made her way across the carpet to his bed. He lay motionless, resting on his left side, his face cradled in his bowed left arm, his right arm comfortably tucked beside his neck. His face was smooth, devoid of the tension of life. She groped for the telephone, stabbing at numbers she was too blind to see, dialing randomly. By chance she reached a neighbor and stammered the frantic words, "Nelson, dead."

Mrs. Bell somehow managed to lower herself into her wheelchair and roll into the kitchen. T. W. Wilson was the first to arrive. To his amazement, Mrs. Bell, who had not stood unassisted in three years, was standing beside her wheelchair. She unlocked the kitchen door for him.

"Nelson . . . dead," she whispered.

Wilson gently helped her back into her bed. Ruth arrived, still in her bathrobe. She kissed her mother and went to her father, gently kissing him, too.

She sat beside her mother, held her hands and said, "He's in Heaven now with Nelson Jr."

The family doctor arrived, and Calvin Thielman, and Billy. It appeared, the doctor told Billy, that Dr. Bell had died at dawn.

"That was when he usually got up," Billy said.

"And he did," Ruth added.

Throughout the day, members of the family flew in from all over the country and gathered at the Bell home to reminisce. Mrs. Bell sat regally in her wheelchair, listening, a solitary tear sliding down her cheek when she thought no one was looking. "Late that night when all was still," Ruth wrote. "There's been a lot of laughter. . . . How can one remember Daddy and not laugh? Humor was as much a part of him as his walk and the tone of his voice. And tears spring unbidden too. I sat briefly on the porch, remembering: his hard work, never complaining, enjoying life, his faithfulness . . . , his wonderful sense of fun."

His children dressed him in the navy blazer and gray slacks they had bought for him when he had been elected moderator, his wire-framed glasses tucked in a pocket. He was buried the next day at 3:00 P.M. on a gentle slope facing east, as thunder rumbled behind the mountains and rain began to fall. "Sitting on the porch tonight listening to the katydids, watching the almost full moon emerge thru the clouds above Rainbow," Ruth wrote a week later, "it is hard to realize he is gone."

Billy and Ruth asked Mrs. Bell to move in with them. At first she refused. Her house held memories. It held objects he had touched. She would not let go. For a while friends spent the night there with her. Sometimes Ruth did, sleeping on her father's old bed, listening to the various clocks striking out of sync on the half hour throughout the house. She waited for the sounds he had heard, and thought of her mother's pain.

"I think losing a loved one," she wrote in late August, "must be a little like losing a leg. First there is the shock, then the anesthetic, and the pain killers; the attention of doctors and nurses, flowers and cards and visits from friends. But sooner or later you have to learn to walk without it."

One day, while she was sorting books and papers in her father's study, she stumbled across a leather-bound Concordance she had given him years before. Tenderly, she thumbed through it and found jotted inside, in his unmistakable and unreadable scrawl, a prayer list. "Franklin school," the last item read.

Had Dr. Bell lived a little longer he would have begun to see his prayers answered, not only about Franklin but also about Ned. Rather than returning to Felsted, Ned was attending a private school in New York, where he excelled in martial arts and made a name for himself as a swimmer. His curiosity was voracious, vacillating from literature to philosophy to science. The turning point for his older brother came in the summer of 1974, when Franklin was twenty-two and was asked to help with the preliminary setup for the International Congress on World Evangelization in Lausanne, Switzerland.

It had been planned by various international committees, his father the driving force. Every nation had been invited to send its Christian leaders as delegates. Franklin flew to Switzerland and soon found, for the first time, that he was on his own, with no television in his small apartment, no nightlife nearby, no automobile or motorcycle. He began picking up the Bible and reading in the Psalms, Galatians, Ephesians, and Proverbs, developing an unexplainable interest in the words.

The congress began July 16 with more than four thousand people from more than one hundred fifty nations gathering in the Palais de Beaulieu. Billy arrived, and one night he sat down with Franklin for a father-to-son talk.

"Franklin," he said, "I don't know when it will be but I know that at some point the Lord is going to get hold of you. I love you very much, but you are going to have to make a decision. I believe the Lord has something for you to do, but you are going to have to choose Him, and you are going to have to go all the way out for Him. You won't be able to ride the fence or rock back and forth."

Franklin listened to him, really hearing for once, and perhaps just a little fed up with the way he had been living. Several weeks after the conference ended, Franklin traveled to the Middle East with BGEA team member Roy Gustafson, a kindly man with a rapier wit who had known Billy for many years. Since his late teens, Franklin had assisted Gustafson in guiding tour groups through the Holy Land.

Gustafson treated him as though he were a son, sure of his talents, even more certain that the young man was destined to contribute something of significance to the world if he would stop running. Gustafson's friendship and example left their mark. One day, in his hotel room in Jerusalem, Franklin felt the urge to throw away his cigarettes. Wadding up the package, he tossed it into the trash and knelt beside the bed.

"I want You to be Lord of my life," he prayed. "I am willing to give up any area that is not pleasing to You. And I'm sick and tired of being sick and tired."

That August, he married Jane Austin Cunningham, who had been his friend and confidante for years. In 1977, almost four years to the day after his grandfather's death, Franklin would graduate from Appalachian State University in Boone, North Carolina, with a degree in business administration. By 1979 he was president of the Boone-based World Medical Missions Inc. and Samaritan's Purse, which recruited Christian doctors for short-term service in Third World countries and sent aid to devastated peoples throughout the world. In 1981 he was ordained as a minister, and in 1996, he would take over his father's ministry.

Eventually, Ruth would have nineteen grandchildren. To them, she was Tai Tai, Chinese for "Great One," and visiting her house on the mountain, as Bunny described, "was like going to Disneyland." Ruth was the ideal grandmother, attentive and, best of all, indulgent. In the same way Billy had let his children break all the rules when he had come home, Ruth threw discipline out the back door when the grandchildren arrived.

Taught at home that they mustn't write on themselves, they were dropped off on the mountain and were soon covered with happy faces drawn by their grandmother. Taught at home that they mustn't get dirty, they were virtually unrecognizable after a day of streaking down the mudslide built by their grandmother, who was usually the first one to try it out. In early October 1974, this playfulness almost ended in tragedy, when Ruth was visiting GiGi, who had recently moved to Milwaukee where her husband was doing graduate work in psychology. Ruth took the grandchildren outside and began rigging up a pipe-slide, a sturdy length of wire threaded through an eight-inch section of pipe.

She fastened the wire between two trees at a sharp angle. The object was to climb the tree at the highest end of the wire, grip the pipe and slide like James Bond over the yard. Ruth wanted to make sure the contraption was safe and decided to test it first. The wire snapped and she plummeted fifteen feet, her heel striking the hard ground first, then her head. She lay motionless on the grass, and GiGi and the grandchildren thought she was playing possum until their dog licked her face and she didn't react.

In the emergency room in Mequon, the doctors could not find a pulse at first. Her left heel was split in five places, and she had a broken rib, a crushed vertebra, and a severe brain concussion. Billy, who had just arrived in Brasília, received a garbled message that prompted him to conclude that his wife had been critically injured in an automobile accident. He telephoned GiGi, who assured him that Ruth was receiving excellent care. GiGi urged him not to cancel his five-day crusade in Rios Maracaña Stadium, and he preached to more than half a million people, sick at heart, not knowing if his wife would survive.

Ruth was in a coma for a week. When she finally regained consciousness, her memory was wiped clean of, among other things, all the Bible verses she had memorized since childhood. Her progress was slow. In October she wrote from GiGi's home, where she was convalescing, "I have had difficulty reading anything, my Bible included, as my mind just wanders or won't absorb. I prayed, Lord, take anything from me, but please give me back my Bible verses. Out of the clear blue this verse came to me: 'I have loved thee with an everlasting love, therefore with loving kindness have I drawn thee.'"

Days later came another, rising out of what seemed a dark side of her mind: "And all of thy children shall be taught of the Lord: and great shall be the peace of thy children." Others came, unfamiliar verses she had no recollection of ever having read, much less memorized. They seemed to come when she needed them most. While she was recovering, her mother suffered another stroke. Ruth flew home in a private jet, to find her mother in the hospital, miserable and furious. Tubes were in her nose and mouth and she was surrounded by attendants who could not decipher her speech. When a nurse glided in to remove her dentures, Mrs. Bell tried to bite her.

Ruth persuaded the cardiologist to let her take her mother home, and at dawn on November 8, Virginia Bell died quietly in her own bed, surrounded by family. Ruth attended the funeral, dizzily swinging down the aisle on crutches. Later, she would not recall the service. The deaths of both parents blended into a single hazy event, and it seemed she had endured one interminable suffering.

According to Mayo Clinic doctors, the fall left Ruth with a mild impairment of short-term memory. It was also probable that the trauma precipitated the various problems she later experienced with the left side of her body, resulting in the replacement of the hip and a portion of the joint in the wrist. Degenerative arthritis in her neck and back, possibly also worsened by the trauma, would eventually lead to the implant of a morphine pump. The procedure was believed to have exposed her to bacterial spinal meningitis, which almost took her life in the early months of 1996.

The loss of Ruth's parents left a heartless void she could not fill. Often she lay awake early in the morning, the usual thoughts rising as they had for decades. She would instantly think of them and of what she could do for them that day. Then, with the feeling one has after waking from a pleasant dream to realize it was just a dream, her spirit would chill. "I awoke this morning after Bill left," she wrote four months after her mother's death, "and lying there I realized Bill was gone, but the comfortable feeling came over me, Mother and Daddy are home. Then I remembered. It comes at unexpected moments, the time to fix a bite for supper, meals they had up here, the back of someone's head that looks like Daddy's, Mother's old wheelchair in the coat closet, Daddy's battered hat on my bookshelf."

To this day, reminders are still thoughtfully scattered throughout Ruth's house. Mrs. Bell's black cane leans against the hearth in Ruth's bedroom, and nearby is her mother's ruffled pillow. Dr. Bell's favorite suit hangs in the hall closet, and his hat is propped on a corner of his framed portrait in Ruth's bedroom. A bowl brought back from China is on the mantel. She would claim in later life that as the years went by, she missed her parents more, not less.

"It's odd," she said in 1996, "but I think of them more now than I used to. For some reason, I think they're down at the house. It seems they are, and I start to call."

In private, Ruth was poignantly sentimental, translating people into symbols when they were absent. The packet of love letters Billy wrote her in their youth is worn and fragile after countless perusals while he was away. In the early years, she slept with his tweed jacket when she was home alone. Stuffed animals, toys, and clothes in the children's empty bedrooms somehow never got packed. One can walk in upstairs rooms now and find remnants of early lives past.

In 1975, when Ruth was in Taiwan for a crusade, she bought slabs of marble for headstones, because she wanted her parents' grave markers to come from China. She was fifty-five now, her children scattered and pursuing their own lives. Her parents were no longer waiting for her visits and phone calls. Billy was busier than ever. Ruth rose in a whirlwind of motion. For starters, she got arrested.

It was a sunny afternoon, May 20, 1975. Spring was sweet as the sun twinkled on the small lake in Charlotte's Freedom Park. Ducks waddled on the shore and paddled through murky water, and yellow flowers bordered benches and dotted the shore. Pooled around the bandshell was a sea of colorful suits, shirts, dresses, some seventy-five thousand people there to celebrate Mecklenburg Independence Day. President Gerald Ford was to deliver a short speech. Senator Jesse Helms was present, as was Billy Graham. Peppering the crowd were the inevitable protesters and their signs:

"GRAHAM AND FORD."

"GOD AND COUNTRY MY ASS!"

"FORD HAS A BETTER IDEA."

"FORD'S A TORY."

On the rise behind the shell, the demonstrators booed. They made loud asides and blew a bugle when anyone got up to speak. Ruth sat in the front row, next to the center aisle, in a restricted area that had been roped off for security. Midway through Ford's speech she noticed heads turning. Beside her in the aisle she spotted a scraggly young man, barefoot, shirtless, short, and wiry. He had slipped under the ropes moments earlier, a cardboard sign tucked by his side. Now, almost to the front he turned to face the crowd, holding his placard high overhead. "EAT THE RICH," it read on one side. "DON'T TREAD ON ME," it said on the other. He did not notice the handsome woman just behind him.

It was a reflex when Ruth snatched the sign from his hands. She sat back down, firmly planting her white pumps on top of it as the protester whipped around like a man whose pocket has just been picked. Ruth seemed oblivious to what she had just done, and was calmly listening to the president when the young dissenter spotted his property. He squatted beside her, and asked her to return his sign. She patted his shoulder in a motherly way, shook her head, and smiled. Police officers briskly escorted him to the other side of the ropes.

"I have been informed that you are Mrs. Billy Graham," an Associated Press reporter leaned over Ruth's shoulder and said. "Will you confirm this?"

She didn't deny a thing, and after the speech was further questioned by reporters. "It was no great matter," she remarked, "it was simply that the sign was rather stupid." She had acted instinctively in removing it. "The man had every right to his opinion," she said. "But when the President of the United

States is speaking it is definitely not the place to express his opinion. I am the mother of five children and disrespect has never been tolerated."[3]

Major television networks covered Ruth's sign-snatching, and former President Richard Nixon telephoned her.

"Good for you!" he said cheerfully.

The next morning the story was in newspapers throughout the United States. The protester, Dan Pollock, was a twenty-eight-year-old member of the antiwar Red Hornet Mayday Tribe, which had recently lost a civil suit charging that the group had been illegally excluded from Billy Graham Day in 1971 when Billy and Nixon had appeared together in Charlotte.[4]

Pollock realized who his assailant was and immediately signed a warrant for Ruth's arrest. He charged her with assault and battery, telling the magistrate that she had shoved him.[5]

"A lawbreaker," Ruth wrote. "Me. Taught from childhood to keep the law. Well, I was taught respect too. Respect for my elders, respect for those in authority. And manners. One didn't interrupt when another was speaking. That is why I have chafed so when demonstrators and hecklers have increasingly disrupted public speeches particularly when the President of the United States is speaking. I get irritated when thousands turn out to hear the President and the cameras panned in on the handful of demonstrators. It is like being at a banquet and someone burps and the press zeros in on the burp."

The Buncombe County sheriff telephoned Ruth at her Montreat home, embarrassed to tell her that it was his task to serve the warrant. He asked to meet her at the BGEA's Montreat office. She knew this probably wasn't a great idea and suggested they meet at the courthouse. The press was on her trail, cameras ready for the sheriff to hand her the warrant. She explained all this over the two-way radio in her car and arranged to meet deputies between two stores in an obscure area of Asheville.

"Now what do I do with it?" she asked her Charlotte lawyer moments after receiving her summons.

"Just mail it back to me," he said. "And don't talk to reporters."

Sadly, the world was cheated out of the press statement she had already written. "The only difference is," part of it read, "if it had been my son, instead of a reassuring pat on the shoulder I'd have given him a resounding whack on the bottom!"

If convicted, she would face a fifty-dollar fine or thirty days in jail.

"I've already made up my mind," she told her lawyer. "If there's a question of a fine or jail sentence, I'll choose the jail sentence. I feel very strongly that what I did was right and paying a fine would be to me an admission of guilt."

She had rolled up her sleeves and was calmly stubborn and ready to fight. "I could get a lot done in thirty days in jail, I think," she mused in her journal. "I'd relish the encounter challenging a law that protects demonstrators of radicalism and immorality instead of patriotic citizens."

The morning of the trial, Friday, August 29, she wrote Pollock a letter, telling him how much God loved him, explaining how he could come to know Christ. She tucked it inside the handsome brown leather edition of the Living Bible she planned to give him. Shortly before 1:00 P.M. she and her lawyer parked beside the Mecklenburg County courthouse. The courtroom was virtually empty when they entered, but it soon filled, reporters lining the walls. A group of admirers from nearby Shelby slipped her a note, telling her that they had come to pay her fine, should she be convicted.

Pollock was sworn in and questioned. When the defense asked him if Ruth Graham had shoved him or in any way touched his person, other than patting his shoulder, he admitted that she had not. Forty-five minutes later, the case was dismissed for lack of evidence. She caught up with Pollock as he headed toward the courtroom door. "I've been praying for you," she said warmly. "Will you accept something from me?"

"That depends on what it is," he replied suspiciously.

She slipped the Bible from her pocketbook and held it out to him, almost shyly. He drew back in disgust.

"No, I'd rather not," he said as he hurried away.

Reporters and photographers surrounded her.

"How would you like it if someone snatched a sign away from you?" one reporter asked, shoving a microphone in her face.

"I wouldn't be carrying a sign," she replied.

"Would you do it again?"

"Yes, I would."

"Why did you object to Pollock's carrying the sign?"

"Because thousands of people were being deprived of their civil rights."

"Did you offer Dan Pollock a Bible?"

"No comment," she answered.

She was drawn back into the safety of the courtroom and the judge angrily swooped to the door. "Now get out!" he barked to all.

That night Nixon called to congratulate Ruth. "It gives me a renewed faith in the American judicial system," he ironically said.

President Ford telephoned her two nights later.

"Don't you want to hire me full time as a sign-snatcher?" she asked him.

"I'll place you in the front row," he replied.

In the spring of 1975, Billy released a statement to the press that read, in part, "Americans have a responsibility to provide humanitarian aid to Indochina and call for urgent negotiations to assure the safety of South Vietnamese whose lives are endangered. . . . With compassionate hearts for the very needy individual and family we Americans have a responsibility to make available medical assistance and food required to heal and sustain life for all Indochina's homeless, needy, and afflicted people."

Shortly afterward, Elizabeth Wilson, a friend of Ruth's, told her that sixteen members of a Vietnamese family were in danger and needed someone willing to sponsor them if they were to be safely evacuated from Vietnam. Nghia, a member of the family, had graduated from Montreat-Anderson College the previous year. Miss Wilson had helped him financially, as much as her meager resources would allow, making it possible for him to finish college. After leaving Montreat, he wrote her an anxious letter, confiding that he feared his relatives would be executed. He wanted Miss Wilson to sponsor sixteen of them. It was something her small pocketbook could not manage.

"Hold on a minute," Ruth told her after hearing the story.

She put down the phone and walked into her husband's office, stopping at the edge of his desk. "Did you mean what you said?"

"What do you mean?" Billy puzzled.

She reminded him of his press statement and told him Nghia's story.

"BGEA will sponsor the family," he replied, simply.

Days later a man telephoned Billy, saying he had a list of one hundred and fifty refugees that the Christian and Missionary Alliance was willing to sponsor. He needed to get the list to the White House, but with his every attempt, it seemed, he was connected to the wrong secretary. Billy called President Ford, and within several weeks the Christian and Missionary Alliance group and Nghia's family were transported by aircraft carrier to Guam and the Philippines.

"We have, each one of us," Ruth wrote at the time, "felt like we were a small part of a miracle, and though we have been sitting on pins and needles, it has been thrilling to watch God at work."

Through it all, she seemed unperturbed. Without flinching, it seemed, she bore the loss of parents, the separation from children, the arrest, the escalating pressures of not only her husband's ministry but her own. There was always someone who needed her, and now she was grappling with the deadline for her first book of poetry.[6] She was traveling more than ever; and the interruptions and responsibilities were always there.

She made it seem easy because in fact she hid it all so well. Ruth was placid on the surface, like the Chinese she had grown up with, impossible to read and, in her own way, proud. The first visible manifestation of stress had occurred some twenty years before when she had developed a chronic cough. It was an affliction that doctors had never successfully diagnosed, much less cured, for they could find no physical cause. She suffered severe headaches. By the late seventies, she began experiencing numbness in her legs and feet, and sometimes in her hands. Again, the cause seemed to be stress.

In January 1976, she experienced what she thought was a heart attack when a breathtaking tightness gripped her chest and her fingers began to tingle. A friend rushed her to an Asheville hospital, and she was kept in the coronary unit for several days. Billy returned home to be at her side. Though the media reported she had suffered a heart attack, the doctors found no cause for her symptoms. Still in pain, she was released and flew with Billy to Mexico for a rest. A week later, the symptoms were gone.

Obviously, vacations were a matter of necessity, and it was ritual for the Grahams to take at least one lengthy rest each year. Usually they left the country, traveling to places where he was less likely to be bothered. Most often they stayed in Mexico in a condominium owned by a Dallas businessman, or they traveled to Europe. Sometimes they stayed in Jamaica with singers June Carter and Johnny Cash, whom they had met in the late sixties when Billy asked Cash to write a Christian song for young people.

June and Ruth met shortly afterward and became deep friends. "It was as though I'd always known her, it was as though she had always known me," June reminisced on a rainy morning in her office just outside Nashville. "She was girlish and lithe in a loose pink sweater, black slacks, and knee-high boots. Honest, we're buddies," she said. It was typical of her and her husband to intervene when the Grahams were exhausted and whisk them off to a secluded spot. The Cashes furnished a special wing for them in their Jamaican home, including a handmade seven-foot-long mahogany bed and antiques.

On February 1, 1976, the Grahams' vacation in Mexico was interrupted when they were jolted awake at 5:20 A.M. by an earthquake. It was mild, inflicting no more damage than cracked plaster and windows. Three days later, some five hundred miles south, Guatemala suffered what at that time was the worst earthquake in the history of Central America. More than twenty thousand people were killed and seventy-five thousand injured. Thousands of the homeless were sleeping on the ground. Thousands more had moved into lean-tos made of cardboard, plastic, and fragments from leveled buildings. Eight inches of silt blanketed cities.

Adobe houses were flattened, and bodies were bulldozed into mass graves as the threat of epidemic loomed. Billy was informed that supplies had been donated for relief, but no money for transport. He replied that the BGEA would guarantee the necessary funds. Next, he began telephoning influential friends who donated planeloads of high-protein bread and medical supplies. Billy agreed to meet with Guatemalan church leaders to discuss the rebuilding of the country.

On February 13, the Grahams boarded a friend's Lockheed Jetstar and followed the coastline, passing over volcanoes and rugged mountains, into Central America. Guatemalan President Kjell Laugerud García was at the airport when they arrived and asked to see them immediately. They were driven across the airfield to a small building where they found him, dressed in fatigues and surrounded by armed soldiers, journalists, and government leaders. He greeted the couple warmly and placed two military helicopters at their disposal. His twenty-seven-year-old son Luis would fly them to fifteen of the three hundred cities that had been most devastated.

The helicopter landed in a pasture in San Martín, where several small boys leaned against a barbed wire fence, their grimy faces furrowed with tears. Beyond lay ruins where four thousand people had died. Those left needed food, salt, and medical supplies. People wandered about aimlessly, numb with shock. Ruth stopped several of them and through her interpreter heard stories of entire families wiped out. Old graves had been split open, and new ones had been dug. The stench of death rose from rubble.

Numerous small tremors occurred while the Grahams were there, one coming in the midst of a talk Billy was delivering in a church in Guatemala City. Oblivious to trembling lights and walls, he was startled when members of the congregation jumped to their feet. Assuming they were reacting to something he said, he toned down his message. Assuming that he knew what he was doing, the congregation didn't move for the remainder of the service. Afterward, he looked up to find the ceiling literally dangling over their heads.

The visit to Guatemala ended just as abruptly as it had begun, and the Grahams again boarded the small jet, their hearts heavy. They felt inadequate and older than their years. Ruth was depressed, wanting to help and unable. She was sickened by suffering she could not heal. The aid the BGEA had financed and instigated seemed insignificant among so many homeless people. Midway into the flight, their pilot began talking to another pilot flying several hundred yards below them. He mentioned that Billy Graham was on his plane, returning from Guatemala.

"Tell him," crackled the reply over the radio, "that I was converted at one of his crusades."

1. Ruth Bell Graham, *Sitting by My Laughing Fire* (Waco, Tex.: Word Books, 1977), 225.
2. January 25, 1969, Private Papers of Virginia Leftwich Bell, Montreat, North Carolina.
3. Fran Schumer, "Mrs. Billy Graham Grabs, Keeps Protester's Sign," *Charlotte Observer*, May 21, 1975.
4. Ibid.
5. Ibid.
6. *Sitting by My Laughing Fire* (Waco, Tex.: Word Books, 1977).

19

CHAPTER

Lighting the Darker Places

Russ Busby, BGEA

Russ Busby, BGEA

TOP: THE CHILDREN'S HEALTH CENTER MISSION

BOTTOM: ON THE PLATFORM, 1995

There is little love in prison and Ruth had been an angel of mercy, lighting the darker places where no light, hope, or love had been.

—Marvin King

The front door was heavy wood, dark and lustrous, with a stained-glass window at the top. Along the tree-shaded street, the townhouse was no different from many others in Detroit's Palmer Woods residential section near Sherwood Forest. It was a breezy early evening, Friday, June 27, 1976. Two police officers paused on the porch, summoned there by a hysterical man who had dialed 911 twenty minutes earlier to report that he had just killed someone. The officers drew their revolvers as they entered.

They found Marvin King kneeling on the living room carpet, his head bent, eyes glassy and empty. He was a handsome man, in his early twenties, six foot two with a lean, muscular build. He seemed in shock; all that he had ever worked for had been obliterated in a violent moment. He was an accomplished pianist who loved Beethoven and Bach. He was a college graduate, well versed in Dickens, Yeats, and Shakespeare, vulnerable and shy, and prone to stutter. His accomplishments were prodigious for a dirt-poor black born out of wedlock in rural North Carolina. But with each mile along the tracks, he had been unwittingly heading for a break in the rails, an instability in his foundation yawning ahead. On this day, he lost it all in an explosion of rage.

Marvin King did not look up when the uniformed legs flanked him as he slumped over the bloody blue carpet. At his knees lay his best friend, Jim, killed by the repeated and frenzied blows of a kitchen knife.

"I am the murderer," he stammered, reeling with nausea.

They slipped guns back into holsters and cuffed his hands behind his back. They led him out into the night.

King was born in a one-story clapboard house, south of Fort Bragg. His father had vanished before his son was born. Mrs. King was a sharecropper's daughter and, too poor to feed her son, she put him up for adoption when he was five. His grandmother interceded and raised him in Red Springs, twelve miles from the place of his birth. After high school, he applied to Montreat-Anderson College and was enrolled in the fall of 1969. He began attending Ruth's Sunday school class and was struck with her personality, her essence.

"It is scintillating," he would later say from prison, "almost contagious." She liked him, sensing his gentleness and quick mind. She reflected his worth to him. "She was able to give me what my mother couldn't," he would say. His graduation was delayed a year when both uncles were killed in an automobile accident and he returned home to take care of his grandmother. He was vice president of the honor society and graduated in 1972 with a three point five grade point average.

In 1974, King moved to Detroit where he lived with a family he had met at a Baptist church there. A year later, holding jobs at both a hospital emergency room and General Motors, he moved into the townhouse. That was when trouble began. He became involved with Jim, the blue-eyed, dark-haired son of a General Motors lawyer. A heroin addict, Jim moved in with King and began his predation, manipulating King's emotions and borrowing money he rarely repaid. The combination of the drug influence and the intensity of the relationship increased King's instability and paranoia.

In the spring of 1976 King lent Jim two thousand dollars, ostensibly so his friend could travel to Holland. Jim was to meet a woman, his Dutch fiancée, he explained calmly. He wanted to marry her. It was a cruel lie, a scam to rob King of more money. When by chance he saw Jim on the street weeks later, King was wild with pain and anger. They argued in the apartment.

"I never cared about you," Jim told him coldly. "I've just been using you all along."

Convicted of second-degree murder, King was sentenced to seven and a half to fifteen years. "I was suicidal," King recalled. "I was suicidal until she came to see me."

In mid-October, Billy Graham was holding a crusade in Detroit. A friend flew Ruth in a private plane to the State Prison of Southern Michigan at Jackson. She was led into a large glass-walled visiting room where she saw a man sitting in a far corner, his face hidden by a heavy beard. She recognized the eyes watching her fearfully as she approached.

"Marvin," she said, hugging him with feeling.

Since late June he had been touched only by the hands that restrained him.

He was lifted and moved by her warmth, and would later say that the idea of her still caring after what he had done was overwhelming. Most people would have consigned him to oblivion, he was certain. It was a paradox of her existence that she was clear and no-nonsense when dealing with the concept of anything the Bible labels as wrong. This sort of cataloging was easy enough until a sin became embodied by a human being, until she came face to face with the adulterer, the thief, the murderer, or the friend or child who had gone astray. Then Ruth was no judge, but a friend, the first to say someone was wrong, but loved and worthwhile.

She was often the first to visit the lawbreaker or appear at the crime scene, her impulse, like her physician father's, not to punish, but to heal and help. Years later, a Montreat woman would sneak into a neighbor's home and kill herself with a shotgun. Ruth arrived with towels to help clean up the gory mess. She moved the family up to her house for the night, and paid to have the room repainted and refurnished, to obliterate reminders of what had happened there.

"What does God say to a Christian who's committed suicide?" a member of the woman's family asked.

"I once heard someone say," Ruth replied tenderly, "'God did not call her home, but He welcomed her.'"

"What about punishment?" she was often asked. "God does not punish us for our sins but by them," she would say.

When a young friend dropped out of college and was hospitalized for an eating disorder, Ruth was the first neighbor to call and take her out for an afternoon. As they drove to Asheville, she gave her young friend encouragement. There was no humiliating and invasive probing, no quizzing as to why the young woman wanted to quit college and slowly die. Ruth offered no quick offers of easy fixes, no advice. She voiced no judgment when marriages fell apart, and did not nag about smoking or alcohol. In truth, no matter what she preached in her Sunday school classes, it was the reality of those who knew her that she could not think in rules when faced with people who had lost their way.

Guards in black slacks and kelly green jackets stood sentry, bored and cynical that afternoon in Jackson. They eyed Marvin King and his guest with mild curiosity.

"Isn't that Billy Graham's wife?" one whispered loud enough for King to hear.

"Why should this black convict be having such famous company?" the other asked in a loud sarcastic tone.

She sat in an upholstered chair, King across from her on a bench.

"You were wrong," she told him. "But you still have a chance. The Lord can forgive you. You can be a witness."

"I have been living disobediently," he told her quietly. "But I have truly repented, and though I cannot undo this horrible deed I am grateful I can at least pay my debt to society. I can accept God's forgiveness but it's hard for me to forgive myself."

"Marvin, let me tell you a story," she said. "Some fishermen in the highlands of Scotland came back to an inn for tea. Just as the waitress was serving them, one of the men began describing the day's catch in the typical fisherman's gestures, and his right hand collided with a teacup. The contents splashed all over the whitewashed wall and an ugly brown stain emerged."

"I'm so terribly sorry," the fisherman apologized repeatedly.

"Never mind," said a man who jumped up from a nearby table.

"Pulling a crayon from his pocket, he began to sketch around the tea stain, and there emerged a magnificent royal stag with antlers spread. The artist was Sir Edwin Henry Landseer, England's foremost painter of animals. If an artist can do that with an ugly brown stain, what can God do with my sins and my mistakes if I but turn them over to Him?"

Later, he watched her leave, walking gracefully. She carried her black leather Bible, dull and soft from use, with pages so swollen and fragile that she now bound the book with a black leather belt, her Bible belt, she jokingly called it. He felt a tightness in his chest, and would recall her words continually, month after month. Periodically he received letters from her and classical music tapes. Two and a half years later he was transferred to Muskegon Correctional Facility in Michigan, and two and a half years after that was granted an early parole.

"I sometimes find it hard to forgive myself," he reflected years later. "But Ruth was a woman God chose to use in keeping the candle of hope and love burning when fate had plunged me into the abyss of guilt and despair."

In the fall of 1976 the administrators at Montreat-Anderson College and Calvin Thielman planned what they called the Fall Festival of Faith. The guest singers were Armenian brothers Dennis and Danny Agajanian. Ruth drafted them, forming a roving band that began showing up at such places as the Juvenile Evaluation Center, the Veterans Hospital, the Alcoholic Rehabilitation Center, local high schools, the Orthopedic Hospital, and the county jail.

Without the demands of home, she immersed herself in the suffering of others, carrying with her the message of love and forgiveness. In the Orthopedic Hospital, she stopped by the bed of Cindy, a five-year-old girl who had once been pretty, with delicate features and curly brown hair. Two years earlier her mobile home had caught fire, and she received third-degree burns over most of her body, her features melted away like wax. She was hideous to look at, her head smooth like a cabbage. Life to her was broken in half. "There was the time before I was burned," she would whisper, "and there is now." When hospital attendants passed out little presents, she always chose costume rings, though she had no fingers.

Through two tiny holes she glanced shyly at this woman hovering over her. A hand lightly touched her shoulder. The face was soft and smiling.

"Honey," Ruth said to her, "what would you like this man to sing to you?"

"Jesus . . ." Cindy began to cry mutely, small drops trickling down her scarred face, as Dennis Agajanian bent down to her eye level and played "Jesus Loves Me" on his guitar.

At the city jail a female inmate also wept as the Agajanians sang. Ruth talked to her, touching her through the bars. "Perhaps the Lord Jesus allowed you to come to a place like this so you could learn of Him."

Ruth befriended a twenty-year-old convicted murderer named Carol, a bright, green-eyed blonde from Kingsport, Tennessee. By Carol's fifteenth birthday she had been arrested on drug charges and sent to a rehabilitation center in Asheville. By twenty, her drug habit was costing her five hundred dollars a day. On December 28, 1976, she borrowed her boyfriend's .357 Magnum revolver. She tucked her hair beneath a dark blue ski mask and attempted to rob an Asheville beauty salon. She claimed it was an accident when the gun discharged and killed the shop's seventy-four-year-old receptionist. Three months later, Ruth visited Carol in the county jail. Ruth wrote her and called when Carol began serving a sixty-year sentence in Raleigh's Correction Center for Women.

"I had a lot of people that tried to get in the jail to see me, the more or less want-to-save-your-soul type people," Carol recalled from prison. "Most of them were trying to cram a whole Bible down my throat in fifteen minutes, typical for this section of the country anyway. . . . I was hearing so much of how I was being damned and going to hell. But Ruth wasn't like that. She wasn't judgmental. She didn't try to push me."

The stories weren't always warmly poignant. There were days when the world snapped at Ruth and her partners. One day they visited war veterans in a local hospital, and as soon as the guitar began to play, an old man jabbed a finger in each ear and rolled his wheelchair out of the room, disgusted. On another afternoon as Ruth, Calvin, and the Agajanians headed back to Montreat, they stopped the car at Pack Square in downtown Asheville to run an errand, inadvertently parking in front of a pornographic bookstore. Without a word, Dennis left the car and sauntered inside.

"Dennis," remarked Ruth to the others, "has no idea what kind of shop that is."

Moments later he burst out the door, shouting. He climbed up on the car hood and had just begun to strum his guitar when a short, portly police officer waddled up, looking a bit like an overdone Christmas pudding, as Ruth described him, and rather angry.

He ordered Dennis to stop singing. "I always obey the law," Dennis replied, climbing down.

Then the officer ordered him not to move until he radioed for his supervisor. Ruth and Calvin boiled from the car. "This amounts to false arrest!" they objected hotly.

Another officer arrived, informing them matter-of-factly that if they wanted to have a street meeting, they'd have to get a permit.

"All right," Ruth said. They promptly drove to City Hall where, much to her amusement, she was issued a slip of paper that read: "Mrs. Billy Graham has permission to sing at Pack Square."

The next day Ruth, the Agajanians, and a busload of Montreat-Anderson students unloaded at Pack Square. They held their street meeting, abruptly awakening the Christmas pudding officer who had been sitting inside his Cushman beneath the obelisk. He stepped outside to investigate, walking with uncertainty, when a six-foot-seven, three-hundred-pound college student with bushy brown hair billowing over his shoulders lumbered toward him.

"God bless you," the giant said, handing the befuddled officer a tract.

The student, who most of his life had been known as "Moose," was one of the Agajanian brothers' converts. Of course, he was one of Ruth's newly acquired friends. Malcolm Winger was born in Spartanburg, South Carolina, son of a mill executive. Winger's mother had died of cancer two days before Christmas when he was twelve. "And I pretty much made up my mind then that I was going to be my own man," he recalled years later in an interview. "I never agreed with my father and I was going to be totally different from him."

A talented guitarist, Winger succumbed to the enticements of rock and roll and the self-destructive lifestyle that often goes with it. After high school he washed up on the shores of Montreat-Anderson College, and on a fall night in 1976, he and several friends were walking in the rain, popping a mixture of speed and heroin called MDA. Drenched and dazed, they slogged through the puddled sidewalk flanking Anderson Auditorium, a massive native-stone building between the lake and the post office. The auditorium's windows glowed and the applause inside sounded like the rain beyond. The concert ended and Billy and Ruth Graham moved into a receiving line in the lobby to greet guests. Winger and friends peered in from a side door, eyes glazed with chemicals and mischief.

"I dare you to go in there and shake hands with Billy Graham," one of the fellows nudged Winger with a laugh.

"Just watch," he replied.

Clad in tattered T-shirt, patched blue jeans, and a twenty-year-old Pendleton jacket, his long wet hair plastered to his meaty back, he pushed through the door. Strolling through a sea of tuxedos and evening gowns, he boldly made his way to the line. He shook the Grahams' hands simultaneously. Ruth smiled.

"I was there to shock everybody. But she wasn't upset. She wasn't shocked,"

Winger would later say. "She was radiant and friendly. It was like I was in a tuxedo."

Weeks later, he met the Agajanians, and Dennis brought him to Ruth's house. "When I walked in," Winger recalled, "I expected this very staunch prude. But you can't get past her laughing eyes. You immediately become attracted to her."

They became friends. She wrote and telephoned, advising him as if he were a son. She played pranks at his expense, and invited his friends to her home for pizzas and discussions. But what meant most to Winger was that she took an interest in his music. He and a friend named Rodney "Flash" Ferrell had formed a band. Ferrell, from Johnson City, Tennessee, was five foot ten and weighed a hundred and thirty pounds, a rowboat to Winger's *Titanic*.

Ferrell had earned the name "Flash" during high school football days when he would wind and weave to avoid being tackled. A guitarist, Ferrell had been entrusted with a set of keys to the college choir room where the public address system and various amplifiers were kept. The equipment, which rested neatly on the Montreat Presbyterian Church platform on Sunday mornings, made the rounds on the weekends, when Ferrell and Winger would sneak it out of the choir room and use it for their barroom acts.

Their ear-shattering rock and roll was complete with original Christian lyrics like "Jesus help me quickly, I'm sinking in the sewer." In the spring of 1978, just before they graduated, they invited Ruth to one of their concerts, certain she wouldn't come. She surprised them by arriving at the opening song and sitting through it all, a good sport who wished she had remembered to take aspirin before leaving the house. When the last note died away, she approached them.

"How would you like to attend this Bible school in Colorado?" she asked, referring to Ravencrest Chalet in Estes Park.

"Well," Winger said with a good-natured shrug, "why not?"

She sent both of them there.

Most people she tried to rescue were not transformed overnight, if ever. After Bible school Winger began playing the bar circuit. Ferrell drifted. Tony Mendez disappeared, leaving his battered gray Oldsmobile rusting on the Graham mountain until weeds pushed through the floorboard and Ruth had it towed away. When he reappeared in the spring of 1982, it was in a red Cadillac with white leather seats. He owned an arcade of slot machines and video games in Barbados, he told her. He added brightly that he was merely saving his money until he could afford to become a minister and join the mission field.

"Tony, in one gambling city, our security guard told us that those big hotels with the casinos in them have separate elevators to carry out the corpses," Ruth said to him. "There's nothing wrong with making money. It's how you make it and what you do with it."

They stood in the driveway, pausing before he left again.

"I guess one of the first things I need to do is sell that car and get a small one," he said, his face pained as he looked lovingly at the red Cadillac.

"I think it would be a very good idea, because, Tony, you don't want to drive up outside of a little country church in that long, bright red Cadillac."

"You know, Ruth," he said, "I guess that's my ghetto mentality."

Later, he would wind up in the hotel business in Las Vegas.

20

CHAPTER

Darkness Over the Face of the Earth

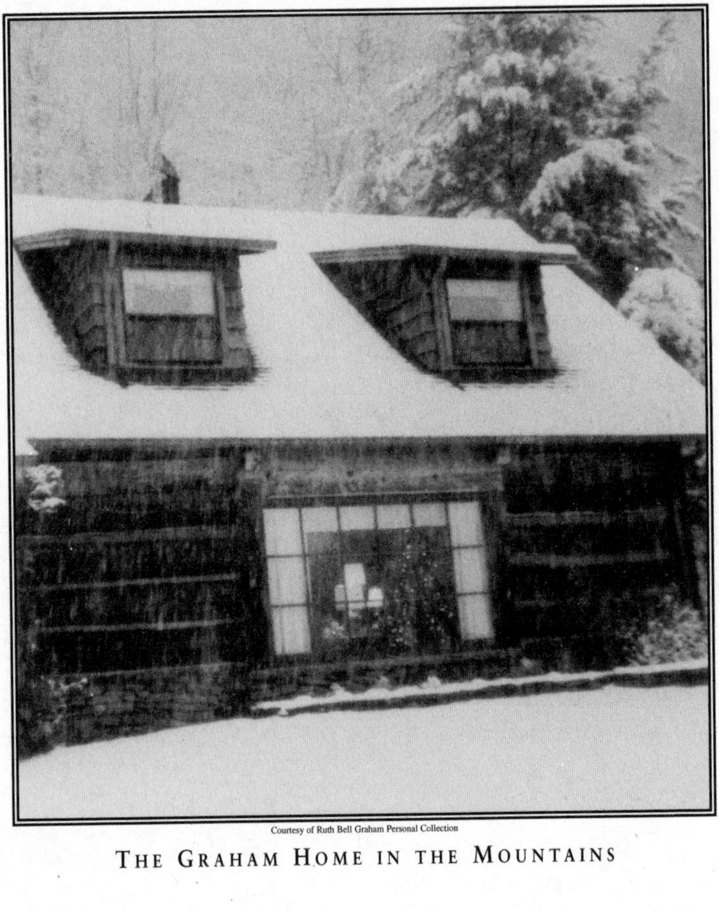

Courtesy of Ruth Bell Graham Personal Collection

THE GRAHAM HOME IN THE MOUNTAINS

At last, you have come, and you have brought the sunshine with you.

—Polish girl to Ruth, 1978

Between 1977 and 1980, Ruth traveled around the world twice, following her husband throughout the United States and then to Hungary, Poland, Sweden, and the Philippines. When the trips were over, she was weary beyond remedy, and determined to stay on her mountain as much as possible for the rest of her days. Billy's taking her on the road, she decided, was rather like a general taking his wife to battle.

In early February of 1978, the couple traveled to Las Vegas for a five-day crusade, their arrival coinciding with a macabre event that was being bruited about in the press. A beautiful young Spanish-American woman named Maria Torres had hacked off her left hand with a machete, claiming that Jesus had told her to do it. Reporters seemed interested in linking the story with the Billy Graham crusade. "What would Satan love better," Ruth commented at the time, "than to have her do something hideous like that and blame it on Jesus?"

At the first press conference a reporter asked Billy if he planned to visit Maria in the hospital. Ruth wouldn't hear of it. She reminded him, "It's sure to be turned into a media event, which would defeat the purpose of the visit." That afternoon she went in his stead. A nurse told her that Maria was sleeping and promised to telephone her when the young woman was ready to see her.

The call came the next day. In the hospital room Ruth was greeted by a lovely face with wide, brown eyes. Ruth sat beside her and gently touched the reattached left hand, bound at the wrist and resting on a pillow. It was black and as cold as death. For the first time since the young woman's self-inflicted mutilation, she began to talk. After an hour of rambling about Old Testament massacres, a previous drug addiction, and her recent live-in boyfriend, she told Ruth why she had cut off her hand.

She was reading the Old Testament, she said, when suddenly, "I realized I was not living the way I should and I heard a voice saying 'Because you are not living the way you should I want you to take a knife and cut off your left hand.' The voice kept saying, 'Cut it off! Cut it off! Cut it off!'" She tried a carving knife and then the machete. "I screamed and I screamed. But I hacked and I hacked and I finally got the thing off."

At that moment, a doctor arrived to wheel Maria to the operating room, where the hand was to be reamputated. Ruth bent over her and said, "Jesus never told you to cut off your hand. It was the Devil. He can quote the Bible, too. Jesus loves you. Whenever you need Him, call. He'll be right there."

Later Ruth asked some doctors, "Could Maria possibly have experienced a drug flashback?"

"No," they said.

Two days later Maria was transferred to a psychiatric ward in another hospital. Again, Ruth went to see her, carrying an inscribed New Testament to substitute for Maria's Gideon Bible. "I wanted to get her out of the Old Testament," she later explained, "especially the Old Testament massacres, because there is no way she would understand them." Ruth found her sitting cross-legged in the center of her bed, her open Bible in her lap, cradled between her right hand and the freshly bandaged stump.

"Maria," Ruth said, "look, I brought you another Bible."

Her eyes remained riveted to an Old Testament passage, her body rigid, slightly swaying like a cobra. Slowly, she lifted her head, staring at Ruth with dull, unblinking hate.

"Maria," Ruth repeated, "I've brought you a new Bible."

Lightly placing her fingers on Maria's forearms, she attempted to lift them and replace the Bible with the New Testament. They were like iron pipes. Ruth could not budge them. She placed the New Testament next to Maria and talked for an hour while the unblinking eyes bored into hers. Ruth quoted Scripture.

"I can't help you," Ruth finally said, "but God can."

Maria began panting and then slowly fell backward. Ruth caught her before she tumbled over the edge of the bed. She eased her around, resting her head on the pillow.

"Remember, Maria," she said as she left, "Jesus loves you and if you call for Jesus He will be here and He will help you."

Maria's eyes closed and a single tear slipped down her cheek. Ruth took the Gideon Bible and left, meeting the ward supervisor outside the room. Ruth wondered aloud if this could be a case of demon possession.

"Well," the woman said coldly, "I just don't happen to believe in demons."

"Well," Ruth said, "my father was a medical missionary for twenty-five years in China and had personal experience with them. The Chinese had separate words for having a devil and being crazy. Once he was called out to see a woman who was demon-possessed. It was winter. He had on his long johns and an overcoat. He told the woman when he went into her room that he couldn't help her but Christ could and only Christ could. And at the mention of His name, she went absolutely livid and grabbed his arm and bit him and broke the skin through all that clothing. It was superhuman power."

Years later a chaplain from Las Vegas, who was working as an usher at a crusade Ruth was attending, approached her. "I have the New Testament you gave Maria Torres," he said.

"Where did you find it?" Ruth asked, surprised.

"In the trash at the hospital."

Eight months after the Las Vegas crusade, Ruth traveled to Eastern Europe. Her first stop was Sweden, then Poland, where three years later General Wojciech Jaruzelski would impose martial law, interning thousands as the government attempted to crush the trade union movement called Solidarity. On September 25, she boarded a plane in Charlotte and flew to Stockholm. She waited there two days while her husband preached to a crowd of twenty thousand people in Oslo and endured the assaults of the Heathen Society, whose members were determined to upset the services. A young woman struck him with a ball of a red doughy substance and then shinnied up a pole and unfurled a banner which read, "WHEN CHRISTIANS GET POWER THEY KILL PEOPLE." A man climbed up after her and ripped it down to the wild applause of the crowd. Billy preached without pause.

From September 27 to October 1 he visited Stockholm, conducting services which were broadcast in Norway, Sweden, Denmark, and Iceland. On the night of the first meeting, Ruth was asked to address the wives of the men helping with the crusade. She sat between two interpreters from the Salvation Army. One was a woman named Gunvar Paulsson, who had been badly injured the summer before when terrorists attacked a mission station in Rhodesia. Two missionaries had been murdered. She was presumed dead and left facedown in the dirt. Now, in a black dress and bonnet, her left arm permanently crippled from bullets, she sat quietly on the platform, translating Swedish to English for Ruth.

"How honored I am to sit beside you. I have never had to suffer for my Lord the way you have," said Ruth, whose childhood prayer for martyrdom remained unanswered.

"Believe me," Miss Paulsson replied with a smile, "it was a joy. You know, I had never had to suffer for my Lord before this happened. And in spite of the horrors going on all around me at the time, there was such a sense of the presence of the Lord Jesus Himself that it was a pure joy."

The Grahams rested three days in a hotel in Copenhagen, where red tile and oxidized copper roofs stretched from their balcony to the Baltic Sea. On the raw, drizzly morning of October 6 they boarded a DC-9 and flew to Poland, passing low over wet black earth and fields of cabbages and three days earlier landed in Warsaw. Cardinal Karol Wojtyła had left from the same airport.

Pope John Paul I had died the week before after serving only thirty-four days, and Cardinal Wojtyła would soon be named his successor. A sliver of history slipped by unnoticed as a Polish cardinal on his way to becoming the first non-Italian head of the Catholic Church in more than four centuries crossed paths with an American Protestant permitted by the Communist government to proclaim the Gospel in a land more than ninety percent Catholic.

The Grahams would travel through Poland for ten days. On their way to their hotel, Billy laid wreaths on two monuments. Ruth, wearing a black coat, followed several paces behind him, the rain steadily falling on her bare head until a young Pole loped out of the crowd and held an umbrella over her. On Saturday, October 7, the sun broke through the overcast sky, dispelling the dark, wet weather for the first time in well over a week. Billy conferred with an ecumenical group of clergy in a Baptist church while Ruth and an interpreter met with a group of women. Ruth was expected to lecture. As she often did on such occasions, she opened the floor to questions.

"How can we be sure our children will grow up believers?" a woman worried, for in Poland, both parents worked, their children turned over to state day care centers.

"Samuel's and Moses' mothers kept them until they were weaned and we know that in primitive societies today, this can be three or four years," Ruth replied. "I would think that Pharaoh's court could hardly be described as an ideal place for a child to be raised. And Eli's temple was even worse since, under the guise of religion, his sons had turned it into a cesspool of iniquity. And yet both Moses and Samuel grew up to be men of God."

As she left the meeting a young woman with plump cheeks, a babushka, and steel teeth approached her and said she had come from Russia. "And Christians from my town knew that I was coming and why," she said, tears streaming down her face. "And they asked me to deliver a request. Will you pray for us?"

"We have not ceased praying for Russian believers," Ruth assured her.

On a foggy Sunday, October 8, the Grahams, their associates, and Dr. Denton Lotz, brother of Anne's husband Danny Lotz, departed for Bialystok, northeast of Warsaw and just short of the Russian border. Billy was to preach in an outdoor service at a Baptist church. He rode in a sedan, while Ruth followed in a bus loaded with BGEA team members and American journalists.

Ruth had been told that in Poland when the bus made a comfort stop it meant the passengers were let out in the woods and left to their own devices. She didn't understand what this meant, nor did it make sense to her when a young preacher-photographer named George Boltniev grinned at her and remarked, "I can't wait for the rest stops so I can get a picture of Ruth Graham picking mushrooms."

At last, the bus lumbered to a halt, and passengers were set loose at the edge of a wooded area, thick with trees but disturbingly lacking in underbrush. Others ambled off in different directions, looking neither left nor right, each furtively in search of a fat tree, preferably with low, foliated branches. Ruth headed for a ramshackle privy, changing her mind six feet downwind of it. She was saved by her voluminous black raincoat. Unbelted, it settled around her like a tent. She picked a handful of mushrooms on her way back and, with mock solemnity, placed them in George Boltniev's lap as she returned to her seat.

There had been no advertising for the Graham crusades. Nonetheless, the news spread as Christians on foot and on bicycles relayed information by word of mouth. Eight hundred people attended the service that afternoon, standing stolidly in a chilly wind and listening intently to the message. Each face, Ruth observed at the time, was a sermon in itself, especially the older faces on which seemed to be etched centuries of suffering. Billy asked those who wanted to commit their lives to Christ to raise their hands. One-third of the audience did.

After the closing prayer a distinct click-click-click-click rippled through the audience.

"What was all that tongue clucking?" Billy asked Ruth later, when they were back in their hotel room. "Did I say something that offended them?"

"No, you nut," she said, laughing. "Those were tape recorders being switched off."

Late that day as dusk fell and pockets of fog scudded over the bus's windshield, the small caravan headed toward Treblinka, a concentration camp where more than half a million Jews had been exterminated during World War II. Billy had an appointment there with a West German film crew.

"Doesn't it seem ironic," Ruth asked an Associated Press reporter, "that it should be a German film crew that had insisted on Bill's coming to this particular extermination camp?"

"Some elements of the liberal German press," the man replied, "are doing all they can to keep the memory of these extermination camps fresh in people's minds and to play them up whenever possible."

"That," Ruth wrote at the time, "made me do some thinking. These places should never be forgotten, nor the horrors committed there. But, at the same time, I wonder if they could be used as a sort of diversionary tactic to keep our attention off what is happening in the world today."

The morning of October 10, a rosy mist veiled the old city of Poznań, and loud crows peppered the sky as the Grahams and team members boarded the buses for Wroclaw. It was the harvest season for sugar beets and potatoes, and they passed carts heavily laden and fishtailing behind straining horses. Ruth had awakened that morning exhausted, sick with a cold and looking it. Harold Lindsell, who since his Wheaton days had edited the *Lindsell and Harper Study Bibles*, was traveling with the BGEA on this trip. He studied his former girlfriend closely.

"Ruth, I have a confession to make," he remarked. "I have been praying for Bill on this trip, but as I sit here looking at you I realize it's you I need to pray for."

"Thank you, Harold," she replied. "It's all right to tell a woman you're praying for her but you don't have to say she looks like she needs it."

On the Grahams' first day in Poland they had attended a workers' luncheon at the headquarters of the Polish Ecumenical Council where the heads of different churches rose to make lengthy extemporaneous speeches. Each expressed the same concern: a very real and deep fear of World War III.

"When the United States dropped the atomic bomb," one man said, "they looked for a flat place where it could do the most harm. Poland is a flat place."

"One could not but have deep sympathy for these who have suffered so much in the past and have a very real fear of going through it all again," Ruth wrote at the time.

On Thursday, October 12, she was granted a gut-wrenching view of the symbols of their pain in the grisly archive of Auschwitz. The bus turned off a main road onto a circuitous dirt lane and deposited the group in a parking lot packed with tour buses. Beyond were railroad tracks, a depot, and a simple archway with the German words for "Work Liberates" in wrought-iron letters. Inside were the red brick barracks built decades ago by the people who later died there.

Their tour began with original films of the prisoners' arrival, grainy, ghostly, and soundless save for the steady clicking of the reels. Darkly clad figures with pale faces pinched with pain, hollow-eyed men and women clutched their bags and filed into the camp. Some leaned on friends, others held babies. Suitcases, many bound in rope, were painstakingly marked with former addresses. They were merely relocating, they had been told. One day they would be reunited with their belongings, with their families and friends. The men who had invaded their homes weeks earlier had emphasized the importance of clearly marking the bags.

Nazis, mouthing silent commands and gesturing mechanically on film, separated men from women. They hurried each line into the bleak, barren showers and ordered the prisoners to disrobe. After their ablutions, they were told, they would find fresh outfits awaiting them, new clothes for their trips to their new locations. Naked and naive, they herded beneath the nozzles that were connected to poison gas lines.

Within an hour, all were dead, their bodies carried on conveyor belts to the next floor. Hair was shaved for mattress and furniture stuffing. Some would be woven into cloth. Gold fillings were extracted from teeth. Bodies, unadorned and pillaged, were again loaded on conveyor belts and fed into raging crematorium ovens. There and in the distance, the black smoke billowed from stacks, signaling the darkest evil of the human heart.

Chilled and shaken, the Grahams were shown three bolts of the human-hair cloth, rough like homespun wool. They were taken to a cell where some prisoners awaiting death had been detained. On one of the walls, preserved behind a glass plate, was the outline of Christ's head that a prisoner had etched with a thumbnail. Billy and Ruth moved past expansive glass showcases filled with clothing, shoes in adult and child sizes, eyeglasses, the carefully addressed suitcases, photographs, and hair, now bleached and gray with age.

In a courtyard where prisoners had been lined up in front of a brick wall and shot, Billy placed a wreath before the wall, his throat tight with emotion, his wife beside him. Together they knelt in soil that had once been so soaked with blood that the Germans had tried to replace it bucket by bucket before the Allies arrived. The couple prayed silently, while camera shutters clicked around them, eerily sounding like the cocking of guns. Ruth rose, queasy and in a cold sweat.

Later that day Ruth visited a home in Kraków run by the Catholic Order of Caritas for children with speech defects. On the second floor, children sat around small tables in a sun-washed room. When Ruth appeared at the door, they jumped to their feet.

"Good day!" they said in unison.

Ruth smiled as she seated herself. Through an interpreter, she asked the children if they would like to hear a story. They eagerly gathered around her feet, gazing up with wide eyes.

"A little boy and girl had gone to the country to visit their grandmother," she began. "The first day they were there the little boy was throwing some rocks and accidentally hit his grandmother's pet duck, killing it. He looked all around to see if anyone was watching. He saw no one. So he quickly buried the duck.

"That night after supper when the grandmother suggested he and his sister clear the table and wash the dishes, his sister said, 'I don't feel like washing the dishes but my brother would love to.'

"Angrily the little boy whispered, 'What do you mean you won't wash the dishes but I would love to?'

"Whereupon the sister whispered in his ear, 'I saw what happened with the duck. I was looking out the window. If you don't do what I say, I will tell Grandmother.'

"So the little boy had to clear the table and wash the dishes. The next morning when the grandmother called them to breakfast, the same thing happened again and the little boy found himself doing the dishes while his sister played.

"At lunchtime, the grandmother called them to come in and set the table and help with lunch. Again, the little girl said she didn't want to but that she knew her brother would love to. When he started to object she whispered, 'Remember the duck.'

"At dinnertime it was the same way. This went on for several days, and his vacation was being ruined. Finally he went to his grandmother and told her exactly what had happened and how sorry he was for it. She listened to him kindly, then with a smile she said, 'I was wondering how long it would take you to tell me. You see, I was looking out the kitchen window and saw just what happened. I was wondering how long you were going to let your sister make your life miserable for you. Now that you have told me what happened and how sorry you are, of course I forgive you!'

"God," Ruth told the children, "sees everything we've ever done and He's willing to forgive. But we must confess to Him."

21

CHAPTER

Return to China

Courtesy of Ruth Bell Graham Personal Collection

NIXON WOULD LATER OPEN DOOR TO CHINA

Beyond those hills
lie yesterday
the silenced now
and a tomorrow.
The clouds
that wrap those hills
like shrouds
are free to come and go
at will:
no guns can frighten them away
nor stop the moon
and stars, nor say
the sun must shine.
No manifesto tells the rain
where it must fall,
how much
and when . . .

—*Ruth Bell Graham, 1973*[1]

June 8, 1973, a Friday afternoon, was cool and clean like glass. Ruth sat in a restaurant on a rise above the Hong Kong harbor, staring hypnotically out the window. The charred hull of the *Queen Elizabeth* lay on its side like a dead whale, dwarfing scores of multicolored boats quietly rocking nearby. The former luxury liner had burned and sunk the year before. Why no one hauled it away, she didn't know.

She could see Deep Bay bridging mainland China and the Portuguese province of Macao. Thousands of Chinese had swum across its waters to freedom since 1949, or died in the attempt. Far beyond, the mountains of China's Guangdong province formed a chalky blue smudge across the bright sky. It was the closest she had been to the land of her birth since she had sailed from Qingdao thirty-six years earlier.

The month before, she and her husband had traveled to the Orient where he was to hold several crusades. The sights and sounds stirred her, dislodging memories of her childhood and creating a yearning that overpowered her one night in a room in Tokyo's Imperial Hotel. She lay awake until dawn, the thought of returning to China possessing her.

The next day she placed telephone calls, then drafted a letter to the Chinese Travel Service in Beijing, requesting permission to visit Tsingkiang, or Qingjiang, as it was now spelled. In part, she was just as afraid of being told yes as she was of hearing no.

Two weeks had passed since then, and now she sat in this Hong Kong restaurant surveying the Kowloon peninsula and listening to two Australian tourists sitting behind her argue about whether the body of water below them was Pearl Harbor. She had heard no reply to her request to return to her birthplace. The desire began to fade. It is too far to go back, she decided at the time.

It was too far in years and memories, not miles. Where she had grown up was a lost civilization, a place devoid of her parents and the missionaries she had loved, perhaps destitute of the faith they had sacrificed their lives to carry there. It was possible, however, that Ruth might find remnants, whispering sounds of her past and the solitary dream of the Christian career that she had left behind. Ruth wasn't sure she could face any of it.

The next day, June 9, the day before her fifty-third birthday, she boarded a plane to Bangkok, passing over Vietnam shortly after takeoff. Tears in the thick layer of clouds revealed a land pockmarked by shell craters and charred tree trunks. Life had not changed so much from the days of bandits and the Long March. Two and a half hours after takeoff she landed and caught a Swissair flight to Geneva, where she was to speak to a group of women in Lausanne. Donald Hoke, a retired missionary whom Ruth had known since her college days, and his wife, Martha, were there setting up the International Congress on World Evangelization. Hoke persuaded Ruth to visit the Chinese consul in Geneva to again ask permission to travel to Qingjiang.

The Chinese consul lived in a large old house in a quiet section of the city.

Trees bordered the narrow, winding streets, and most of the homes were surrounded by walls or hedges. Crumpled paper and other bits of trash fluttered over the gravel drive around the consulate like tumbleweeds in a forgotten town. On the morning of June 12, Hoke and Ruth were greeted at the door by a short, unsmiling houseboy who eyed Ruth with suspicion when she told him she had an appointment with the consul. The houseboy shut the door in the visitors' faces and conferred with people inside. Several minutes later the door was again opened, this time by an older Chinese man dressed in cloth shoes, ill-fitting dark gray cotton trousers, and a pale gray rumpled shirt that bulged over his corpulent middle. His unshaven face was impassive as Ruth briefly explained her mission.

With a slight nod he turned and led them through the entrance hall, around a corner, and into a reception room with pale gray walls, several tapestries, and a few Chinese objets d'art. Draped across one wall was a scroll bearing Chairman Mao's sayings. The savory odor of cooked cabbage and garlic permeated the airless rooms. Ruth and Hoke seated themselves in Chinese chairs with plush red cushions. They were soon joined by a young Chinese woman, dressed in the familiar comrade's garb of loose gray trousers and jacket. The pink collar of a Western-style blouse peeked out at her neck, and her short black hair was parted low on one side and fastened with a barrette. She was silent throughout the conversation, her eyes passing back and forth between the consul and Hoke, and never focusing on Ruth.

"My father had the honor of serving the people of China for twenty-five years as a doctor of medicine," Ruth explained. "He is in his seventy-ninth year and not well, and if possible, we would like to return home for a visit. This would be a strictly private and personal pilgrimage, not to Shanghai or Beijing but to Qingjiang, Jiangsu."

"How long ago did you leave China?" the consul asked Ruth.

"Thirty-six years ago," she replied.

"There should be no difficulty," he said. "When do you wish to go?"

"Perhaps sometime within the year?" she queried.

He left the room and returned with forms which he advised, with a faint smile, that Ruth and her father should complete and mail to a committee in New York. On June 18, Ruth flew home and asked Dr. Bell to return with her to China. Despite his wife's frantic disapproval and his own failing health, he eagerly embraced the plan. Ruth gave him the form, which he never completed because soon afterward it mysteriously disappeared. Two months later he died. After his wife died the following year, the form was found among her belongings, where she had hidden it.

Two years of loss and change and silence passed. There was no response to Ruth's requests. With renewed interest she read histories of China and analyses of what had happened to the culture, the people, and their faith since the 1949 Communist takeover. Her concern for the Chinese people became an avocation, a subject she frequently impressed upon those she talked with.

"It's the oldest continuous civilization in the world," she would say. "It's the third largest country in the world. And it has by far the world's biggest population. We cannot ignore it." In later years, she often mentioned a symbol that was of great importance to her, the Chinese character for "ten" superimposed over the Chinese character for "four." It meant the tenth for the fourth, an encouragement to people to set aside the tenth day of each month to pray for a fourth of the earth's people.

In the fall of 1975 Ruth and Billy returned to Hong Kong and Taiwan for crusades. The urge to return to her birthplace grew. She was asked to address a large group of women in the Great Hall in Taipei, Taiwan, October 29. "While I was growing up," she wrote at the time, "I planned to return to China to preach and to teach the Gospel. God had other plans. Now the committee has me scheduled to address a group of women (they hope many unbelievers) and I, accustomed to raising children and teaching an American college Sunday school class, am faced with a slight fulfillment of my childhood dream. And I am asking God to give the right message, anoint it that someone might be converted to Christ who may someday go back to China and carry the Gospel of Christ as I have longed to do."

The Wednesday of the talk arrived. Dressed in tweed, she entered an auditorium filled with brightly attired Chinese women. For a week Ruth had labored fruitlessly on the speech, wanting it to be the best ever and paralyzed by the personal symbolism of the occasion. The harder she tried, the less productive she became. Days passed and she produced nothing. Amid tiers of expectant faces she now mounted the podium. She had no notes, no prepared talk, her dream dissolving into a nightmare. Through an interpreter, she extemporaneously told of her parents' mission work and her own childhood in China, closing with a description of Wang Nai Nai, her Chinese nanny.

"Her Christian life had such an impact on us children," she said. "She taught herself how to read the Bible after becoming a Christian, and she loved the old hymn 'There Is a Fountain Filled with Blood.' Only after we were grown were we told the evil life she had lived before becoming a Christian. She and her husband were engaged in the Chinese version of white slave traffic, procuring young girls for sale in Shanghai.

"Then I understood why she so loved that old hymn, especially the last verse: 'The dying thief rejoiced to see / That fountain in his day / And there may I, though vile as he, / Wash all my sins away.'"

An elderly woman hurried forward afterward and hugged Ruth. "I too Qingjiang person," she said with glowing eyes. Ruth held the woman's hand as they walked along an aisle and kissed her at the exit. "Such a small link," she wrote that night, "and it leaves one speechless."

The first week in November Ruth flew to Hong Kong. On Sunday, November 9, she addressed another group of women, reliving the horror of mounting the platform with no prepared speech. Afterward she wrote, "A year ago today Mother was buried. Perhaps it was significant that today at 3:00 I spoke to two thousand mostly Chinese women in the largest Baptist church in Hong Kong. I never had a harder time speaking. It was as if I had spiritual laryngitis."

Three days later she was out of bed at 6:30 A.M. to catch the hydrofoil to Macao. There was a bleak, unassuming memorial somewhere on that six-square-mile province, and it called to her. In a tiny Spartan cemetery filled with plain stone markers, weathered and covered with moss, she found the grave of Robert Morrison, the father of Protestant mission work in China. A Presbyterian minister, he had arrived in Guangzhou in 1809 and died there twenty-seven years later, after translating the New Testament and a dictionary into Chinese and making but ten converts. His wife and child were buried with him.

One man had sacrificed so much for what seemed so little. Ten converts. One would have been enough, at least to Ruth. "The popular thing today is to criticize the early missionaries who went to China and point out their many mistakes," she wrote that night. "Even Robert Morrison. I thought about this as I stood beside his grave. At least they went. They went, carrying with them the Living Word and the written Word. And the gates of hell have not prevailed against it."

Her last evening in Hong Kong, November 16, shortly before midnight, she sat in her hotel room alone. Billy had left for the United States earlier that day. She would fly to Korea the next day to visit her sister Virginia, a missionary. Like the shadow of the Guangdong Mountains on the mainland, the past seemed within reach but was untouchable. She was drawn to the patch of earth where her parents had worked and where she had played as a child. Those seventeen years in Qingjiang had shaped her more than anything that had happened to her since. They were her fabric. She could take the regular tours to China, as thousands of sightseers had, but that would bring her no closer to the place of her birth, which was on no tourist route. In any event, she doubted that anything from her early years remained. This is perhaps the closest I will ever get to the land of my childhood, she decided.

Through the cool darkness of her room, she moved to the window and drew back the draperies for a last look at the Hong Kong harbor. Boat shadows gently bobbed in the glow of lamps along the dock. A seaworn junk silently glided past, its wide sails round with breeze.

Montreat, January 1980. Billy pushed the lighted button on his telephone and picked up the receiver. He was greeted by the familiar voice of Richard Nixon. The former president was preparing to leave for another visit to the People's Republic of China.

"Is there anything I can do for you?" Nixon asked him at the end of the conversation.

"Yes," Billy replied, "I think Ruth should go back to her birthplace."

"It's no problem," Nixon replied. "I'll arrange for it when I'm in China."

Nixon kept his promise, and without delay Ruth received word that the Chinese-American Friendship Association would officially receive her and the other immediate members of the Nelson Bell family. They would be given a special tour of their old home. Aside from the tediousness of completing numerous applications and writing letters, the plans for the trip went smoothly until the day before Ruth was to leave in the spring of 1980.

Billy decided he wanted movie producer Irwin Yeaworth to travel with the party and film the event. Yeaworth, who had produced many secular films, including actor Steve McQueen's first movie, *The Blob*, had worked for Billy in the past. Again, Nixon's name was needed to gain clearance, but he was somewhere in Germany and even his daughter Julie didn't know how to reach him. Finally, several days before the party was scheduled to meet in Tokyo, Yeaworth managed to obtain permission to travel with the group.

Ruth, her two sisters, and her brother left from different locations for the long pilgrimage home. Yeaworth hastily packed his bags and rushed to join them as their chronicler. On April 29, 1980, Ruth met her older sister, Rosa Bell Montgomery, in Los Angeles. Rosa was married to Don Montgomery, an engineer at the Atomic Research Laboratory in Los Alamos, a small, isolated city on the Pajarito Plateau of New Mexico. Rosa had lived in the arid climate of New Mexico since first arriving there with tuberculosis almost forty years earlier.

The next day, the two sisters flew to Honolulu and were reunited with their brother Clayton Bell, senior minister of the Highland Park Presbyterian Church in Dallas, Texas, one of the largest Presbyterian churches in the country. At forty-eight he bore a striking resemblance to the young Nelson Bell, though he was much taller and heavier. On May 6, the three arrived in Tokyo, where they were joined by their younger sister, Virginia Bell Sommerville, married to a university professor in Korea, where they had been Presbyterian missionaries for more than twenty years.

It was a rare and happy family reunion made even more unusual by its purpose. The next day, May 7, the family landed in Beijing at 2:10 in the afternoon. They were greeted by members of the Chinese-American Friendship

Association and introduced to their government companion, Yao Jin Rong, a linguist who had been in charge of the U.S. press corps during Richard Nixon's 1972 visit. Yao would be their companion for the next fourteen days, a subtle reminder that the Bell children were semi-official guests of the government. They were to travel in tan limousines with filmy curtained windows and be treated to excellent food and accommodations. "Things were scrubbed as they'd never been before because of Nixon," Yeaworth recalled.

Their first afternoon in Beijing, May 8, they had tea with Madame Soong Ching-ling, the widow of Sun Yat-sen, the father of the Republic of China. It was a bit of historical irony that Madame Soong and her sister Soong Mei-ling had spent a summer in Montreat in 1912 while in America attending school. They stayed at a lodge next door to the house the Bells would live in some thirty years later. When the Communists drove the Nationalists off the mainland in 1949, Soong Mei-ling, who had married Nationalist leader Chiang Kai-shek, followed her husband to Taiwan, and Soong Ching-ling stayed behind.

Madame Soong, ninety, without a wrinkle on porcelain skin, spoke impeccable English. The visitors stayed for an hour in the old one-story gray brick house enclosed in rings of courtyards. Madame Soong spoke of her sister and their American friends, and about the social organizations she aided, such as the Children's Palace, which trained exceptional children.

Ruth and her family stayed in Beijing two days, touring the usual places—a primary school, the imperial palaces in the Forbidden City which had been converted into museums, a cotton textile mill, and a factory commune. They wandered through the Ming Tombs, and along the Great Wall where Ruth, whose arthritic left hip caused her pain when she walked, cheerfully slid down the steel railing, heedless of the masses swarming through the wide thoroughfare. Over her navy turtleneck sweater, she wore a gold cross. It attracted attention.

"Do you wear this cross as a symbol or a decoration?" one young man stopped on the Great Wall and asked her in broken English.

"As a symbol," she replied, smiling.

"Of Christian?" he asked. "Do you believe in Christian?"

After six days of touring, the Bell children were to fulfill the purpose of their trip halfway around the world. On Tuesday, May 13, early in the morning, they were driven toward Qingjiang. It was a clear day and the limousines thrummed along a two-lane road, their drivers honking frequently, swerving through crowds of bicyclists, pedicabs, pedestrians, and horse-drawn wagons. Beekeepers had set up shop beneath blooming locust trees on either side of the packed-clay thoroughfares. Bamboo cages swung by the sides of old men walking their birds. Scattered throughout the noisy throng were guards wearing green caps with the familiar red star above the bill.

Brother and sisters traveled through small villages, and the sights became more familiar as they passed mud-walled cottages with thatched roofs, a lone water buffalo loitering over a murky pond, drab walls and shops, and landscapes splashed with brilliant red, pink, and yellow azaleas and roses. Eyes followed the limousines, the people wondering about the important passengers. When the cars stopped at one point, the party was immediately surrounded. The Chinese laughed in delight when Rosa spoke Mandarin, and they beamed when Ruth soothed a frightened little girl by producing a tiny stuffed koala from her luggage and presenting it to her.

They approached Qingjiang from the west, and Ruth knew they were almost home when they crossed a bridge over the Grand Canal. The water and the junks and sampans looked as they had when she was a girl. But there were no children frolicking in the murky water, no women washing rice on the banks. Years ago, the first sight upon entering the city had been the chimney of the Qingjiang mint. It was gone. The corrugated red tin roofs of the mission compound arched above the skyline were not to be found. Now there were smokestacks, and billboards advertising Coca-Cola. Sidewalks were as wide as streets used to be. The ancient city gate and the wall where the heads of criminals had once been impaled were no longer.

The limousines passed through an arch of sycamore trees and parked at the Qingjiang Guest House, a two-story building with private rooms, hot water, electricity, and flush toilets. After a sumptuous lunch, the Bell family returned to the cars. A black limousine joined them and led them toward their old home. "This," Ruth recorded at the time, "was really an embarrassing way to arrive home as we would have so loved to walk in like ordinary folks."

The ancient mud wall on top of which Ruth once had walked, heading to school each morning, was gone, replaced by a wide road. Gone also was the foreign cemetery where her baby brother Nelson Jr. had been buried. They passed a gray brick wall to Ruth's right and then a building. After a hard right turn through wide gates, the cars halted. The house Ruth had been raised in stood before them, ravaged and sad like the face of a forgotten old woman. A red banner had been draped above its front porch: "AMERICAN FRIENDS, YOU ARE WARMLY WELCOMED BY THE PEOPLE LIVING IN YOUR BIRTHPLACE."

It seemed so much smaller. The yard, once spacious enough for a tennis court, was a balding scar between the house and the lot next door where the James Woodses had lived. Where Ruth had grown up was shutterless and chimneyless, and the old tin roof had been replaced with artificial gray tile. Drainpipes were orange with rust, and the brick wrought-work balustrade that had once surrounded the downstairs porch had crumbled and now littered the backyard.

Their house wore the death mask of neglect. Inside paint-peeled frames, the windows gaped like empty eye sockets. The door to the central gable that once had led to the sleeping porch had vanished, leaving a wide orifice frozen into a yawn. What Ruth saw sadly symbolized much more than the demise of her parents and the passing of time in her own life. The scene before her seemed a dismal monument to an age that had been completely obliterated. There were no more missionaries. Most Chinese were too young even to remember the courageous foreigners who had carried the promise of salvation and Western culture across the world to share. Ruth wondered if the missionaries, many of whom had died there, had left no more than this.

The Bell children got out and explored. In the backyard Virginia discovered the crumbled balustrade and inquired if they could each have two bricks from it to take back with them. Ruth headed straight toward the eight-foot-high gray brick wall at the edge of the yard.

"I wonder if it's the same wall," she muttered to herself. "I wonder. Right along here . . ."

"What was there?" Yeaworth asked her.

"My little pet dog," Ruth said, referring to Tar Baby, the mongrel she'd buried among the irises half a century before. "My first one and the one I loved most," she said as she took slow steps, absorbed in an unsuccessful search.

Inside, whitewashed walls were mottled like greasy butcher's paper, and naked lightbulbs dangled from twisted cords. It was time for tea, and they were led upstairs into a room dominated by a large table. They were seated in what had once been their parents' bedroom.

"I'm sure our father would be very, very happy to know that we his children have come back here," Rosa told their hosts. "He always loved the people in Qingjiang. He dreamed about them many, many times."

"People here," a Chinese man replied in English, "still have very good memory of your father and they knew that many of them were treated by your father and they knew that your father had done good things."

There was more exploring, and reminiscing out loud and squabbling about the previous location of furniture and whose bedroom had been where. The nook in the house Ruth wanted to see most was her favorite attic bedroom over the kitchen wing. But it was impossible, their Chinese host told her, for the occupants had locked the door and he did not have a key. The party was told it was time to leave. Reluctantly, the Bell family headed for the cars. The only visible sign that they had ever lived there were two hooks in the porch ceiling where the swing had once hung.

As they continued the tour of the compound, they found that all of the buildings they had known as children were standing except for the Woodses' home, the boys' school and the men's hospital. The women's hospital and administration building were missing entire floors and had been converted into classroom buildings. The hospital where Dr. Bell had practiced surgery was now a technical school. The Chinese-style house where Ruth had been born still stood, as did the schoolhouse where Lucy Fletcher had taught Rosa, Ruth, Sandy Yates, and the Talbot boys each morning.

"The walk to school," as Ruth remembered it, "had been long." But now she was surprised at how close it was to the house. It seemed that time shrank distance and buildings as well as people. The schoolhouse had been newly whitewashed and each room was filled with industrious young students, with heads bent intently over books while a portrait of Chairman Mao watched them from above the blackboard. The family toured several former missionary homes. All were overcrowded. Porches had been bricked in to make extra space, and entire families lived in one room. The Chinese guides could not contain their amazement that this American family had once had an entire two-story house to themselves.

"What," the interpreter asked Rosa, "did you do with all that room?"

By afternoon it was time to leave. Ruth, Rosa, Virginia, and Clayton took more photographs of their old house and climbed back into the limousines, preparing to drive to a nearby garment factory for another tour. When they emerged from the brick gate, they found the street lined with hundreds of Chinese applauding and waving. An elderly man rushed toward the car and grabbed Clayton's hand through the open window, shaking it warmly and with recognition. When Nelson Bell had left China he had been the same age his son was now. Ruth wondered who among the crowd along the roadside remembered her parents. She would never know.

On May 15, at a sandalwood factory in Suzhou, Ruth bought a fan for ten dollars because its spicy fragrance stirred up memories of her mother fanning herself and perhaps a nearby child during church services and prayer meetings in the stifling hot Qingjiang summers. In an open market downtown she spotted an old Chinese peasant loitering beside his cart. She began bartering with him over the *bian dan* propped beside him, holding up one, two, and finally five yuan. He took the money and handed her the split bamboo pole which the Chinese had used for centuries to carry burdens across their shoulders. As she picked up her new purchase, the crowd began to yell at the old man, claiming he had cheated her.

"You charged her too much," a young soldier shouted. "You should give her some back."

The man sheepishly handed one yuan back to Ruth.

"She could have gotten it for sixty cents in the country," a peasant woman muttered as Ruth walked away.

Ruth returned to her group and found the interpreter laughing. He explained that the money she had paid the old man was special money issued by the government to tourists and worthless to the natives.

"Well, anyone crooked enough to charge me so much will find a way to spend it," Ruth replied.

The morning of May 18, the family attended a Sunday service at the Mo An Church. The sanctuary was filled and they were told that people had begun lining up at three o'clock that morning to get seats. Entering the old Gothic building, they were greeted by the piano playing "This Is My Father's World." Other traditional hymns and a sermon followed. That night, a retired Chinese schoolteacher approached Ruth. He was the son-in-law of the former pastor of the Chinese church the Bells had attended so many years ago in Qingjiang. The man told Ruth that he had once had a badly infected foot and had visited Dr. Bell.

"Your father not only healed my foot," he said, "he led me to Jesus Christ and I am a Christian today. I am your father's fruit."

That afternoon Ruth asked their government companion if she could visit a Chinese man and his wife, a couple known and loved by friends of Ruth's in the States. The man, a former pastor, had been released the previous March after twenty-two years of imprisonment with hard labor. His wife had spent fifteen years in another camp. Permission was granted and she took a taxi to the quiet street, finding the cramped, two-story house where the couple lived. The doorman told Ruth that the man and his wife were not in. In broken Chinese Ruth left the message that she would be back at five o'clock that afternoon. She returned to her hotel, disappointed and frustrated.

"You know I needed to see them," she prayed silently. "I need to learn from them. We who have never been through what they have been through need to hear how You supported them. It may help prepare us for what lies ahead." The words floated through her mind, "Look to the Rock from whence you were hewn."

Later, she wrote, "We are so prone to look to one another for help which we can only get from Him. When our time comes, He will sustain us, not with what He used to sustain these dear Christians necessarily, but He will sustain us Himself in whatever way He sees we need the most." When she returned to the apartment several hours later, her desire, she recalled, was to go in, "not in order to get, but to give."

The doorman led her upstairs and, without knocking, opened the couple's apartment door. Ruth found herself facing a thin, balding man squinting at her curiously. "His eyes were almost blind with cataracts. His wife was younger and almost as blind. 'At least,' the wife pointed out, 'she had more teeth than her husband had.' He has five teeth, it was her wont to tease, only two of which meet."

Ruth introduced herself and the man's mouth spread into a wide grin. Weeks earlier, several Chinese friends in the United States had asked Ruth to visit the elderly couple. One woman had suffered in a labor camp with the wife. She asked Ruth to deliver a letter and photographs to the couple. The pastor held the photographs close to his nose and talked excitedly when he recognized the figures. Ruth produced the letter and, mindful of the couple's deafness, read it at the top of her voice, though she was sure that anyone outside the apartment could hear every word.

"Once," said the pastor toward the end of the visit, "your father invited me to Qingjiang to hold meetings for the hospital staff and the patients who could walk and the families of the patients. But," he paused apologetically, "I was too busy."

"That's understandable," Ruth assured him.

She left them, somehow learning what she had wanted to know. There was no bitterness or complaining, no hatred for those who had caused their suffering. There was peace. The husband and wife were grateful because they had been given the strength to bear it all. At 4 Quinsan Road, when Ruth found the old four-story Mission Home, she remembered a young girl on top of the sheets in the stuffy darkness, crying because she did not want to leave home. She remembered preferring death to the pain of separation. She remembered being given the strength to endure it all.

Ruth would return to China twice more before arthritis and other ailments would render such arduous travel impossible. She had become the missionary she had always wished to be, but somehow could never quite see it. She had built her life ruggedly and alone, really, on the Roof of the World on top of her mountain. She had healed and left her mark on others as privately as she might have on a compound in another land. Ruth had loved a man who needed her, and lives were changed in a world that did not seem much better.

1. Ruth Bell Graham, *Sitting by My Laughing Fire* (Waco, Tex.: Word Books, 1977), 226.

Little Piney Cove, 1996

Courtesy of Ruth Bell Graham Personal Collection

RUTH AND BILLY GRAHAM

Many years have passed for the house on the mountain and the woman who built it. Time has weathered old wood, and, last I checked, the rail fence around the yard had been chewed up by scary dogs that bark at air and lick. All that training in Germany, I always think as they wag their tails when people drive in. Chester the cat recently passed on, and I feel very guilty since I've teased Ruth for years about how enormously fat he was. In my letters to her, I used to draw rather rude cartoons of him ballooning bigger than the Graham mountain.

He was so inflated with self that when he sat in Ruth's lap, she complained she could not breathe. I witnessed this on a number of occasions while we were visiting before the fire in her living room. Chester would silently sneak in and up he'd jump. When she would gently put him down and check to see if her bones were intact, it sounded like a medicine ball thudding on old heart-of-pine flooring.

There is now a new Chester, this one much smaller, although I know it is simply a matter of time. Ruth's house is still well stocked with field mice that scratch inside the walls at night, causing me to sit straight up in bed, my heart crazed with fright. Since I wrote her biography, my emotional landscape has been dramatically changed by shadows and morbid things. She says she drove me to murder.

She claims it is hard for her not to take it personally that my first activity after writing her book was to find a morgue and immerse myself in homicide for the rest of my days. I am often asked about what seems an incongruous and jolting transition in my career, but it really does make sense. Ruth is good. She is love and life. Knowing her inspired me to create a character who wants to leave the world a little better than she found it.

Besides, after the biography, I missed her. For years, I had Ruth by my side, even when she wasn't there. Then my work with her was done. I decided I had to find some other remarkable person who would put up with me for more than one crime. That's the genesis of Scarpetta, the heroine of my series. It is Ruth's fault. She is responsible for people around the world knowing a lot more about blood spatter patterns, autopsies, and DNA.

It's hard to know Billy's thoughts. I remember he came home from a crusade and found his wife wearing a necktie she had gotten from me. I have a photograph. I can prove it. He's suspicious about what other mysteries I might bootleg up there, and fixes me in a blue stare as intense as the light sources my scientists use.

"What are you doing to my wife?" he said. "I come home and she's wearing a tie."

"It's very stylish," I nervously replied.

He thinks about this, trying to be open-minded as he pries the lid off a big tin of popcorn.

"Want some?" He offers it to me as he helps himself.

Ruth is in another part of the house, and the dogs start to bark. I can hear her slippers along the polished old brick hall. It is dark out, and the canary in its cage over her favorite chair starts to sing. Ruth walks in, tightening the sash around her robe; she is seventy-six and still beautiful, as life continues to sculpt her into something finer.

"They're hungry," Billy says to her as their two-hundred-pound German shepherds continue to bay pitifully.

He goes out with treats, and the silence lasts maybe fifteen minutes before he goes out again with more biscuits.

"Honey," Ruth says, "now you've made sure they'll bark all the time."

She's always been the one who disciplines people and pets. Billy is simply incapable of that. A humble, unaffected human being, he walks into a room in jeans, his shirt half tucked in, telling Ruth he can't find his glasses (because he has them on). He acts as if I'm doing him a favor whenever I spend my time with them. He's always seemed to think that other people are more famous than he is.

I was to join them in a small European seaside city several years ago, and by the time I arrived he had let everyone know. He was bragging about me to people who mostly spoke French. Billy is fascinated by what other people think, it doesn't matter who. Some months back, we were watching one of his crusades on TV. Ruth and I were mesmerized, and he kept trying to change the channel while the canary competed with his preaching.

"We don't need to see this," he kept complaining, pointing the remote control from his recliner chair.

"Yes, we do," Ruth said.

She never could take her eyes off him. She asked her bird to stop singing, and it wouldn't, so Billy unfolded his considerable length. He unhooked the cage from a rough exposed beam and carried the protesting bird to another room.

"I hope I did the right thing," Billy worried when he returned.

But the canary wasn't on his mind as he sat back down with a troubled sigh. A Christian rock band had begun to play, and the drummer had long hair and was serious with his sticks.

"I think it's great," I chimed in.

"You know," he went on, "I never would have allowed anything like this back in the old days."

"Bill," Ruth replied. "Look. There must be thirty thousand young people in the stands watching this instead of playing games on the Internet or reading trashy books."

"Are you working on a new one?" he asked me, by the way.

Ruth has not so subtly suggested over the years that I use too many cuss words. I explain it's the characters who talk like that, not me. She once wrote me a note: If I would clean up my language, she thought my crime novels would sell like hotcakes. She doesn't read them, probably has never read a single one, and I pay her back whenever I can. For example, in *The Body Farm*, which is set near Montreat, several of the characters make mention of their legendary neighbors Billy Graham and his wife. They whisper rumors they hear.

Before I give Ruth a lovingly signed copy of my latest novel, I secretly draw little boxes throughout its pages, and pencil in, "Check here if you're still reading." Of course, she never is. I once tried reading aloud to her. We sat on her porch in the gnarled rocking chairs that LBJ gave them, and I read, skipping over anything with four letters that I knew she wouldn't like. I was very patient as she listened with a sweet smile, rocking, looking out at sun shining on the Blue Ridge mountains.

I skipped over another word or two, and got surprised by a love scene I had forgotten was there. I quickly flipped past pages that Ruth didn't seem to miss.

"Patsy, how about some tea?" She got up right in the middle of the most exciting part. "You certainly have a way with words. Always did, but I don't want to tire you out."

She gave me my first leather-bound journal and told me I should be a writer when I was just a young girl down the road. When I used to walk to the tennis courts or post office, let's say, and she would pass me going the other way, I'd wait a bit and turn around. Later, she'd reappear, and since we were both heading the same direction now, she'd open the door and let me in. I always ended up right back where I started from, usually at my house. I'd wait until she disappeared in a swirl of exhaust, and head out again to wherever I was supposed to be going. Sometimes I had to run the entire way, because I was late.

I did anything to be with her for even a minute. She always admired my brother's hand-me-downs, asked about my mother and what I was learning in school. When she wanted to read my poetry, I didn't believe it was true. I found out she wrote poems, too, and painted funny creatures on the shutters of log cabins and cupboards. Maybe that's where I got the idea to collect smooth rocks from the stream behind my house and turn them into silly painted birds that I glued to deadwood and moss. I gave her those and words.

I thought she was the loveliest, kindest person ever born. I still do. I thought there must be something special about me, too. Why else would she notice that I played baseball and tennis better than the boys, or wrote poetry and songs and was lonely?

I judge someone by how he treats children and those who are wounded and don't have much. I remember a brilliant fall day when I arrived for a visit and walked into her house, calling out her name while the guard dogs licked me and nudged my legs. I couldn't find Ruth anywhere, and I carried my bags to the room upstairs where I always stay. She had left a note on my pillow, distinctively penned by a hand that curls almost backward when it writes.

"Patsy, I'll be right back," it said. I sat on a bed not of this century and so high I have to climb up steps to get to it. I looked at the note for a long time as leaves blazed beyond the window beneath a perfect sky. I reread the words and stared, knowing I would always keep the scrap of paper somewhere. I felt like crying, but never told her.

U.S.S. Chau
while in Yokohama

If I marry—
1. He must be so tall that when he is on his knee
as one has said, he reaches all the way to hea
2. His shoulders must be broad enoug
the burdens of a family.
3. His lips must be strong enough
firm enough to say "no" and tender enough
kiss.
4. Love must be so deep that it takes its stand in
and so wide that it takes the whole lost w
in.
5. He must be active enough to save sou
6. He must be big enough to be gentle and
great enough to be thoughtful.
7. His arms must be strong enough to
carry a little child.

Courtesy of Ruth Bell Graham Personal Collection

If I Marry...

Credits

First I must honor Ruth herself for her assistance in the preparation of a book that now stretches over fifteen years.

I thank her for entrusting me with some two thousand pages of her private letters and diaries. Without their artistry and remarkable detail, the fabric of this biography would be painfully thin and colorless. I am indebted for the countless hours she spent with me in person and over the telephone, and for letting me excavate through cartons of photographs, only to return in 1996 with friend and *Washington Post* journalist Laura Stepp to dig some more.

I thank Ruth's brother the Reverend Clayton Bell, of Dallas, Texas, for granting me access to some thirteen hundred letters written by Nelson Bell in China. I thank Virginia Bell Sommerville, of Taejon, Korea, for turning over Mrs. Bell's China diaries, discovered in a basement. I thank Rosa Bell Montgomery for sharing several days in her former home in Los Alamos, New Mexico.

I thank Mary, Sarah, and Margaret McCue of Mount Sidney, Virginia, for showing me Belvidere and sharing family letters.

I am grateful to Irwin S. and Jean Yeaworth of Valley Forge Films for allowing me to view the footage of Ruth's first return to China and indulging me in mulled cider and Peking duck while I did so.

I dearly love Billy Graham for his ever sweet, unassuming, and gracious attention, and, most profoundly, for not disappointing me up close. You are better than your legend and bigger than your name.

I am grateful to Billy's family for their time: his mother, Morrow Graham, who died in the fall of 1981; his late brother, Melvin, and sisters Jean

Graham Ford and Catherine Graham McElroy. I thank the Graham children Anne, Bunny, Franklin, and Ned for their patient interviews. To the oldest child, GiGi, I give my heart.

GiGi, what would I have done without you? I wish you were my sister.

I thank employees of the Billy Graham Evangelistic Association office in Montreat: Evelyn Freeland, Maury Scobee, Karlene Aceto, Sally Wilson, and Stephanie Wills. All are surely sick and tired of hearing my voice over the telephone and picking me up at the airport. I thank other BGEA employees and friends of the Grahams: Mrs. Cliff (Billie) Barrows; former public relations director Gerald Beavan; actress Joan Winmill Brown and her husband, Bill Brown, president of World Wide Pictures; writer Colleen Townsend Evans; singer George Beverly Shea; and associate evangelist Grady Wilson.

I am grateful to my old friends at the *Charlotte Observer* who gave me access to the paper's library. I will never forget that it was editors there who gave me my first job in journalism.

I appreciate everyone, and there are too many people to mention, who granted me interviews, shared letters with me, or gave me suggestions. I especially appreciate the contributions of Gay Currie Fox and of Hampton Talbot (who died in the fall of 1982), for without their vivid recollections much that is in the chapters on China would not be remembered.

I can't say enough about my adopted dad, the Reverend Calvin Thielman, Montreat Presbyterian Church. Someday I will write you another poem.

I am greatly indebted to the scholars who read my manuscript or donated bits of their learning to it: Dr. Mary D. Beaty, assistant librarian, Davidson College, Davidson, North Carolina; Dr. John H. Leith, professor of theology, Union Theological Seminary, Richmond, Virginia; Dr. Arthur S. Link, editor, the Papers of Woodrow Wilson, Princeton University, Princeton, New Jersey; Eileen Moffett and Dr. Samuel H. Moffett, professor of missions and ecumenics, Princeton Theological Seminary, Princeton, New Jersey; and my instigator and personal editor, the late Charles E. Lloyd, professor emeritus of English, Davidson College, Davidson, North Carolina.

I am honored by the following people who took hours from their frenetic schedules to write, telephone, or see me in person: William F. Buckley Jr., Barbara Bush, June Carter Cash, Julie Nixon Eisenhower, Paul Harvey, William Randolph Hearst Jr., Senator Jesse Helms, Lady Bird Johnson, Bob Jones Jr., Dr. Harold Lindsell, Dan Rather, and, of course, Billy Graham.

Finally, I offer my warmest thanks to my agent, Esther Newberg.

I haven't forgotten my former husband, the Reverend Charles L. Cornwell, who had to live with this project back then. You were a great encouragement.

If I have left anyone out, and of course I have, I beg forgiveness.

It would be impossible to footnote every quotation. Therefore, one can assume that all unattributed quotations in the text came from private papers and my interviews with Ruth and others.

In keeping with her wishes, many of the names in the book are fictitious to protect those she always did.

To you, Ruth, the cricket sang.

Index